GOD WHO CREATES

GOD WHO CREATES

Essays in Honor of
W. SIBLEY TOWNER

Edited by

William P. Brown and S. Dean McBride Jr.

WILLIAM B. EERDMANS PUBLISHING COMPANY
GRAND RAPIDS, MICHIGAN / CAMBRIDGE, U.K.

© 2000 Wm. B. Eerdmans Publishing Co.

Wm. B. Eerdmans Publishing Co.
255 Jefferson Ave. S.E., Grand Rapids, Michigan 49503 /
P.O. Box 163, Cambridge CB3 9PU U.K.
www. eerdmans.com

Printed in the United States of America

05 04 03 02 01 00   7 6 5 4 3 2 1

Library of Congress Cataloging-in-Publication Data

God who creates: essays in honor of W. Sibley Towner /
edited by William P. Brown and S. Dean McBride Jr.
          p.   cm.
Includes bibliographical references.
ISBN 0-8028-4626-2 (pbk.: alk. paper)
1. Creation — Biblical teaching.
I. Towner, W. Sibley (Wayne Sibley), 1933-
II. Brown, William P., 1958-
III. McBride, S. Dean (Samuel Dean), 1937-

BS680.C69 G64 2000
231.7′ 65 — dc21

00-022302

Unless otherwise noted, quotations from the Bible are the authors' own
translations. Biblical quotations marked NRSV are from the New Revised
Standard Version of the Bible, copyright © 1989 by the Division of Christian
Education of the National Council of Churches of Christ in the U.S.A., and
used by permission.

Contents

CONTENTS

PSALMS AND JOB

PROPHETS

vi

Contents

Contributors

James Barr
Distinguished Professor of Hebrew Bible, Emeritus
Vanderbilt University Divinity School;
Regius Professor of Hebrew, Emeritus
Oxford University

David L. Bartlett
Dean of Academic Affairs and
J. Edward and Ruth Lantz Professor of Christian Communication
Yale University Divinity School

E. Carson Brisson
Associate Professor of Biblical Languages
Union Theological Seminary and Presbyterian School of Christian
Education

William P. Brown
Professor of Old Testament
Union Theological Seminary and Presbyterian School of Christian
Education

Walter Brueggemann
William Marcellus McPheaters Professor of Old Testament
Columbia Theological Seminary

John T. Carroll
Dean of the Theology Faculty and Professor of New Testament
Union Theological Seminary and Presbyterian School of Christian
Education

Dusty Kenyon Fiedler
Pastor
Covenant Presbyterian Church, Roanoke, VA

Thomas W. Mann
Pastor
Parkway United Church of Christ, Winston-Salem, NC

James L. Mays
Cyrus M. McCormick Professor of Hebrew and Old Testament
Interpretation, Emeritus
Union Theological Seminary and Presbyterian School of Christian
Education

S. Dean McBride Jr.
Cyrus H. McCormick Professor of Hebrew and Old Testament
Interpretation
Union Theological Seminary and Presbyterian School of Christian
Education

Patrick D. Miller Jr.
Charles T. Haley Professor of Old Testament Theology
Princeton Theological Seminary

David L. Petersen
Clifford E. Baldridge Professor of Biblical Studies
Iliff School of Theology

CONTRIBUTORS

Karen Pidcock-Lester
Pastor
First Presbyterian Church, Pottstown, PA

Gene M. Tucker
Professor of Old Testament, Emeritus
Emory University

Steven Tuell
Associate Professor of Religious Studies
Randolph-Macon College

Marsha M. Wilfong
Assistant Professor of Homiletics and Worship
University of Dubuque Theological Seminary

Robert R. Wilson
Hoober Professor of Religious Studies and Professor of Old Testament
Yale University

Preface

The title of this volume, *God Who Creates*, identifies a tectonic shift in emphasis that has taken place in the theological study of the Bible over the past several decades. The outcome has challenged core theological assumptions about the nature of divine providence and the scope of theological ethics. In a nutshell, this change marks nothing short of a paradigm shift from a once exclusive stress upon the mighty interventions of God in history to God's formative and sustaining ways in creation. Moreover, as the title indicates, the God attested in the Scriptures of ancient Israel and the early church not only created the world, filling it with manifold life, but continues to create — sustaining, reconciling, renewing, and bringing new things into existence. As the biblical canon makes clear from beginning to end, divine sovereignty is a matter of benevolent vocation rather than imperious dominion. Scripture also confesses such sovereignty to be a mandate, which the God Who Creates shares with those created in the divine image, empowering women and men to participate in an ongoing struggle against forces that threaten to overwhelm the created order and, thus, the well-being of life.

In 1952, G. Ernest Wright published a series of lectures entitled *God Who Acts: Biblical Theology as Recital*, which charted a new course for his generation of biblical theologians.[1] Abjuring the entrenched positions of

---

1. G. Ernest Wright, *God Who Acts: Biblical Theology as Recital*, SBT 8 (London: SCM, 1952). Cf. Patrick D. Miller, "Editorial: Revisiting the God Who Acts," *ThT* 54 (1997): 1-5.

Fundamentalism and Modernism in American religious thought, Wright sought to redirect American Protestants, especially those identified with the Reformed tradition, toward what he perceived to be the historical dynamic of biblical faith itself. In his view, this faith was principally grounded neither in the stability of the natural order nor in Scripture's oracular "words," but in the communal experience of God's providential work in human history. It was Wright's aim to restore theological integrity to a historically grounded faith over and against attempts, ostensibly on behalf of the modern church, to impose an artificial structure of thought on "the variety, change and flexibility" of the biblical evidence.[2] Ancient Israel, and later the early church, articulated theology not as a system of propositional dogma — treating issues related to God, human nature, sin, and salvation as matters of doctrine — but as a narrative "recital" of God's mighty deeds in history. The key events that constituted the "core of Biblical Theology" were the deliverance of Israelite slaves from Egyptian bondage and their formation into the people of God, enacted through the covenant at Sinai.[3] Exodus and covenant established both the foundation and the framework of Israel's faith. Moreover, this confessional tradition was eventually adopted and supplemented by the early church. In Acts 13:16-25, for example, Paul's preaching at Antioch narrates the benchmarks of the faith: God's choice of Israel's ancestors, the exodus, the conquest, the election of David, and the fulfillment of the promised Savior, Jesus Christ.[4]

Prominently missing in these summaries of the faith, Wright pointed out, is God's work as creator. For Wright, the biblical view of creation focuses essentially on human creation, with humanity's glory and honor serving as "the aim and climax of God's creative work."[5] Consequently, "Israel was little interested in nature [*per se*], except as God used it together with his historical acts to reveal himself and to accomplish his purpose."[6] As the earliest confessions of the church were Christological rather than Trinitarian, so the primary confessions of faith, Wright observed, focused on history to the exclusion of nature or creation. Any outline of biblical

---

2. Wright, *God Who Acts*, p. 11.

3. Ibid., p. 59.

4. Ibid., p. 70.

5. Ibid., p. 89; cf. Wright's treatment in "Schöpfung II. Im AT," *Die Religion in Geschichte und Gegenwart* (Tübingen: J. C. B. Mohr [Paul Siebeck], 1961), 5:1473-77.

6. G. Ernest Wright, *The Old Testament against Its Environment*, SBT 2 (London: SCM, 1950), p. 71.

theology, thus, must begin with the paradigmatic events of election and covenant, to which any discussion on the subject of God's creation can be included only secondarily.[7]

That Wright relegated creation to ancillary status within the purview of biblical theology was by no means unprecedented. Sixteen years earlier, Gerhard von Rad asserted that the "doctrine of creation" was not only peripheral to the theological purview of the Old Testament, "but a magnificent foil for the message of salvation."[8] Von Rad's position reflected the Confessing Church's struggle against the rise of National Socialism, which sought theological legitimization in the form of a theology of creation.[9] That struggle was articulated most sharply in the work of Karl Barth, the author of the German church's statement of resistance in the Barmen Declaration of 1934. Barth categorically set the revealed knowledge of Scripture, embodied in Christ, over and against all forms of natural theology.[10] Any doctrine of creation, von Rad contended two years after Barmen, was at best a marginal matter in Scripture and, at worst, tainted with the superstitious myths and rites of Canaanite fertility religion.

Although the cultural and theological factors behind Wright's relativizing of creation's role within biblical theology were different, both Wright and von Rad regarded the authors and tradents of biblical literature as primarily *historical* theologians who, in effect, let the drumbeat of history drown out the music of the celestial spheres. The "God Who Acts"

7. Wright, *God Who Acts*, p. 114. See also Wright's fuller discussion of this point in *The Old Testament and Theology* (New York: Harper & Row, 1969), pp. 70-96.

8. Gerhard von Rad, "The Theological Problem of the Old Testament Doctrine of Creation," in his *The Problem of the Hexateuch and Other Essays*, tr. E. W. Trueman Dicken (London: SCM, 1966 [originally published in 1936]), p. 134.

9. See Norbert Lohfink, "God the Creator and the Stability of Heaven and Earth: The Old Testament on the Connection between Creation and Salvation," in his *Theology of the Pentateuch: Themes of the Priestly Narrative and Deuteronomy* (Minneapolis: Fortress, 1994), p. 118; W. Brueggemann, "The Loss and Recovery of Creation in Old Testament Theology," *ThT* 53 (1996): 177-78; R. Albertz, *Weltschöpfung und Menschenschöpfung untersucht bei Deuterojesaja, Hiob und in den Psalmen* (Stuttgart: Calwer, 1974), p. 174.

10. See Emil Brunner and Karl Barth, *Natural Theology*, tr. P. Fraenkel (London: G. Bles, 1946). The alleged polarity between natural theology and revelatory faith, however, has been most vigorously questioned in the 1991 Gifford Lectures of James Barr, who discerns a positive place for natural theology in Scripture and finds no necessary connection between natural theology and ideological accommodation, on the one hand, and revealed theology and resistance, on the other (*Biblical Faith and Natural Theology* [Oxford: Clarendon, 1993]).

was primarily the divine judge and savior of Israel, rather than a universal sovereign who creates, nurtures, and guides the world toward its consummation.

Since Wright's important work, the focus of theological study of the Bible has split into innumerable refractions, one of which is the study of creation and ecology in the Bible.[11] It is not without a degree of irony that von Rad himself, 28 years after his aforementioned essay, concluded that nature and history were inseparably and fruitfully bound together in the Hebrew corpus.[12] On the one hand, intense concern with the natural environment in the face of pollution and dwindling resources has generated much interest in the biblical views of creation. Within comparative scholarship, on the other hand, the work of Frank Moore Cross and others has demonstrated that the allegedly sharp dichotomy between nature and history, and concomitantly between Israelite faith and Canaanite religion, is not so sharply drawn in the Scriptures of ancient Israel as had been assumed.[13] In addition, the prominent portrayal of creation in the wisdom corpus of the Old Testament and in other biblical traditions, as noted particularly by H. H. Schmid,[14] has led some to regard creation as the very foundation upon which all other dimensions of biblical faith rest (e.g., election, covenant, salvation, and eschatology).

11. For an overview of the rise of creation theology in biblical scholarship, see W. Brueggemann, "The Loss and Recovery of Creation in Old Testament Theology," *ThT* 53 (1996): 177-90; W. Brown, *The Ethos of the Cosmos: The Genesis of Moral Imagination in the Bible* (Grand Rapids: Eerdmans, 1999), pp. 4-10.

12. Gerhard von Rad, "Some Aspects of the Old Testament World-View," in his *The Problem of the Hexateuch and Other Essays*, tr. E. W. Trueman Dicken (London: SCM, 1966 [originally published in 1964]), pp. 154-55.

13. See particularly Frank Moore Cross, "The Song of the Sea and Canaanite Myth," in his *Canaanite Myth and Hebrew Epic: Essays in the History of the Religion of Israel* (Cambridge: Harvard University Press, 1973), pp. 112-44; idem, "The Redemption of Nature," *PSB* 10 (1989): 94-104. See also Theodore Hiebert, *The Yahwist's Landscape: Nature and Religion in Early Israel* (New York/Oxford: Oxford University Press, 1996); Ronald Simkins, *Creator and Creation: Nature in the Worldview of Ancient Israel* (Peabody, MA: Hendrickson, 1994).

14. Hans Heinrich Schmid, *Wesen und Geschichte der Weisheit: Eine Untersuchung zur altorientalischen und israelitischen Weisheitsliteratur* (Berlin: A. Töpelmann, 1966); idem, *Gerechtigkeit als Weltordnung: Hintergrund und Geschichte des alttestamentlichen Gerechtigkeitsbegriffes* (Tübingen: J. C. B. Mohr [Paul Siebeck], 1968); "Creation, Righteousness, and Salvation: 'Creation Theology' as the Broad Horizon of Biblical Theology," in *Creation in the Old Testament*, ed. Bernhard W. Anderson (Philadelphia: Fortress, 1984), pp. 102-17.

The debate about the place of creation in biblical theology is, of course, not confined to biblical scholars and historians. At its most fundamental level, the issue revolves around how knowledge of God is to be attained. The Scriptures aver that knowledge of the Divine is discernible from the created order. The psalmist, for example, proclaims, "The heavens are telling the glory of God," with day and night declaring "knowledge" (Ps. 19:1-2). Employing a form of the cosmological argument, Paul claims that divine nature is "understood and seen through the things [God] has made" (Rom. 1:20). Creation's role in religious epistemology became even more pronounced as biblical tradition encountered a Hellenistic environment. In the apocryphal Wisdom of Solomon, a startling claim is found: "For from the greatness and beauty of created things comes a corresponding perception *(analogos)* of their Creator" (13:5). In early Eastern Orthodoxy, as illustrated in the writings of the Three Cappadocians — Basil of Caesarea, Gregory of Nyssa, and Gregory of Nazianzus — natural theology was employed as an apologetic, no less, for dogmatic theology.[15] Drawing from Basil, Calvin himself claimed that creation provides ample evidence of God's wisdom, power, justice, and goodness.[16] But whether as an apologia, a reason for praise, or a framework for theological reflection, creation, as a source of revelation, cannot be demoted, much less expunged, from Scripture. Indeed, the biblical view of creation underscores God's triune nature. God has created the world as much as God has intervened in the world to redeem a people. God is Creator and Savior, Redeemer and Sustainer. Both natural theology and revealed theology, in turn, point to the same comprehensive worldview in which justice and mercy, faith and life, are to flourish. The Bible, in short, presents nature and redemption, history and creation, as a seamless whole, never to be rent asunder.[17] Indeed, just as it marks the beginning of the biblical drama, the affirmation of God as creator is the starting point for defining Christian faith, as the

15. See the comprehensive discussion in Jaroslav Pelikan's 1992-93 Gifford Lectures, *Christianity and Classical Culture: The Metamorphosis of Natural Theology in the Christian Encounter with Hellenism* (New Haven and London: Yale University Press, 1993), esp. pp. 3-39, 57-73, 90-106.

16. John Calvin, *Institutes of the Christian Religion*, 1.14.20-22, ed. John T. McNeill (Philadelphia: Westminster, 1940), pp. 179-82.

17. See G. von Rad's more nuanced remark: "The Old Testament draws no such distinction between nature and history, regarding them as one single area of reality under the control of God" ("Some Aspects of the Old Testament World-View," pp. 154-55).

Nicene and Apostles' Creeds attest. Such an affirmation, in turn, denotes the end point of the biblical drama, the consummation of life itself, which decisively informs Christian practice. As W. Sibley Towner aptly notes, "Biblical renditions of the future of nature come to us not as metaphysical claims but as moral ones. . . . The value of these texts lies not in their capacity to predict cosmic or human history in advance — that they cannot do — but in their capacity to *shape* our behavior now toward each other and the other denizens of the earthly ecosystem."[18]

While acknowledging the considerable extent to which theological and ethical reflection has shifted since Wright's day, the following collection of essays confirms Wright's insistence on the Bible's irreducible variety by eschewing any kind of uniform, systematic presentation of creation in the Bible. It is the conviction of both the editors and contributors that the very diversity of biblical perspectives on creation is more blessing than bane for modern readers of Scripture.

This volume sets itself apart from most studies of creation, which examine the various traditions to determine either their ancient Near Eastern mythological precursors or their compatibility with modern ecology and science. Written by biblical scholars and church leaders, the essays presented in this volume explore the various perspectives of creation within their native theological contexts, including literary and historical. Early on in the development of this volume, the editors determined that in addition to essays written by scholars, homiletically oriented essays were vitally needed in order to provide a well-rounded, accessible volume for theological use and discussion. While a systematic presentation is avoided in this collection, an attempt is made to provide some canonical breadth through the variety of contributions included. Naturally, one would expect to find some overlap of treatment with certain foundational creation texts, such as those found in Genesis and the Psalter. That these same texts are interpreted in different ways attests in no small measure to their hermeneutical power.

This volume honors one who has contributed significantly to the study of the "God Who Creates." W. Sibley Towner's various writings on creation, from scholarly essays to curricula and sermons, are well known to the church and the guild. As one contributor aptly puts it, "Sib's love of God is nurtured by his love affair with God's world." Bearing witness, in

18. W. Sibley Towner, "The Future of Nature," *Int* 50 (1996): 30-31.

his own words, to "the great big 'Good!' that God uttered over creation in the beginning still echoing around the edges," Sib has led a life of loving concern for creation.[19] Moreover, Sib's concern for God's world is reflected in his deep reverence for God's word. Throughout his active career, Sib's passion for interpreting Scripture in provocatively relevant ways has never waned. Winsome colleague, inspiring preacher, effective teacher, caring mentor, and treasured friend, Sib has led countless students and church leaders into the strange and vital world of the Bible. As Sib's work continues to be a labor of love for the church, so this volume is offered as a source of theological reflection and dialogue.

The editors wish to thank the various contributors who made this rich volume possible. Many thanks go to them for their diligence and cooperation. Equally acknowledged are Jon Pott and Allen Myers of William B. Eerdmans Publishing Company, who eagerly agreed to publish this *Festschrift* in a time when such works are all too often deemed unprofitable ventures. Special thanks go to our skilled faculty secretaries, Jill F. Torbett, who helped in the tedious work of formating and proofreading the contributions, and Jean Hayes, who developed the index.

WILLIAM P. BROWN
S. DEAN McBRIDE JR.

---

19. W. Sibley Towner, "The View from the Screened-in Porch," *Pulpit Digest* 68, no. 490 (March/April 1988): 119. This sermon won first place in the "the best sermon competition" in the doctrine/theology category.

Abbreviations

AB	Anchor Bible
ANET	J. B. Pritchard, ed. *Ancient Near Eastern Texts Relating to the Old Testament*, 3rd ed. with supplement. Princeton: Princeton University Press, 1969.
AnOr	Analecta orientalia
Ant	Josephus, *Jewish Antiquities* (= *Antiquitates Judaicae*)
ASORMS	American Schools of Oriental Research Monograph Series
ATD	Das Alte Testament Deutsch
BA	*Biblical Archaeologist*
BDB	F. Brown, S. R. Driver, and C. A. Briggs. *A Hebrew and English Lexicon of the Old Testament*. Oxford: Clarendon, 1907.
BHT	Beiträge zur historischen Theologie
BLS	Bible and Literature Series
BTS	Biblisch-theologische Studien
BWANT	Beiträge zur Wissenschaft vom Alten und Neuen Testament
BZ	*Biblische Zeitschrift*
BZAW	Beihefte zur Zeitschrift für die alttestamentliche Wissenschaft
CAT	Manfried Dietrich, Oswald Loretz, Joaquin Sanmartin, eds., *The Cuneiform Alphabetic Texts*, Abhandlungen zur Literatur Alt-Syrien-Palastinas und Mesopotamiens 8; 2nd ed. Münster: Ugarit-Verlag, 1995.
CBQ	*Catholic Biblical Quarterly*
CBQMS	Catholic Biblical Quarterly Monograph Series
ConBOT	Coniectanea biblica: Old Testament Series
CTA	A. Herdner, *Corpus des tablettes en cunéiformes alphabétiques dé*

	couvertes à Ras Shamra-Ugarit de 1929 à 1939. MRS 10. Paris: Imprimerie Nationale, 1963.
EvT	*Evangelische Theologie*
FOTL	Forms of the Old Testament Literature
HAT	Handbuch zum Alten Testament
HBT	*Horizons in Biblical Theology*
HSM	Harvard Semitic Monographs
HTR	*Harvard Theological Review*
HUCA	*Hebrew Union College Annual*
ICC	The International Critical Commentary
Int	*Interpretation*
IntBC	Interpretation: A Bible Commentary for Teaching and Preaching
IRT	Issues in Religion and Theology
JAOS	*Journal of the American Oriental Society*
JBL	*Journal of Biblical Literature*
JEA	*Journal of Egyptian Archaeology*
JEvTS	*Journal of the Evangelical Theological Society*
JR	*Journal of Religion*
JRT	*Journal of Religious Thought*
JSOT	*Journal for the Study of the Old Testament*
JSOTSup	Journal for the Study of the Old Testament Supplement Series
JTS	*Journal of Theological Studies*
KAT	Kommentar zum Alten Testament
KEH	Kurzgefasstes exegetisches Handbuch
KTU	M. Dietrich, O. Loretz, and J. Sanmartin, *Die Keilalphabetischen Texte aus Ugarit*. AOAT 24; Kevelaer: Butzon und Bercker/ Neukirchen-Vluyn: Neukirchener, 1976.
LCL	Loeb Classical Library
LXX	Septuagint
MT	Masoretic Text
NCBC	New Century Bible Commentary
NJPS	New Jewish Publication Society Version
NRSV	New Revised Standard Version
OBT	Overtures to Biblical Theology
OTL	Old Testament Library
OTS	Oudtestamentische Studiën
PSB	*Princeton Seminary Bulletin*
PRU	*Le Palais Royal d'Ugarit*
RB	*Revue Biblique*
RestQ	*Restoration Quarterly*, Abilene, TX
RSV	Revised Standard Version

ABBREVIATIONS

SB	Stuttgarter Bibelstudiën
SBLDS	Society of Biblical Literature Dissertation Series
SBT	Studies in Biblical Theology
SP	Sacra pagina
SR	*Studies in Religion/Sciences religieuses*
STDJ	Studies on the Texts of the Desert of Judah
TEV	Today's English Version
ThLZ	*Theologische Literaturzeitung*
ThT	*Theology Today*
TZ	*Theologische Zeitschrift*
UF	*Ugarit-Forschungen*
VT	*Vetus Testamentum*
VTSup	Vetus Testamentum Supplements
WBC	Word Bible Commentary
WMANT	Wissenschaftliche Monographien zum Alten und Neuen Testament
ZAW	*Zeitschrift für die alttestamentliche Wissenschaft*

PENTATEUCH

Divine Protocol:
Genesis 1:1–2:3 as Prologue to the Pentateuch

S. Dean McBride Jr.

I. Introduction

Pentateuchal Torah is a composite work, an archive or collage of traditional materials. Varied in literary type, date, and provenance though the components may be, the whole has a coherent structure and purpose. To state the matter succinctly, the Pentateuch is a theopolitical charter, designed to establish not only how but why descendants of the patriarch Jacob were incorporated, under his alternate name Israel, to be a uniquely sanctified people among the world's nations. Torah professes that Israel's sanctification is a principal means by which the beneficent providence of God who creates is to be made known in and for the whole realm of creation.

By ancient Near Eastern standards, biblical Israel was an upstart nation, a latecomer and, even then, a minor player in an arena of international politics and culture dominated principally by Egypt, Assyria, and Babylon. Pentateuchal traditions acknowledge the seniority of such neighbors in making Israel's latter-day claim to a weighty role in the universal scheme of divine sovereignty. The case is developed through an extended genealogical narrative that bridges millennia of antiquity, joining the age of Moses with primeval times.[1] Initial segments of the narrative, in Gene-

---

1. On genealogical narrative as a literary feature of Genesis, see Robert R. Wilson, *Ge-*

sis 2:4–9:29, outline a natural history in which creation itself is repeatedly endangered, usually by acts of human perversity, with God reactively intervening to correct and stabilize nature's course. Larger narrative segments thereafter trace Israel's pedigree from the primal ancestors — especially Noah and his son Shem, followed in nearer generations by Terah, Abraham, and Isaac — which it shares with other ethnic and national lineages. The epoch of Israel's political formation, whose onset is signalled in Genesis 37:2, begins with the Joseph narrative and continues through prolonged accounts of the sojournings of Jacob's clans, first in Egypt and then, after the drama of the exodus, in the wilderness of Sinai. The final narrative segment, introduced in Numbers 3:1, is also complex and lengthy but even more narrowly defined: it treats the need for Israel's internal governance by legitimating successions of authoritative leadership that institutionalize the prototypical roles of Aaron and Moses.[2]

---

nealogy and History in the Biblical World, Yale Near Eastern Researches 7 (New Haven and London: Yale University Press, 1977), esp. pp. 9, 189-95, 201-2. Cf. also Karin R. Andriolo, "A Structural Analysis of Genealogy and Worldview in the Old Testament," American Anthropologist 75 (1973): 1657-69; and Robert B. Robinson, "Literary Functions of the Genealogies of Genesis," CBQ 48 (1986): 595-608. I use Wilson's designation more broadly here to describe the editorial segmentation of pentateuchal narrative traditions, as demarcated especially by the so-called Toledot rubrics: "[And] these are the generations of . . ." ([wĕ]'ēlleh tôlĕdôt) in Gen. 2:4; 6:9; 10:1; 11:10, 27; 25:12, 19; 36:1, 9; 37:2; Num. 3:1; and "This is the book of the generations of humankind/Adam" (zeh sēper tôlĕdôt 'ādām) in Gen. 5:1. The import of these superscriptions in the "Priestly [P]" edition of Genesis was underscored by Frank M. Cross, Canaanite Myth and Hebrew Epic: Essays in the History of the Religion of Israel (Cambridge: Harvard University, 1973), pp. 301-5. On the structural significance of the rubrics, see also Sven Tengström, Die Toledotformel und die literarische Struktur der priesterlichen Erweiterungsschicht im Pentateuch, ConBOT 17 (Uppsala: CWK Gleerup, 1981); Howard N. Wallace, "The Toledot of Adam," in Studies in the Pentateuch, ed. John A. Emerton, VTSup 61 (Leiden: E. J. Brill, 1990), pp. 17-33; and Terje Stordalen, "Genesis 2,4: Restudying a locus classicus," ZAW 104 (1992): 163-77.

2. I.e., the seemingly peripheral Toledot rubric in Num. 3:1 serves as the heading for the remainder of the Pentateuch; it refers, quite properly, to the "generations" of both Aaron (the priest, whose heirs are empowered in the rest of Numbers) and Moses (whose legacy and principal legatees are described, e.g., in Num. 11–12 and especially in Deuteronomy). That the rubric here, as also in Gen. 2:4, 6:9, and 37:2, is a secondary editorial or redactional device only underscores its structural import. (It is unfortunate that both NJPS and NRSV, following not a few commentators, have misconstrued the contextual sense of Num. 3:1. They render the formula in the singular — "This is the line/lineage of Aaron and Moses" — as though it referred only and awkwardly to the summary list of Aaron's immediate offspring, separately introduced by "These are the names . . . ," which follows in vv. 2-4.)

While the metahistorical character of the genealogical narrative is evident throughout, theological intentionality is highlighted by a series of five covenants, centered on the elaborate portrait of Israel's constitution at Sinai-Horeb.[3] The central covenant, certainly, but each of the others as well, secures an aspect of God's providence within the temporal realm. As the series progresses, from the comprehensive covenant with "every living creature of all flesh" in the time of Noah through the pact enacted with Moses' heirs in the land of Moab, it provides closer rationale for Israel's peculiar sociopolitical identity and mandates its sacral vocation.

The present essay will sketch the world-ordering significance of these five covenants, examining them through the lens ostensibly crafted for this purpose in the Pentateuch's initial pericope.

II. The Protocol of Genesis 1:1–2:3

Whatever its antecedent history may have been, the Priestly "creation account" in Genesis 1:1–2:3 functions admirably as a cosmological prologue to the whole Pentateuch.[4] This text's purview crosses the boundaries of lit-

---

3. See my brief overview (which will be developed in the present essay): "Perspective and Context in the Study of Pentateuchal Legislation," in *Old Testament Interpretation: Past, Present, and Future. Essays in Honor of Gene M. Tucker*, ed. James L. Mays, David L. Petersen, and Kent H. Richards (Nashville: Abingdon, 1995), pp. 53-55.

4. For our present purposes, the literary design and hermeneutical function of the pericope are much more important than disputed issues of its sociocultural origins, its connections with and departures from other ancient Near Eastern traditions of creation, and its precise relationship to and role within the work of the Priestly school. Indeed, the witness of the text is attenuated and misunderstood when the pericope is principally construed, for example, as an originally independent liturgical tradition, adapted to serve as a sophisticated alternative to the folkloristic account of human origins in Gen. 2–3 or as a secondary theological preface to a "primeval history" that extends to and ends in Gen. 11. The function of the text as "prologue" to the broad scope of pentateuchal traditions was succinctly described by Frank Cross: ". . . the [P] creation account is a prologue attached to an epic account of the call of the fathers, the victory of the Divine Warrior in the exodus and conquest, and the creation of the covenantal political order at Sinai" ("The 'Olden Gods' in Ancient Near Eastern Creation Myths," in *Magnalia Dei/The Mighty Acts of God: Essays on the Bible and Archaeology in Memory of G. Ernest Wright*, ed. Frank Moore Cross, Werner E. Lemke, and Patrick D. Miller Jr. [Garden City: Doubleday, 1976], pp. 335-36, as reprinted with minor revisions in Frank M. Cross, *From Epic to Canon: History and Literature in Ancient Israel* [Baltimore and London: Johns Hopkins University

erary sources, epochs of the genealogical narrative, and individual pentateuchal books. The theological commitments of the text affect the interpretation of more mundane and parochial traditions, including those that belong to other compositional strata, drawing them into its own grand vision of God's cosmic rule. Both the form of the pericope and the allusive quality of its contents support this understanding of an expansive function.

The pericope is "densely structured."[5] Formulaic language is used to delineate a sequence of creative acts, displayed in seven panels, each panel a paragraph *(pārāšâ)* in the received Hebrew text. These panels correspond to the six days of God's active work and the culminating seventh day, which is discretely hallowed by and for divine rest.[6] The completeness of the design is schematic rather than fulsome. With the conspicuous, though only partial, exception of what is reported in 1:26-29 about the creation of human life, the account is succinct, even abbreviated. It resembles an itemized list more than a true narrative. We are not told much at all about the physical features of the universe, for example, or how they operate, either separately or in concert; even the taxonomy of the world's nonhuman life

---

Press, 1998], p. 83). Cf. now also Gordon J. Wenham, "The Priority of P," *VT* 49 (1999): 254-58; and, for a brief review of current critical positions on the compositional character of P, Anthony F. Campbell, "The Priestly Text: Redaction or Source?" in *Biblische Theologie und gesellschaftlicher Wandel: Für Norbert Lohfink, SJ,* ed. Georg Braulik, OSB, and Sean McEvenue (Freiburg, Basel, Wien: Herder, 1993), pp. 32-47.

5. See especially the detailed analysis of William P. Brown, *Structure, Role, and Ideology in the Hebrew and Greek Texts of Genesis 1:1–2:3,* SBLDS 132 (Atlanta: Scholars Press, 1993), pp. 59-112 and 249 (where the text is characterized as the most "densely structured in the Hebrew Bible"). Cf. also Bernhard W. Anderson, "A Stylistic Study of the Priestly Creation Story," in *Canon and Authority: Essays in Old Testament Religion and Theology,* ed. George W. Coats and Burke O. Long (Philadelphia: Fortress, 1977), pp. 148-62 (revised in Bernhard W. Anderson, *From Creation to New Creation: Old Testament Perspectives,* OBT [Minneapolis: Fortress, 1994], pp. 42-55); and Odil Hannes Steck, *Der Schöpfungsbericht der Priesterschrift: Studien zur literarkritischen und überlieferungsgeschichtlichen Problematik von Genesis 1,1–2,4a,* Forschungen zur Religion und Literatur des Alten und Neuen Testaments 115 (Göttingen: Vandenhoeck & Ruprecht, 1975).

6. The seven pertinent panels are Gen. 1:1-5, 6-8, 9-13, 14-19, 20-23, 24-31, and 2:1-3. There is no paragraph division in the Hebrew "Massoretic [𝕸]" textual tradition between 1:25 and 26. The break often introduced at this point, according to putative sense (e.g., in NRSV), obscures the visual impact of the seven-part structure and disfigures the parallelism between the twofold work accomplished on the third and the sixth days (1:9-13 and 1:24-31).

remains skeletal here (1:24-25, 29-30).[7] This terseness may, at least in some instances, reflect a guarded approach to mythological motifs.[8] More often, however, the language seems to be intentionally cryptic, not in an effort to conceal antecedents deemed problematic but rather to entice interest in particular themes, suggesting that their significance is yet to be unveiled.

The term "protocol," in its chief literary and diplomatic senses, may suit these facets of the pericope. The text is an initial memorandum — minutes or, more formally, an authoritative chronicle of God's primordial work. As a protocol, moreover, the chronicle not only documents what happened at creation "in the beginning"; it also epitomizes divine procedure and purpose, setting an agenda that previews the creator's continuing relationship to an ordered but still malleable cosmos.

There are three complementary features of the protocol that especially merit closer attention in order to clarify how the text functions as a prologue to the rest of the Pentateuch.

Identity and Character of the Divine Creator

The seven constituent panels of the pericope are tightly focussed on the sequential acts of a divine being who is designated throughout, often and exclusively, by the generic appellation "God" (*'ĕlōhîm*).[9] Usage of the appel-

7. Such brevity cannot easily be explained as due to either ancient Israelite or Priestly disinterest in such matters; compare, for example, the following passages: Lev. 11; 1 Kgs. 4:33; Job 38–39; Prov. 30:24-31.

8. The depiction of primordial conditions in 1:2, with God's "wind" (*rûaḥ*) stirring the surface of abysmal waters, has often been interpreted as an attenuation of a myth of cosmogonic combat, comparable to theomachies attested in the Ugaritic "Ba'l Cycle" and the Babylonian epic *Enuma Elish* (cf. the review in Claus Westermann, *Genesis 1–11: A Commentary,* tr. John J. Scullion, S.J. [Minneapolis: Augsburg, 1984], pp. 28-33). Yet there is no hint of such combat in this text, whose content Cross has more aptly compared with Phoenician and early Greek theogonic traditions of cosmic origins (*Canaanite Myth* [n. 1], pp. 40-43, 120; *Magnalia Dei* [n. 4], pp. 329-38 [*Epic to Canon* (n. 4), pp. 73-83]). The theogonic genre is also compatible with Brown's analysis of animate or personified sea and earth as collaborators with God in creation of life-forms (*Structure* [n. 5], pp. 145-205); compare *Genesis Rabbah* 12.7-8. A useful overview of pertinent theogonic and cosmogonic traditions is provided by Richard J. Clifford, *Creation Accounts in the Ancient Near East and in the Bible,* CBQMS 26 (Washington, D.C.: Catholic Biblical Association of America, 1994).

9. Although this divine appellative is indicative especially of P texts in Genesis (most notably 1:1–2:3 and 9:1-17), it does not suffice to label the term a "proper name" represent-

lation here — thirty-five times without qualifying epithet, honorific title, or adjectival modifier — is stark. It anticipates, if only by way of contrast, the more constructive and sometimes overtly speculative predications of deity elsewhere in the Pentateuch. Already in Genesis 2:4, which introduces the first major part of the genealogical narrative, the generic appellation is joined to the personal name "Yahweh" *(yhwh)* in order to declare that the creator is indeed Israel's tutelary deity.[10] Later, in the report of Abram's encounters with the king of Sodom and with Melchizedek, priest and king of Salem (apparently proto-Jerusalem [cf. Ps. 76:1-2]), association is carefully made between Yahweh and "'El 'Elyon," who is identified as "creator [*qōnēh*] of heaven and earth" (Gen. 14:17-24).[11] Similarly, a series of Priestly texts develops an emblematic equation in which "'El Shaddai," as divine patron of Israel's itinerant ancestors, is the transitional persona between "God" who creates and Yahweh as disclosed to Israel through Moses.[12] At the close of the Pentateuch, Deuteronomic theologiz-

---

ing the "latest stage" of a complex semantic development (cf. Westermann, *Genesis 1–11* [n. 8], pp. 100-101, referring to Ludwig Köhler's work). The P usage, connoting divine creatorship, is a studied component of a dispensational scheme: see Cross, *Canaanite Myth* (n. 1), pp. 296-98; and, with a somewhat different perspective, Israel Knohl, *The Sanctuary of Silence: The Priestly Torah and the Holiness School,* tr. Jackie Feldman and Peretz Rodman (Minneapolis: Fortress, 1995), pp. 124-25, 147-48, 168-69.

10. Use of the designation *yhwh 'ĕlōhîm* (NRSV: "the LORD God") throughout the garden story in 2:4b–3:24, except for the dialogue between the serpent and the woman in 3:1b-5 (where *'ĕlōhîm* appears), has redactional significance, serving to link the P prologue of 1:1–2:3 (using only *'ĕlōhîm*) with the Yahwist's genealogical narrative (preferring *yhwh*) in Gen. 4. However, the usage is neither unique nor ad hoc, though it may be late (see Exod. 9:30; Jon. 4:6; Pss. 72:18; 84:12[11]; 1 Chron. 28:20; 29:1; 2 Chron. 1:9; 6:41-42; 26:18). The ostensible sense is "Yahweh [who is] God"; compare "Yahweh the God" (*yhwh hā'ĕlōhîm*) in 1 Chron. 22:1, 19; 2 Chron. 32:16; cf. Neh. 8:6 as well as the passages listed in note 13 below. The issues are reviewed by Jean L'Hour, "Yahweh Elohim," *RB* 81 (1974): 524-56.

11. Compare "Yahweh, maker [*'ōśēh*] of heaven and earth" in Pss. 115:15; 121:2; 124:8; 134:3; cf. 146:6. See also Deut. 32:8 (associating Yahweh with 'Elyon) and Ps 89:6-9 (identifying Yahweh with 'El). On this and other epithets of 'El, and their relationships to Yahweh in pentateuchal traditions, see Cross, *Canaanite Myth* (n. 1), pp. 44-75; and J. J. M. Roberts, "El," in *The Interpreter's Dictionary of the Bible, Supplementary Volume,* ed. Keith Crim (Nashville: Abingdon, 1976), pp. 255-58.

12. See Gen. 17:1-8; 28:3-4; 35:9-15; 48:3-4; Exod. 6:2-8. On the meaning of "'El Shaddai" see Cross, *Canaanite Myth* (n. 1), pp. 52-60. The theological equation "'Elohim > 'El Shaddai > Yahweh" provides foundational support for a continuity of revelation within Scripture that was summarized as follows by Dale Patrick: "The first chapter of Genesis introduces the God who is recognized in Scripture, and at no place in the Pentateuchal narra-

ing reasserts that Yahweh, whose unique sovereignty has been demonstrated in the singular events of the Israelite exodus from Egypt and the law-giving at Horeb, is the only viable claimant "in heaven above and on the earth beneath" to the appellation "God," which here too designates the universal creator (Deut. 4:32-39).[13] In the protocol of Genesis 1:1–2:3, however, the more intimate, personalized identities of "God" who creates are not specified by name, but they are adumbrated through verbal asseverations of God's work which certify characteristic modes of divine agency in the pentateuchal traditions that follow.

Above all, the protocol attests that created order emerged incrementally, without hint of conflict or caprice, in obedient response to the *articulated* will of the creator. God who creates acts by speaking.[14] Conversely, divine speech and its dramatic consequences together model God's sovereign character.[15] The ten archetypal injunctions — introduced in

---

tive do the human personae lose knowledge of this God. He does reveal his name and designs to various figures at important junctures, but there is no suggestion that these revelations re-establish a knowledge that has been interrupted" ("The Rhetoric of Revelation," *HBT* 16 [1994]: 20).

13. See also Deut. 32:7-9, 39; 2 Sam. 7:22, 28; 2 Kgs. 19:19; Isa. 45:21; Jer. 10:10; Ps. 100:3. Cf. Gen. 24:3; Deut. 7:9; Josh. 22:22; 1 Kgs. 8:60; 2 Chron. 2:11[12]; Neh. 9:6. Philo of Alexandria reflected as follows on the principal connotations of the divine appellations *theos* (= Hebrew *'ĕlōhîm*) and *kyrios* (= Hebrew *yhwh*): "His creative potency is called God, because through it He placed and made and ordered this universe, and the kingly is called Lord, being that with which He governs what has come into being and rules it steadfastly with justice" (*De Vita Mosis* 2.99); compare, however, Ps. 47:8-9[7-8].

14. Notations in the chronicle that God "divided" (*wayyabdēl* [1:4; cf. 1:6, 7, 14, 18]), "made" (*wayya'aś* [1:7, 16, 25]), "fixed" (*wayyittēn* [1:17]), and "created" (*wayyibrā'* [1:21, 27]) report results of God's performative speech (compare, e.g., Num. 23:19-20 and Ps. 33:6-9); they do not support the critical hypothesis of an earlier or variant "deed-account" (*Tatbericht*) of creation overlaid by a "word-account" (*Wortbericht*). A review of scholarship and cogent analysis of the textual evidence are provided by Anderson, "Stylistic Analysis" (n. 5), who also observes (*From Creation* [n. 5], pp. 45-46) that Gen. 1 provides the archetype of the "command-execution" pattern, which is so important elsewhere in P narrative (e.g., Gen. 6:13-22 and Exod. 39:32-43).

15. I.e., the protocol establishes God's superlative credentials to rule and to legislate through direct decree (e.g., Gen. 9:1-17; 17:4-8) but also through mediated speech (e.g., Exod. 4:10-16; 19:7-9; 20:22; Deut. 5:1-5; 18:15-22). See James W. Watts, "The Legal Characterization of God in the Pentateuch," *HUCA* 67 (1996): 1-14; and now also E. Theodore Mullen Jr., *Ethnic Myths and Pentateuchal Foundations: A New Approach to the Formation of the Pentateuch*, Semeia Studies (Atlanta: Scholars Press, 1997), p. 95. On the biblical creation accounts as witnesses to God's "mastery," see Jon D. Levenson, *Creation and the Persistence of*

each instance by "then God said" — not only invoke structural cosmos out of chaos but elicit congruous forms of life, also endowing them with the capacity to flourish in their respective realms.[16] Divine speech that assigns names to the foundational structures (1:5, 8, 10) and that blesses manifold life, to commission its increase (1:22, 28), reinforces the sense of a program whose design is finished on the sixth day but still unfulfilled (see 2:1-2). This sense is further strengthened by the sevenfold declaration that God "saw" both emergent parts and the whole of creation, assessing them to be "good."[17] While these are no doubt aesthetic judgments, they also attribute an ethos to creation, underscoring that its order reflects deliberate decisions generated in the will or "moral imagination" of the creator.[18]

The measure of divine satisfaction with the work of creation is an implicit plan, which later interpretive traditions identify as "wisdom," preexistent "Torah," and "Logos."[19] In the context of the Pentateuch, though, it suffices to recognize that the plan, initially exhibited in the implementation of God's efficacious words, continues to unfold, revealed especially through subsequent acts of divine speaking that both respond to and shape the course of world events. The protocol establishes that cosmos, since it is wholly contingent on God's uncontested

---

Evil: The Jewish Drama of Divine Omnipotence (San Francisco: Harper & Row, 1988), pp. 4-13.

16. Gen. 1:3, 6, 9, 11, 14, 20, 24, 26, 29 (all with the formulaic introduction *wayyo'mer 'ĕlōhîm*) and 1:28 (with *wayyo'mer lāhem 'ĕlōhîm*). Hence the maxim in *Mishnah 'Abot* 5.1: "By ten words the world was created." Implicit here may be comparison with the Decalogue, the ten foundational "words" of God that define the ethos of Israel's covenantal society (cf. Exod. 34:27-28; Deut. 4:13); the association is explicit in *Pesiqta Rabbati* 21.19, though Gen. 1:28 is not counted and 2:18 is paired as the tenth "word" with the prohibition of coveting (tr. William G. Braude, *Pesikta Rabbati: Discourses for Feasts, Fasts, and Special Sabbaths*, Yale Judaica Series 18 (New Haven and London: Yale University Press, 1968), 1:444-46.

17. Gen. 1:4, 10, 12, 18, 21, 25, 31. God's "seeing" is a major trope in pentateuchal theology, usually connoting attentive oversight and judicious discernment; compare, e.g., Gen. 6:5, 12; 11:5; 16:13-14; 22:14; 29:31-32; Exod. 2:25; 3:7; 32:9; Deut. 32:19-20; cf. 1 Sam. 16:7.

18. Compare, e.g., Pss. 19:2; 97:6. See William P. Brown, *The Ethos of the Cosmos: The Genesis of Moral Imagination in the Bible* (Grand Rapids: William B. Eerdmans, 1999), esp. pp. 46-52; and, with particular attention to Job 38–41, Carol Newsom, "The Moral Sense of Nature: Ethics in the Light of God's Speech to Job," *PSB* 15 (1994): 9-27.

19. See, e.g., Prov. 3:19-20; 8:22-31; Sir. 24:1-29; John 1:1-5; *Genesis Rabbah* 1.1. These and other pertinent sources are surveyed in James L. Kugel, *Traditions of the Bible: A Guide to the Bible As It Was at the Start of the Common Era* (Cambridge and London: Harvard University Press, 1998), pp. 44-45, 65-70.

decrees, bears enduring witness to the providence of the creator. This witness is thus an entitlement which, if inchoate here, will later be validated in Israel's hymnic profession that "Yahweh reigns forever and ever" (Exod. 15:18).[20]

Cosmos as Temple

What takes material shape in response to God's speaking is a palatial abode — fashioned over the course of six days and completed on a seventh. While the edifice teems with created life, its architecture is inhabitable on a more sublime scale. Cosmos as epitomized in the protocol of Genesis 1:1–2:3 is suited for the creator's own residence. Philo of Alexandria, in the earlier first century CE, described the basic structure and some of its accoutrements as follows:

> The highest, and in the truest sense the holy, temple of God is, as we must believe, the whole universe, having for its sanctuary the most sacred part of all existence, even heaven, for its votive ornaments the stars, for its priests the angels who are servitors to His powers. . . .[21]

20. See also Balaam's testimony about the theopolitical uniqueness and independence of Jacob/Israel in Num. 23:21: "Yahweh his God is with him, acclaimed as king by him." Otherwise, pentateuchal traditions seem reluctant to use conventional language of kingship to acknowledge Yahweh's ineluctable sovereignty over the cosmos, the world of nations, and even the people Israel — perhaps to aver thereby that the role of "God" transcends the status of any and every "king" (compare, e.g., Exod. 6:28–7:1; 19:5-6; Deut. 10:14-18). Psalms, on the other hand, attests the importance of kingship language (which is often associated with themes of creation) in Israelite theology and liturgy: e.g., Ps. 29:10; 93:1-2; 96:10; 97:1; 99:1; 145:1, 10-13. See James Luther Mays, "The Language of the Reign of God," *Int* 47 (1993): 117-26; and Bernd Janowski, "Das Königtum Gottes in den Psalmen," *Gottes Gegenwart in Israel: Beiträge zur Theologie des Alten Testaments* (Neukirchen-Vluyn: Neukirchener, 1993), pp. 148-213.

21. *De Specialibus Legibus* 1.66 (tr. F. H. Colson, *Philo*, LCL [London: William Heinemann; Cambridge: Harvard University Press, 1937], 7:137). This description introduces Philo's review of pentateuchal legislation that treats the place and practices of Jewish worship (matters which he understands to amplify the decalogic commandment prohibiting idolatry [Exod. 20:4-6; Deut. 5:8-10]). Although Philo makes no direct reference here to Gen. 1:1–2:3, nor does he develop the temple imagery in his treatment of creation in *De Opificio Mundi*, both works provide ample witness to what Levenson calls "the homology of Temple and world" (*Creation* [n. 15], pp. 78-99). See also Jon D. Levenson, "The Temple and

The protocol configures this macrocosmic "temple of God" (*hieron theou* in Philo's Greek) in temporal as well as spatial terms. Although the dimension of time complicates visualization, it is not only indicative of biblical cosmology in general, but also, in the context of the Pentateuch, predictive of the cultic-liturgical significance of emergent cosmic order.[22] Space is arranged into vertical layers, which are delineated chronologically in a pattern of symmetrical triplets (days 1-3 and 4-6) plus the asymmetrical seventh day.

Light is introduced as the "first distinction" in the construction of cosmic space and periodic time (1:3-5).[23] Its invocation, appearance, and

the World," *JR* 64 (1984): 139-58; Martin Metzger, "Himmlische und irdische Wohnstatt Jahwes," *UF* 2 (1970): 139-58; Othmar Keel, *The Symbolism of the Biblical World: Ancient Near Eastern Iconography and the Book of Psalms,* tr. Timothy J. Hallet (New York: Seabury, 1978), pp. 171-76. On biblical and other ancient Near Eastern traditions of both divine and royal temple-construction, see esp. Victor (Avigdor) Hurowitz, *I Have Built You An Exalted House: Temple Building in the Bible in Light of Mesopotamian and Northwest Semitic Writings,* JSOTSup 115, ASORMS 6 (Sheffield: Academic Press, 1992); his remarks on p. 242 indicate the relevance of these traditions for understanding the creation account in Gen. 1:1–2:3.

22. I.e., the seven-day week of creation, culminating in God's rest, models the basic sacral structures of both time and space (exemplified especially in Sabbath observance and the Tabernacle cultus) that will define Israel's existence as a holy people. Overviews of these structures are given by Frank H. Gorman Jr., *The Ideology of Ritual: Space, Time, and Status in the Priestly Theology,* JSOTSup 91 (Sheffield: JSOT Press, 1990); Eric E. Elnes, "Creation and Tabernacle: The Priestly Writer's Environmentalism," *HBT* 16 (1994): 144-55; and Brown, *Ethos* (n. 18), pp. 71-132. Still important in the discussion are earlier studies that identified the principal conceptual and intertextual connections between Gen. 1:1–2:3 and the accounts of the revelation and construction of the Tabernacle in Exod. 25–40: Joseph Blenkinsopp, "The Structure of P," *CBQ* 38 (1976): 275-92; Peter J. Kearney, "Creation and Liturgy: The P Redaction of Ex 25–30," *ZAW* 89 (1977): 375-87; Michael Fishbane, *Text and Texture: Close Readings of Selected Biblical Texts* (New York: Schocken, 1979), pp. 11-13; Moshe Weinfeld, "Sabbath, Temple, and the Enthronement of the Lord — The Problem of the Sitz im Leben of Genesis 1:1–2:3," in *Mélanges biblique et orientaux en l'honneur de M. Henri Cazelles,* ed. A. Caquot and M. Delcor, Alter Orient und Altes Testament 212 (Kevelaer: Butzon & Bercker; Neukirchen-Vluyn: Neukirchener, 1981), pp. 501-12; Peter Weimar, "Sinai und Schöpfung: Komposition und Theologie der priesterschriftlichen Sinaigeschichte," *RB* 95 (1988): 337-85; and Bernd Janowski, "Tempel und Schöpfung: Schöpfungstheologische Aspekte der priesterschriftlichen Heiligtumskonseption," in *Schöpfung und Neusschöpfung,* ed. I. Balderman et al., Jahrbuch für biblische Theologie 5 (Neukirchen-Vluyn: Neukirchener, 1990), pp. 37-70 (reprinted in Janowski, *Gottes Gegenwart in Israel* [n. 20], pp. 214-46).

23. The initial act of creation, in which divinely invoked light pierces the darkness of

immediate approbation portend all subsequent acts of divine discrimination. Darkness and light, normalized in sequence as "night" and "day," veil the structural habitat formed on day one. Architecture becomes visible only on the second day, when the dome of sky is set in the midst of primordial waters, bisecting them into upper and lower deeps (1:6-8); and again on the third day, when oceanic and terrestrial zones are differentiated beneath the dome with its atmosphere (1:9-13). In this initial triplet of days, cosmic construction takes place from the top down, in tiers that descend from the supernal realm of light and darkness, to the celestial hemisphere, and then to the foundational region where seascape and landscape are ordered topographically. In the parallel triplet of days four through six, the three cosmic realms already distinguished are outfitted from top to bottom with "all the host" of heaven and earth (see 2:1).[24] Astral bodies are formed and set in regulated motion "in" the dome of sky, to serve as temporal signs and sources of light (1:14-19); aquatic life and birds are let loose to adorn the expanses of seas and of the air between earth and sky (1:20-23); and many other varieties of creatures, including human beings, are created with earth as their habitat (1:24-31).

The repetitive, formulaic language used to structure the chronicle of the creator's work on days one through six is missing in the protocol's final paragraph. Absent here too is divine speech. The account of the sixth day already includes God's own retrospect on creation, declaring everything that has been made to be "very good" (1:31). The summary notice at the beginning of the final paragraph (2:1) looks back further, behind the invocation of light in 1:3 to the preface in 1:1-2, reporting that "heaven and earth" with their attendant host now "were complete." Even so, as we are told in 2:2-3, the overall work of creation was not "completed" until God

---

space, thus establishes what Jan Assmann (developing George Spencer Brown's "first Law of Construction") cogently identifies as "the most fundamental of all distinctions, the distinction between God and the world" (*Moses the Egyptian: The Memory of Egypt in Western Monotheism* [Cambridge and London: Harvard University Press, 1997], p. 8). This differentiation between creator and creation is the crux of what Assmann labels "the Mosaic distinction" (pp. 1-8, 168-207). Characteristic of both ancient Egyptian and Mesopotamian cosmologies, on the other hand, is the consubstantiality of creator and creation that yields pantheism; see note 31 below.

24. The locution "all their host" *(kol-ṣĕbā'ām)*, with "host" extended to include the fullness of created life beneath the celestial realm, is unusual (cf. Ps. 33:6; 148:1-6; Isa. 45:12; Neh. 9:6); Westermann (*Genesis 1–11* [n. 8], p. 169) cites Isa. 34:2 as the closest parallel. Compare the terminology in Ps. 24:1; 69:34; 96:11-12; 146:6.

ceased from all labor on the seventh day. What is more, the seventh day was wordlessly blessed by God, to set it apart from the preceding six as sanctified. This day of silent divine rest is a consummation of all that has gone before because it inaugurates God's residence within the cosmic temple.[25]

Although specifically located only in hallowed, sabbatical time, the resting place must be the chamber that Philo identified as the temple's heavenly "sanctuary" *(neōs)*.[26] Its microcosmic counterpart is the inner or upper adytum of an earthly temple.[27] The celestial prototype, as we may

25. See esp. 1 Kgs. 8:1-11; these rites, and the primal Sabbath of Gen. 2:2-3, may be compared to the Egyptian ceremony of "Ceding the Temple to Its Lord" *(swḏ k3t n nb.s),* which was celebrated on the eve of the New Year. See A. M. Blackman and H. W. Fairman, "The Consecration of an Egyptian Temple according to the Use of Edfu," *JEA* 32 (1946): 75-91 (reprinted in *Gods, Priests and Men: Studies in the Religion of Pharaonic Egypt by Aylward M. Blackman,* ed. Alan B. Lloyd [London and New York: Kegan Paul, 1998], pp. 326-42); and E. A. E. Reymond, *From Ancient Egyptian Hermetic Writings,* Mitteilungen aus der Papyrussammlung der Österreichischen Nationalbibliothek (Papyrus Erzherzog Rainer) Neue Serie 11 (Wien: Brüder Hollinek, 1977), pp. 28, 104-5. On the association of sabbatical rest with God's enthronement in early Jewish liturgical traditions, see Weinfeld, "Sabbath" (n. 22), pp. 508-10; and Levenson, *Creation* (n. 15), pp. 119-20. According to Philo, the weekly Sabbath is, or ought to be, a universal, "public" celebration of the birth of the cosmos (*De Opificio Mundi* 89). On themes of divine rest and enthronement in ancient Near Eastern lore, see Bernard F. Batto, "The Sleeping God: An Ancient Near Eastern Motif of Divine Sovereignty," *Biblica* 68 (1987): 156-66; and Hurowitz, *Exalted House* (n. 21), pp. 330-31.

26. This heavenly sanctum, which is sometimes designated "the abode of [God's] holiness" (*mĕʿôn qodšô* [Jer. 25:30; 2 Chron. 30:27; cf. Deut. 26:15]), bears at least generic resemblance to the celestial chambers built for Baʿl Haddu in Ugaritic lore (a central theme of Tablets 3-4 of the "Baʿl Cycle" [*CAT* 1.3-4]) and by Marduk for his own supernal rest in the Babylonian *Enuma Elish* (Tablet 4.141-45; cf. 1.70-84). For recent translations, see Mark S. Smith, *Ugaritic Narrative Poetry,* ed. Simon B. Parker, Writings from the Ancient World 9 (Atlanta: Society of Biblical Literature/Scholars Press, 1997), pp. 105-41; and Benjamin R. Foster, *Before the Muses: An Anthology of Akkadian Literature* (Bethesda: CDL, 1993), 1:356-57, 377.

27. I.e., the "most holy [place]" *(qōdeš haqqŏdāšîm),* whether of the Tabernacle (Exod. 26:34) or of Jerusalem's Solomonic and Herodian Temples (1 Kgs. 6:16, 19-20, 23-28, 31; 8:6-8; 2 Chron. 3:8-9; *Mishnah Kelim* 1.9; cf. Josephus, *Jewish War* 5.219). In describing the Tabernacle complex as a microcosm, Josephus likened the curtained *neōs* or *adyton* to the inaccessible realm of heaven (*Ant.* 3.123-25, 180-81). Compare the description of the upper stage of the Babylonian temple-tower (with an imageless *neōs*) in Herodotus 1.181; see also Keel, *Symbolism* (n. 21), pp. 166-71 (with particular attention to Egyptian evidence).

suppose on the basis of other biblical data, is a pavilion of thick darkness in the realm of pristine light.[28] Its construction should therefore be God's work hidden in day one. But the protocol leaves these matters veiled. It does so with the knowledge that what is most important about them will be revealed in due course — in divine word and vision to Moses atop Sinai (Exod. 25–31) — when Israel, reclaimed by its divine patron from Egyptian servitude, may be ready for constitution as a sanctified people among the nations, to be set apart like creation's archetypal shrine of the Sabbath for the creator's indwelling presence.

God's Image in Humankind

According to the protocol's chronicle of divine work, human beings, expressly both "male and female," were fashioned after other species of terrestrial life in a second, distinctive act of creation on the sixth day. They were also given a unique blessing, commissioning them not only to reproduce (cf. Gen. 1:22) but to exercise jurisdiction or guardianship over other creatures who inhabit with them the hemisphere that is roofed by the dome of sky and has the earth as its platform (1:27-28). The creator's plan to this effect is first voiced in council (1:26), addressed to an unnamed cohort that Philo understood to be the angelic servitors of the celestial sanctuary:[29]

> Let us make humankind ['ādām] in our image, according to our likeness, so that they may have dominion over the fish of the sea, over the birds of the sky, and over the beasts — over the whole earth and over everything that moves upon the earth.[30]

28. Compare Exod. 24:10; 1 Kgs. 8:12-13; Isa. 40:22; Ezek. 1:22-28; Ps. 104:1-4, 13; Job 38:19-21. See also the texts collected in Kugel, *Traditions* (n. 19), pp. 713-14.

29. *De Specialibus Legibus* 1.66; cf. *De Opificio Mundi* 72-75; and *De Confusione Linguarum* 168-79; cf. *Genesis Rabbah* 8. Compare the assembly convened by Enlil to design and create humankind in the Babylonian *Atrahasis Epic*, Tablet 1.99-305 (tr. Foster, *Before the Muses* [n. 26], 1:162-68); and also the divine assemblies portrayed esp. in Isa. 6:1-3; 1 Kgs. 22:19-22; Ps. 89:6-8[5-7]; Job 1:6; 2:1; Dan. 7:9-10. Cf. E. Theodore Mullen Jr., *The Divine Council in Canaanite and Early Hebrew Literature*, HSM 24 (Chico: Scholars Press, 1980).

30. So 𝔐, with *wĕyirdû* (simple conjunction + imperfect, following the cohortative *naʿăśeh*) understood to express purpose: "that they *may* have dominion." On the syntax, see Theophile J. Meek, "Result and Purpose Clauses in Hebrew," *Jewish Quarterly Review* 46

Both here and in the following report of the plan's implementation, the protocol supposes the singular "image" *(ṣelem)* to constitute a discriminable "likeness" *(dĕmût)*, a formal resemblance that is shared by divine and human pluralities ("us . . . our . . . they") to the apparent exclusion of all other cosmic entities, including other earth-creatures of flesh and blood.[31] Moreover, this unifying image in humankind has a sacramental as well as an essentially corporeal function: Adamic beings are animate icons; they are empowered by the "image" and its correlative blessing to be a terrestrial counterpart to God's heavenly entourage.[32] The peculiar purpose for their creation is "theophanic": to represent or mediate the sovereign presence of deity within the central nave of the cosmic temple, just as cult-images were supposed to do in conventional sanctuaries.[33]

The view inscribed in the protocol acknowledges humankind to be an inherently ambivalent species whose temporal existence blurs, by de-

---

(1956): 40-43; and Thomas O. Lambdin, *Introduction to Biblical Hebrew* (New York: Charles Scribner's Sons, 1971), p. 119 (noted also by Mullen, *Ethnic Myths* [n. 15], p. 97 n. 35).

31. See J. Maxwell Miller, "In the 'Image' and 'Likeness' of God," *JBL* 91 (1972): 289-304. Neither the protocol nor any other pentateuchal witness provides support for a more inclusive or pantheistic view of the divine "image," such as the one recently proposed by Langdon Gilkey ("Nature As the Image of God: Signs of the Sacred," *ThT* 57 [1994]: 127-41). In classical antiquity, such a view was attributed to Moses by Strabo (*Geography* 16.2.35): ". . . God is this one thing alone that encompasses us all and encompasses land and sea — the thing which we call heaven, or universe, or the nature of all that exists" (*The Geography of Strabo*, tr. Horace Leonard Jones, LCL [London: William Heinemann, 1930], 7:283).

32. See Ps. 115:16. Egyptian solar theology of the Ramesside period (late 14th-12th centuries BCE) posits a three-tiered cosmos, each featuring an aspect or component of Amun's presence, with earth being the realm of the divine "image" *(ḥnnty* and *'ḫn)*. See Jan Assmann, *Egyptian Solar Religion of the New Kingdom: Re, Amun and the Crisis of Polytheism*, tr. Anthony Alcock (London and New York: Kegal Paul, 1995), pp. 174-77; and Erik Hornung, *Conceptions of God in Ancient Egypt: The One and the Many*, tr. John Baines (Ithaca: Cornell University Press, 1982), pp. 228-29. Cf. Eberhard Otto, "Der Mensch als Geschöpf und Bild Gottes in Agypten," in *Probleme biblischer Theologie: Gerhard von Rad zum 70. Geburtstag*, ed. Hans Walter Wolff (München: Chr. Kaiser, 1971), pp. 335-48.

33. See esp. Thorkild Jacobsen, "The Graven Image," in *Ancient Israelite Religion: Essays in Honor of Frank Moore Cross*, ed. Patrick D. Miller, Jr., Paul D. Hanson, and S. Dean McBride (Philadelphia: Fortress, 1987), pp. 15-32. On the procedures for vivification of cultic statues, see also Aylward M. Blackman, "The Rite of Opening the Mouth in Ancient Egypt and Babylonia," *JEA* 10 (1924): 47-59 (reprinted in Lloyd [ed.], *Gods, Priests, and Men* [n. 25], pp. 102-14); Siegfried Morenz, *Egyptian Religion*, tr. Ann Keep (Ithaca: Cornell University Press, 1973), pp. 150-58.

sign, the otherwise sharp distinction between creator and creation. It is thus important to underscore that the "image" defines a contingent relationship — the physical and functional dependence of humankind upon God.[34] Human beings are identified as a family of earth-creatures who belong to the creator in an intimate, peculiar way. Ostensibly like the angelic host, with whom the creator deliberates about their theomorphic constitution, human beings are instruments of divine providence. They are endowed with attributes that give them the capacity to act on God's behalf; but they are not enfranchised to exercise hegemony as autonomous agents, either to subjugate one another or to tyrannize other created beings with whom they are supposed to share earth's sufficient produce (1:29-30). Similarly, just as the protocol nowhere uses the explicit language of kingship to describe the cosmic role and preeminent status of God who creates, so the divine "image" and the commission to "rule" (1:28) neither require nor preclude a specifically royal interpretation.[35] Once again, the protocol's circumspection seems to be quite deliberate and, in this case, enormously portentous. The crucial question of how iconic humankind will manifest, extend, or imitate the sovereignty of God within the cosmic temple is left open. What remains intentionally ill-defined or unresolved here will unfold as the plot of the Pentateuch's genealogical narrative. As viewed especially through the lens of the protocol, the plot's significance remains ecumenical, even when the narrative begins to focus closely on the offspring of second sons of one particular lineage within the segmented and

---

34. In the words of W. Sibley Towner, the divine image signifies ". . . a relational capacity that makes possible a life-giving partnership with God on the one side and tender, responsible husbandry and friendship with our fellow creatures on the other" ("The Future of Nature," *Int* 50 [1996]: 32).

35. Gen. 1:26-28 may, as now generally supposed, represent a democratization of royal ideology, extending to the whole of humankind the concept (attested especially in cuneiform sources) of the king as created in the "image" of deity, thereby becoming an embodiment of divine power and authority. On this, see esp. Levenson, *Creation* (n. 15), pp. 111-17; Hans Wildberger, "Das Abbild Gottes: Gen. 1,26-30," *TZ* 21 (1965): 245-59; and John Van Seters, "The Creation of Man and The Creation of the King," *ZAW* 101 (1989): 341. Even so, it should not be forgotten that this concept of royal apotheosis is itself an adaptation or extension of the theophanic significance attributed to cult statues of deity: see Peter Machinist, "Literature as Politics: The Tukulti-Ninurta Epic and the Bible," *CBQ* 38 (1976): 467 n. 39; and William W. Hallo, "Texts, Statues and the Cult of the Divine King," in *Congress Volume: Jerusalem 1986*, ed. J. A. Emerton, VTSup 40 (Leiden: E. J. Brill, 1988), pp. 55-66.

widely dispersed human family. The plot will reach its climactic stages when the vocation of those revealed to be the creator's treasured firstborn is announced at Sinai (Exod. 19:3-6) and their institutional transformation into a "sacerdotal dominion and holy nation" commences.

III. Pentateuchal Covenants in Cosmological Perspective

Embryonic though the Adamic job description may be in the protocol, the constitution of humankind to serve as an active, sacramental link between creator and other creatures makes both God and the cosmic ecosystem potentially vulnerable to human initiatives and failings. In this respect the biblical drama is comparable to other ancient Near Eastern cosmological traditions in which theogony, the usually irenic generation of the primal gods, sets the stage for cosmogony, the struggle among the deities to establish and increase their respective hegemonies within the inchoate bounds of creation. The pentateuchal version of cosmogony lacks an individuated theistic cast, but it is by no means benign: it pits God against God's own incarnated image.[36] This multifaceted conflict never comes to complete resolution in the Pentateuch itself (nor is it fully resolved, except in visionary forms, in the extended corpora of Jewish and Christian scriptures). The conflict is mitigated, however. This happens principally through a series of figures whose heroic lives vindicate God's trust in the capacity of at least some human beings to serve as loyal, courageous, and effective instruments of divine rule. These assisted but uncoerced human victories elicit divine accommodations, which involve refocusing or calibration of the commission spoken by the creator to humankind at the time of its creation (Gen. 1:28-30). Each such accommodation is sealed by a covenant. The primordial commission, which is at once solemn command and blessing, has precedence in this broad scheme of divine providence.[37] As im-

---

36. Although rare elements of theomachy do appear in the Pentateuch (see Exod. 12:12; Num. 33:4; Deut. 33:27), only in later Jewish and Christian apocalyptic sources is the pentateuchal cosmogony recast as a conflict between superhuman forces (e.g., Dan. 7; Rev. 20-22; *1 Enoch* 6–11). Divine "image" figures as a crux in Jack Miles's imaginative construal of the broader biblical drama: "The plot begins with God's desire for a self-image. It thickens when God's self-image becomes a maker of self-images, and God resents it" (*God: A Biography* [New York: Alfred A. Knopf, 1995], p. 21; cf. pp. 406-8).

37. See the perceptive remarks of R. Kendall Soulen, who sketches a biblical "theol-

portant as they are in supporting the theological weight of the Pentateuch, the five covenants — with their particular configurations of assurances and responsibilities — are subordinate measures.[38] In forensic terms, the covenants are codicils to an existing relationship rather than new or independent contracts. They are formal instruments by which supplementary decisions are integrated into the cosmic design of God who creates. These supplements are introduced to facilitate and sustain the efficacy of the protocol's benedictory commission, on behalf of all created life and in spite of demonstrated weaknesses in the human agents whose formation in the divine image is endangered but never abrogated.

The Noahic Covenant

A "primeval history," if it is useful to distinguish such within the received text of Genesis, should be limited to 2:4–9:29, comprising the first three interconnected segments of the extended genealogical narrative.[39] The

---

ogy of God's blessing," anchored in Gen. 1:28 (*The God of Israel and Christian Theology* [Minneapolis: Fortress, 1996], pp. 114-34). See also the lucid overview of pentateuchal evidence provided by Bernard Och, "Creation and Redemption: Towards a Theology of Creation," *Judaism* 44 (1995): 226-43. The "kerygmatic" signficance of Gen. 1:28 in the theology of P was identified by Walter Brueggemann, "The Kerygma of the Priestly Writers," *ZAW* 84 (1972): 397-413 (reprinted in Walter Brueggemann and Hans Walter Wolff, *The Vitality of Old Testament Traditions* [Atlanta: John Knox, 1975], pp. 101-3, 143-51).

38. Structurally, the pentad of covenants is the spine of the Pentateuch's genealogical narrative, which joins creation of the people Israel to the prologue's chronicle of world ordering. The work as a whole and in its principal parts is disfigured by either adding to or substracting from the pentad. I.e., disfigurement occurs when a "covenant of works" is identified in Gen. 2:16-17 (which view became a feature of Reformed theology in the seventeenth century [e.g., the "Westminster Confession of Faith," 6.038,101]) or when a primal "covenant with Adam" is posited as implicit in Gen. 1:28–2:4 (Julius Wellhausen, *Prolegomena to the History of Israel*, tr. J. Sutherland Black and Allan Menzies [Edinburgh: Adam and Charles Black, 1885], pp. 338-39). Divine command, promise, and blessing do not in themselves, either individually or in combination, constitute covenantal acts or relationships. However, greater distortion of the received structure and theological coherence of the Pentateuch results when the final two covenants of the pentad — the one granted to Phinehas and his lineage (Num. 25:10-13) and the one enacted with Israel "in the land of Moab" (Deut. 29:1[28:69]) — are severely devaluated or ignored.

39. The chief point is to recognize the epochal significance of the world flood in the narrative structure of Genesis, an import it also has in ancient Mesopotamian mythohisto-

first and second of these segments are complementary (2:4–4:26; 5:1–6:8). Each starts at creation, with a heading that links it into the protocol: "These are the generations of heaven and earth when they were created" (2:4a [cf. 1:1; 2:1]); "This is the book of the generations of humankind . . . made in God's likeness . . . male and female. . . . [God] blessed them and named them humankind in the day of their creation" (5:1-2 [cf. 1:26-28]). Together these segments trace the antediluvian propagation of Adamic beings, emphasizing the male line of descent from Adam through his youngest son Seth, who replaces the murdered second-born, Abel (4:25-26; 5:3-8). The third segment (6:9–9:29) nests into the second, developing the story of Noah and his offspring already adumbrated in 5:28-32 and 6:8. The Sethite scion whose naming by Lamech forecasts only modest consolation for human agricultural labors, to be gained from "the soil that Yahweh has cursed" (5:29 [cf. 3:17-19; 4:11-12]), takes on a much grander role in the third segment. He is reintroduced at the outset as uncommonly "innocent" or "complete" *(tāmîm)*, "a just man" *('îš ṣaddîq)* who apparently alone among his long-lived contemporaries "walked with God" *('et-hā'ĕlōhîm hithallek* [6:9; cf. 5:22, 24]). Through this mature Noah's extraordinary industry — now as boat builder, zookeeper, and navigator rather than viticulturist (cf. 9:20) — remnants of all terrestrial life are enabled to survive the catastrophic, pollution-cleansing waters of the universal flood.[40]

As drafted in Genesis 9:8-17, the covenant initially pledged to Noah, in the context of God's privileged instructions to him concerning the impending inundation (6:18), has a broad ecological significance and constituency.[41] It takes the form of a unilateral divine decree, declaring that

---

riography. On this, see W. Malcolm Clark, "The Flood and the Structure of the Pre-patriarchal History," *ZAW* 85 (1971): 184-211; and Tikva Frymer-Kensky, "The Atrahasis Epic and Its Significance for Our Understanding of Genesis 1–9," *BA* 40 (1977): 147-55.

40. For this understanding of the flood as an act of purgation, in response to the earth-polluting "violence" of bloodshed, see Tikva Frymer-Kensky, "The Atrahasis Epic" (n. 39 above); and "Pollution, Purification, and Purgation in Biblical Israel," in *The Word of the Lord Shall Go Forth: Essays in Honor of David Noel Freedman*, ed. Carol L. Meyers and Michael O'Connor (Winona Lake: Eisenbrauns, 1983), pp. 399-414.

41. Cf. Anderson, *From Creation* (n. 5), pp. 147-64; and Rolf Rendtorff, *Canon and Theology: Overtures to an Old Testament Theology*, tr. and ed. Margaret Kohl, OBT (Minneapolis: Fortress, 1993), pp. 92-113. Especially in light of modern environmental concerns, it is tempting to exaggerate the ecological scope and significance of Gen. 9:8-17, as does Ronald A. Simkins when he identifies the text as God's "covenant with all creation," subordinat-

earth and its creatures will "never again" be wholly annihilated by flood-waters (9:9-11, 15). Although there is nothing to negotiate, the covenantal decree is enacted performatively "with" Noah and family, "with" their posterity, but also "with" every other species of life preserved through Noah's diligent service.[42] The "bow" that appears arched in storm clouds over the earth is, of course, the mnemonic "sign" *('ôt)* of this "everlasting covenant" *(běrît 'ôlām);* it is set both meteorologically and transactionally "between God and every living creature of all flesh that is on the earth" (9:12-17).[43]

This first covenant of the pentad is thus not made with Noah alone, nor is it granted as a reward per se for his superlative fidelity. It is, nevertheless, "Noahic" in a crucial, consequential sense. God's self-limiting deposition — precluding another flood of such devastating proportions — presupposes what Noah has modeled: the disciplined character and capacity to perform the delegated duties of guardianship for which humankind was originally constituted in the creator's own image.[44] Accordingly, the covenantal stabilizing of the terrestrial ecosystem is conditioned by the renovated Adamic charge addressed to Noah and his offspring in 9:1-7. Reiterations of the protocol's benedictory commission ("Be fruitful and multiply . . ." [9:1, 7; cf. 1:28a]) frame a revised job description that concedes or, better, entrusts a greater and more accountable exercise of authority than before (9:2-6; cf. 1:28b-30). The key provisions extend human stewardship within God's cosmic temple to include matters of life and death, especially punishment of homicide — thereby criminalizing the principal form of "violence" that had corrupted "all flesh" and polluted earth itself in the antediluvian epoch (cf. 6:11-13).[45] In effect, the en-

---

ing the role of Noah (*Creator and Creation: Nature in the Worldview of Ancient Israel* [Peabody: Henrickson, 1994], pp. 154-55).

42. In Sir. 44:18 this is apparently interpreted to refer to a series of "covenants" (Greek *diathēkai*) vouchsafed to Noah as deliverer.

43. On the character of this sign, in relationship to others in P pentateuchal traditions, see Michael V. Fox, "The Sign of the Covenant: Circumcision in the Light of the Priestly *'ôt* Etiologies," *RB* 81 (1974): 568-73.

44. Consistent with the protocol's view of humankind in Gen. 1:26-30, the post-diluvian covenant in P is more positively anthropocentric than the resigned, somber position expressed by the Yahwist in 8:20-22.

45. See Philo, *De Specialibus Legibus* 3.83-84, where homicide is defined as "sacrilege" (*hierosylia*) because it is a crime against God's own "glorious image" *(pagkalēs eikonos)* in human form; cf. also *De Decalogo* 132-34. The significance of *běṣelem 'ĕlōhîm* in 9:6 as Adamic empowerment is insightfully treated, with attention to pertinent cuneiform evi-

hanced dominion received by Noah and bequeathed to his posterity inaugurates a rule of law that responds to the primeval devolution of creaturely existence into moral anarchy (cf. 4:4-15, 23-24; 6:5-8).[46] It is this "Noahic" turning point in the history of terrestrial affairs which the creator ratifies in the covenantal deposition of 9:8-17.

The strange concluding episode of Noah's story, in 9:20-27, deserves brief notice because it not only previews the continuing drama of the genealogical narrative but gives conflicted witness to the God-like power that Adamic creatures have acquired.[47] Noah, here a compromised patriarch, passes judgment upon his own heirs. He discriminates their respective destinies by invoking — ostensibly for the first time within the realm of human society — divine sanctions of curse and blessing. If punitive estrangement between humankind and the soil receded with the flood, and was forsworn as an option by the creator (cf. 8:21-22), primordial alienation within the human family seems to have gained a new purchase through Noah's juridical enfranchisement. In any case, the mechanisms of blessing and cursing will need and receive further covenantal adjustment.

The Covenant with Israel's Forebears

According to the broad pentateuchal portrait of divine providence, ancient Israel's formation into the people of God was neither an autochthonous

---

dence, by Jeffrey H. Tigay, "The Image of God and the Flood: Some New Developments," in *Llmd wllmd: Studies in Jewish Education and Judaica in Honor of Louis Newman,* ed. Alexander M. Shapiro and Burton I. Cohen (New York: Ktav, 1984), pp. 174-78. On the thematic and juridical connections between Gen. 9:1-7 and 1:28-30, see Susan Niditch, *Chaos to Cosmos: Studies in Biblical Patterns of Creation,* Studies in the Humanities 6 (Chico: Scholars Press, 1985), pp. 23-24; also Odil Hannes Steck, *World and Environment,* Biblical Encounter Series (Nashville: Abingdon, 1978), pp. 102-13.

46. Gen. 9:2-6, interpreted together with 2:16-17, was construed in rabbinical exegesis as stipulating at least seven commandments — including institution of a judicial system — incumbent upon all of Noah's descendants (i.e., Gentiles as well as Jews); see especially *Babylonian Talmud, Sanhedrin* 56a-60a. The import of this interpretive tradition in later medieval Jewish thought is sketched by Dov I. Frimer, "Israel, the Noahide Laws and Maimonides: Jewish-Gentile Legal Relations in Maimonidean Thought," in *Jewish Law Association Studies II: The Jerusalem Conference Volume,* ed. Bernard S. Jackson (Atlanta: Scholars Press, 1986), pp. 89-102.

47. See Niditch, *Chaos to Cosmos* (n. 45), pp. 50-55.

development nor a private affair between a particular deity and a select company of devotees.[48] Instead, Israel's corporate identity takes shape interactively, through its ancestral connections with and differentiation from other ethnic and political entities that occupy the wider world over which the creator remains sovereign. Although this perspective is certainly attested elsewhere (e.g., Deut. 4:32-39; 26:5-9; Josh. 24:2-18), it is afforded especially by the major "patriarchal" segments of the genealogical narrative (Gen. 11:10–37:1).[49] Set against the backdrop of the dispersion of Noahide families, sketched in the ethnography of Genesis 10:1–11:9, these segments span the chronological chasm between the Noahic and Mosaic epochs of covenantal history. They do so not only in a unilinear, ethnocentric way — featuring the familiar generational sequence of Abram/ Abraham, Isaac, and Jacob/Israel — but also by reaffirming the inclusiveness of the creator's benedictory commission, which was addressed both originally and again through Noah to all humankind.

Divine blessing, conceptualized in terms of vocation, compels the two signal themes of the patriarchal history.[50] The themes are variously articulated, usually in the form of divine first-person promises addressed to the principal patriarchs; they are often conjoined, as is the case in their initial appearance in the imperatival "call" of Abram (12:1-3):[51]

---

48. A somewhat different viewpoint is suggested in Deut. 32:7-9.

49. For a useful overview, see Frank Crüsemann, "Human Solidarity and Ethnic Identity: Israel's Self-Definition in the Genealogical System of Genesis," in *Ethnicity and the Bible,* ed. Mark G. Brett (Leiden, New York, Koln: E. J. Brill, 1996), pp. 57-76. Cf. also Richard H. Moye, "In the Beginning: Myth and History in Genesis and Exodus," *JBL* 109 (1990): 577-98.

50. See the classic study of Hans Walter Wolff, "The Kerygma of the Yahwist" (tr. Wilbur A. Benware), *Int* 20 (1966): 131-58 (reprinted in *The Vitality of Old Testament Traditions* [n. 37], pp. 41-66, 132-38); and also Thomas W. Mann, "'All the Families of the Earth': The Theological Unity of Genesis," *Int* 45 (1991): 341-53. The pertinent themes, which are identified below in terms of Abrahamic political entitlement and Abrahamic benefaction of the world's dispersed families, correspond substantially to what Soulen calls "economies of difference and mutual dependence" (*God of Israel* [n. 37], esp. pp. 116-17). The data are classified and qualified more elaborately by David J. A. Clines, *The Theme of the Pentateuch,* JSOTSup 10 (Sheffield: JSOT Press, 1978), esp. pp. 29-60.

51. Cf. also Gen. 18:18; 22:17-18; 26:3-5; 28:14. In 12:1-3, syntax is of critical importance in recognizing the parallelistic segmentation and complementarity of principal clauses. The "call," or two-part charge to Abram, consists of coordinated imperatives ("Go [*lek-lĕkâ*] . . . and be [*wehyēh*] . . ."), each clause of which is followed by a statement of divine purpose that begins with a simple conjunction plus first-person imperfect subjunctive/

Go from your land, your kin, and your father's house to the land that
I will show you
  so that I may make you into a great nation, bless you, and magnify
    your name;
and be a blessing
  so that I may bless those who bless you, but anyone who
    disparages you I will curse;
  thus, by means of you, all the families of the earth will be blessed.

Here, in 12:1-2a, the political entitlement of Abram's heirs — concretely
expressed as nationhood and sovereign name — is contingent on his own
obedient response to God's command, which directs him to leave one
homeland behind and to be led into discovery of another.[52] The promis-
sory motifs of territorial dominion and national grandeur are also associated with the first theme elsewhere, though numerous "progeny" is usually
emphasized and the formulaic benediction of 1:28 and 9:1, 7 ("Be fruitful
and multiply") is even more directly echoed.[53] The second theme of blessing is an extension of the first. Abrahamic entitlement becomes a prospective means of extramural benefaction, an instrument through which the
creator's gifts of well-being may be shared with other terrestrial "families"
(12:2b-3) or may be distributed anew among all the separated "nations of
the earth" that are implicitly descended from Noah (18:18; 22:18; 26:4;
28:14).[54]

---

cohortative (12:1-2a, 2b-3a); the final clause (3b) expresses the intended result of the divine
initiative that is to be implemented through Abram. This analysis differs somewhat from the
proposals of Wolff ("Kerygma" [n. 50], pp. 137-40); and Patrick D. Miller Jr. ("Syntax and
Theology in Genesis xii 3a," *VT* 34 [1984]: 472-76); cf. now also J. Gerald Janzen, *Abraham
and All the Families of the Earth: A Commentary on the Book of Genesis 12–50*, International
Theological Commentary (Grand Rapids: Wm. B. Eerdmans, 1993), pp. 15-16. On the syn-
tactical distinction between purpose and result clauses in Hebrew, see the works of Meek
and Lambdin cited in n. 30.

52. On the significance of Abram/Abraham as "common ancestor" of kindred na-
tions, allied under the hegemony of David and Solomon, see George E. Mendenhall, "The
Nature and Purpose of the Abraham Narratives," in *Ancient Israelite Religion: Essays in
Honor of Frank Moore Cross*, ed. Patrick D. Miller Jr., Paul D. Hanson, and S. Dean McBride
(Philadelphia: Fortress, 1987), pp. 337-56.

53. See Gen. 17:6, 20; 28:3-4, 13; 35:11-12; 48:4. Cf. Gen. 46:3-4, which previews fulfillment of the promise.

54. On the use of both Nip'al and Hitpa'el forms of *brk* in these passages, see Cross,
Canaanite Myth (n. 1), p. 263; and Mendenhall, "Abraham Narratives" (n. 52), p. 350. The

The benedictory commission as channeled through Israel's ancestors does not negate the the charge given to all Noahides, which was sealed by the creator's covenantal pledge to them (9:1-7, 8-17). Nevertheless, reinvestment of the charge in a particular lineage is a significant accommodation, one that acknowledges the diversity of humankind and also prepares for providential fulfillment of the protocol's agenda of sanctification. Noah's isolated, consequential "walking with God" (6:9) exemplified what Yahweh, in the guise of 'El Shaddai, asks of Abraham and his heirs: "Walk before me and be complete" (*hithallēk lĕpānay wehyēh tāmîm* [17:1; cf. 48:15]). Their physical and spiritual itineracy foreshadows in turn the vita of Moses as well as the discipline of Moses' polity that will enlist some of Abraham's beneficiaries to "walk" together faithfully in Yahweh's revealed ways (cf. Deut. 10:12; 11:22; 26:17). This extraordinary continuity of both divine sovereignty and human vocation, obedient to the creator's decrees (cf. Gen. 18:19; 22:16-18; 26:5), is consolidated in the ancestral covenant of Genesis 17.[55] Although anticipated by the covenantal grant in 15:7-21, which formalizes through enacted oath to Abram the promised endowments of progeny and land, the "everlasting covenant" (*bĕrît 'ōlām*) of 17:7-14 is bolder, both more intensely personal and more sublimely indicative of Israel's future career as God's people.[56] Its crux is the divine pledge to Abram "to be God to you [*lihyôt lĕkâ lē'lōhîm*] and to your descendants after you" (v. 7).[57] And yet this guaranteed relationship with the creator is

---

concept expressed by the command "and be a blessing" (*wehyēh bĕrākâ*, 12:2b) is scarcely unique to this context. Compare esp. Isa. 19:24-25; Ezek. 34:26; Zech. 8:13.

55. See also Exod. 2:24; 6:2-5; Lev. 26:42; cf. Deut. 1:10-11; 7:8-11; Sir. 44:19–45:1. Still important is the study by Walter Zimmerli, who argues that in the scheme of P the covenant of Gen. 17 takes theological precedence over the Sinaitic covenant, which is its communal implementation ("Sinaibund und Abrahambund: Ein Beitrag zum Verständnis der Priesterschrift," *TZ* 16 (1960): 268-79 [reprinted in *Gottes Offenbarung: Gesammelte Aufsätze zum Alten Testament*, Theologische Bücherei 19 (München: Chr. Kaiser, 1963), pp. 205-61]).

56. On the compositional structure of the "Abraham cycle" of narratives in Gen. 11:27–22:24, see Gary A. Rendsburg, *The Redaction of Genesis* (Winona Lake: Eisenbrauns, 1986), pp. 27-52. Especially noteworthy is the bracket formed by 12:1-9 and 22:1-19, both of which exhibit the key terminology of Abrahamic entitlement and benefaction. When 15:1–16:16 and 18:1-15 are identified as an inner bracket (concerned with the births of Ishmael and Isaac respectively), 17:1-17 stands alone at the mid-point of a palistrophic arrangement, centering the two signal themes of blessing in an "eternal covenant."

57. Claus Westerman's assessment of the import of this covenantal promise in P's

expressly reciprocal in its expectations: full participation in the enhanced legacy of blessing is predicated on continuing fidelity, epitomized here by observance of circumcision as the corporeal "sign" *('ôt)* of male membership in the segmentary community of Abraham.[58]

The vocation that Abraham receives in trust for his heirs comes to initial fruition already in the generations of Isaac and, especially, Jacob. Each of the two seminal "nations" represented by the twin sons whom Rebekah bears (25:21-26) inherits from Isaac a share of political entitlement (27:27-29, 39-40; cf. 36:1-41); but it is the ambitious second-born, Jacob, who acquires the additional portion usually associated with primogeniture. Thus, albeit with some reluctance, Jacob becomes a benefactor of cognate lineages (30:26-28; 33:1-17; cf. 47:10) as well as progenitor of offspring who prefigure the tribal "association of peoples" *(qĕhal 'ammîm* [28:3; 48:4; cf. 35:22b-26]) that will eventually reclaim the land of Canaan in which he settles (37:1).[59]

The Mosaic Covenant

The expansive pentateuchal account of Israel's theopolitical transformation — from the sodality of Jacob's household into the formally constituted people of God — exhibits a grand palistrophic design encompassing Genesis 37:2 through the end of Deuteronomy.[60] Principal boundaries of

---

theology is apt: "He will be Israel's God: this embraces the action of the creator, the action of the God who saves, who directs the history of his people, the action of the holy God who acts from the midst of the sanctuary in his *kābôd* and with his blessing, the action of the God who instructs, who commands and it happens" (*Genesis 12–36: A Commentary,* tr. John J. Scullion S.J. [Minneapolis: Augsburg, 1985], p. 262).

58. See Cross, *Canaanite Myth* (n. 1), pp. 270-73; Fox, "Sign" (n. 43), pp. 586-96; and Knohl, *Sanctuary of Silence* (n. 9), pp. 138-42. Note should be taken that Ishmael is specifically included in the Abrahamic renewal of the benedictory commission and, together with Abraham himself and other male members of the household, undergoes covenantal circumcision (17:20-27); yet the continuity of pentateuchal covenants will extend through the line of the second-born, Isaac (17:15-19; cf. 22:15-18; Sir. 44:22-23). For a perceptive analysis of Ishmael's status, see Janzen, *Genesis 12–50* (n. 51), pp. 50-53.

59. I.e., Jacob is the "common ancestor" of the Israelite tribal confederation; cf. Mendenhall, "Abraham Narratives" (n. 52), p. 338.

60. For the symmetrical design, which coordinates narrative and prescriptive traditions around the self-revelation of God to Moses in Exod. 33:12–34:9, see McBride, "Context

this configuration are marked by the testamentary benedictions of the patriarchs Jacob (Gen. 49:1-28) and Moses (Deut. 33), which are set outside the Israelite homeland in the northeastern delta of Egypt and in northwestern Moab respectively.[61] Innermost symmetries are formed by the coordinated narrative and prescriptive traditions in Exodus 19:1 through Numbers 10:10, which portray Israel's encampment in the southern wilderness at "the Mountain of God," Sinai or Horeb, apparently located in the vicinity of Midian (cf. Exod. 3:1; 18; Num. 10:11-32). At the center of the configuration is the peak of the mountain itself, where Moses negotiates on Israel's behalf the decisive self-revelation of Yahweh in Exodus 33:12–34:9. The understanding of God's patient, reliable character and beneficent presence articulated here anchors the bilateral covenant enacted in Exodus 34:10-28 and also the two additional covenants that implement it, completing the pentad.

This palistrophic literary design encourages us to view Israel's corporate formation as a prolonged, episodic pilgrimage that progresses circuitously from Canaan via Egypt to the Mountain of God and then northward through Transjordan to the eastern boundary of the national homeland promised to the ancestors.[62] But the journey is also a perilous

---

and Perspective" (n. 3), pp. 53-56. Some of the key elements in the design were observed a century ago by Julius Wellhausen (*Prolegomena* [n. 38], pp. 342-45) who tried to explain them as due to dislocation in the older "Jehovistic history-book" caused by the insertion of the massive Sinai traditions of P. A more elaborate palistrophic arrangement, extending from Genesis through Joshua, is sketched by Jacob Milgrom, *Numbers*, JPS Torah Commentary (Philadelphia: Jewish Publication Society, 1990), pp. xvi-xviii. See now also Mark S. Smith, *The Pilgrimage Pattern in Exodus*, JSOTSup 239 (Sheffield: Sheffield Academic Press, 1997), pp. 252-57, 285-88.

61. Whatever the historical origins of these collections of tribal epigrams may have been, narrative context accounts for their differing views of "Israel." Jacob's prognostications are more familial as well as ominous, while those attributed to Moses have a decidedly geo-political character, which is emphasized by the hymnic frame in Deut. 33:2-5, 26-29. Cf. the assessments of David Noel Freedman, "'Who Is Like Thee among the Gods?' The Religion of Early Israel," in *Ancient Israelite Religion: Essays in Honor of Frank Moore Cross*, ed. Patrick D. Miller Jr., Paul D. Hanson, and S. Dean McBride (Philadelphia: Fortress, 1987), pp. 318-20; and James W. Watts, *Psalm and Story: Inset Hymns in Hebrew Narrative*, JSOTSup 139 (Sheffield: JSOT Press, 1992), pp. 70, 171.

62. On the theological as well as literary-redactional significance of the itinerary notices that demarcate this journey, see George W. Coats, "The Wilderness Itinerary," *CBQ* 34 (1972): 135-52; cf. also Cross, *Canaanite Myth* (n. 1), pp. 308-17; and G. I. Davies, "The Wilderness Itineraries and the Composition of the Pentateuch," *VT* 33 (1983): 1-13. The con-

odyssey. Each of its two major movements, which are conjoined in the Israelite sojourn at Sinai-Horeb, elaborates a scenario that highlights conflict, victory, and world ordering.[63] The overall effect is to connect the principal stages of Israel's itinerary with the chronicle of God's creational work in the protocol of Genesis 1:1–2:3. Israel's passage through and separation from other nations becomes a cosmogonic drama that vindicates the creator's life-sustaining providence.[64]

The Joseph narrative in Genesis 37–50 is transitional. In continuity with the signal themes of the ancestral saga, Joseph's masterful administration of Egypt's agricultural resources facilitates both well-being for "the whole world" (41:46-57) and a specific prospering of Jacob's family now settled in Goshen (47:1-27). This international state of beatitude ostensibly models fulfillment of the Adamic commission in Genesis 1:28-30 (cf. 47:27; 50:19-21; Exod. 1:7). Its antithesis is the tyrannical nativism — a construct of pharaonic xenophobia that condones genocide and ruthless exploitation — which Yahweh defeats in order to reclaim Abraham's heirs from servitude, thereby demonstrating incomparable sovereignty over even the strongest of the world's nations.[65] However, this victory does not

---

nection of these geographical and chronological data with liturgical traditions of pilgrimage is explored by Smith, *Pilgrimage Pattern* (n. 59), esp. pp. 289-301; his remarks on Exod. 15:1-18 (pp. 205-26) are pertinent to recognition of the literary design that balances the victories of the divine warrior against Egypt and Transjordanian states.

63. On this scenario, which is well attested in ancient myth and epic, see esp. Paul D. Hanson, "Zechariah 9 and the Recapitulation of an Ancient Ritual Pattern," *JBL* 92 (1973): 50-59. Cf. also Michael Fishbane, *Biblical Interpretation in Ancient Israel* (Oxford: Clarendon Press, 1985), pp. 351-68; and Susan Niditch, *Oral World and Written Word: Ancient Israelite Literature*, Library of Ancient Israel (Louisville: Westminster John Knox, 1996), pp. 21-24.

64. Important features of this scheme, which can only be reviewed here in broadest outline, have been identified esp. by Terence E. Fretheim, "The Plagues as Ecological Signs of Historical Disaster," *JBL* 110 (1991): 385-96; "The Reclamation of Creation: Redemption and Law in Exodus," *Int* 45 (1991): 354-65; "'Because the Whole Earth Is Mine': Theme and Narrative in Exodus," *Int* 50 (1996): 229-39; and *Exodus*, IntBC (Louisville: John Knox, 1991), pp. 152-70, 268-76. See also Thomas B. Dozeman, *God at War: Power in the Exodus Tradition* (New York and Oxford: Oxford University Press, 1996), esp. pp. 101-52 ("Exodus and Creation").

65. See esp. Exod. 4:21-23; 7:4-5; 9:13-16; 14:30-31; 18:10-11; 19:3-6; cf. Deut. 4:34-35; 7:6. Jan Assmann has astutely observed that Egypt in the narratives of Exodus is Israel's counterimage and that God the warrior ". . . is much closer to Pharaoh than to Aton or Amun, let alone to Aristotle's unmoved mover, in being a primarily political figure" (*Moses the Egyptian* [n. 23], p. 211).

complete the first major movement of the two-part cosmogony, because Israel itself has yet to be reconstituted through covenant as Yahweh's "first-born" or institutionally sanctified so that it can sustain in its midst the creator's own indwelling presence. For this to happen, the liberated Israelites must be purged of the latent idolatry which, in the golden calf episode (Exod. 32; Deut. 9:8-22), comes to the fore in Moses' absence, threatening their communal rebirth in God's image.[66]

In spite of considerable differences in genre, socio-political perspective, and theological emphasis, the major legislative and ritual corpora assembled in Exodus 19 through Numbers 2 are arranged to convey the interrelated, complementary significance of cult and covenant in normalizing Israel's existence as the discrete people of God. What these varied traditions of cult and covenant share above all is a conviction that Israel, unlike other nations, is obligated not only to honor the creator from afar but to be configured into a corporeal temple, infused with holiness in order to mediate the gracious presence of the cosmic sovereign who delivered it out of Egypt.[67] Becoming such a living sanctuary — being covenantally bonded into a "sacerdotal dominion and a holy nation" *(mamleket kōhănîm wĕgôy qādôš)* — is not as simple as it seems when, at the outset, the Israelite refugees assembled at Sinai-Horeb readily accept the offer that Moses proffers to them on God's behalf (Exod. 19:3-8; cf. 24:3-8). According to the pivotal witness of Exodus 32–34, a sustainable relationship between God and Israel is achieved only through a carefully negotiated compromise, yielding an agreement that responds to the grievous issues posed by the "great sin" *(hăṭā'â gĕdōlâ)* of idolatry (32:30-35).[68]

---

66. See J. Gerald Janzen, "The Character of the Calf and Its Cult in Exodus 32," *CBQ* 52 (1990): 597-607; also Assmann, *Moses the Egyptian* [n. 23], pp. 211-12.

67. See, e.g., Lev. 18:2-5; 20:9-26; 26:9-13; Deut. 4:7; 26:18-19. On the functions of law that nurture and implement covenantal sanctification, see S. Dean McBride Jr., "The Yoke of Torah," *Ex Auditu* 11 (1995): 5-9.

68. On the compositional character, thematic coherence, and theological import of these central chapters in the configuration of Sinaitic traditions, see esp. George W. Coats, "The King's Loyal Opposition: Obedience and Authority in Exodus 32–34," in *Canon and Authority: Essays in Old Testament Religion and Theology,* ed. George W. Coats and Burke O. Long (Philadelphia: Fortress, 1977), pp. 91-109 (reprinted in George W. Coats, *The Moses Tradition,* JSOTSup 161 [Sheffield: JSOT Press, 1993], pp. 57-75); R. W. L. Moberly, *At the Mountain of God: Story and Theology in Exodus 32–34,* JSOTSup 22 (Sheffield: JSOT Press, 1983); Herbert Chanan Brichto, "The Worship of the Golden Calf: A Literary Analysis of a Fable on Idolatry," *HUCA* 54 (1983): 1-44 (revised in Herbert Chanan Brichto, *Toward a*

Key features of the protocol in Genesis 1:1–2:3 have counterparts in the nuanced roles that this agreement articulates for God, as well as for Israel, God's refractory people, and their chief advocate, Moses.

First, the agreement relies on a fulsome disclosure of God's character, unveiling the most intimate attributes of divine ethos and pathos. Victory over Egypt has demonstrated the unrivaled power, discriminating judgment, and trustworthiness of the ancestral God revealed anew to Moses as Yahweh (Exod. 3:1–4:17; 6:1-8; cf. 14:13-14; 15:1-12). But divine wrath, provoked by the apostate cultus of the golden calf or calves, calls into question the viability of a covenantal partnership between such a severe, militant deity and an Israel whose unruliness seems to be congenital (32:1-10; cf. Deut. 9:7; 32:5-6, 20). Through intercession that invokes the merit of his own sublime servanthood (Exod. 32:10-13, 31-32; 33:7-17; 34:8-9), Moses gains from Yahweh not only a pledge of restraint (32:14) but a penetrating view of Yahweh's glorious persona (33:13, 18-23). Yahweh now, and indeed henceforth, is to be known as "God merciful and gracious" (ʾēl raḥûm wĕḥannûn), whose devotion to justice is tempered with a compassionate constancy and an abundant readiness to remove the burdens of human transgression (33:18-23; 34:5-7).[69]

Second, Moses' personal intercession also elicits a commitment that Yahweh's own "presence" (pānîm), rather than an angelic surrogate, will accompany the Israelites on their continuing journey into possession of a national homeland, thereby keeping them distinct "from every [other] people on the face of the earth" (33:14-15; cf. 33:1-3; 34:9, 11).[70] The cove-

Grammar of Biblical Poetics: Tales of the Prophets [New York and Oxford: Oxford University Press, 1992), pp. 88-121, 270-75); and Donald E. Gowan, *Theology in Exodus: Biblical Theology in the Form of a Commentary* (Louisville: Westminster John Knox, 1994), pp. 217-55.

69. Compare the parallel scenario in Num. 14:13-25. See also Deut. 4:31; 7:9-10; Neh. 9:17, 31-32; Ps. 86:15. Ps. 145:8-9 attests to the significance of this divine disclosure for the whole of creation. On these and other major scriptural reverberations of Exod. 34:6-7, see Josef Scharbert, "Formgeschichte und Exegese von Ex 34,6f und seiner Parallelen," *Biblica* 38 (1957): 130-50; Thomas B. Dozeman, "Innerbiblical Interpretation of Yahweh's Gracious and Compassionate Character," *JBL* 108 (1989): 207-23; and James L. Mays, "Psalm 103: Mercy Joined to Loving Kindness," *Austin Seminary Bulletin* 105 (1990): 27-32.

70. See Thomas W. Mann, *Divine Presence and Guidance in Israelite Traditions: The Typology of Exaltation*, Johns Hopkins Near Eastern Studies (Baltimore and London: Johns Hopkins University Press, 1977), pp. 144-63. Cf. Moberly, *Mountain of God* (n. 67), pp. 74-75; and, on the broader issue of the distinctive identity claimed for Israel in biblical traditions, Peter Machinist, "The Question of Distinctiveness in Ancient Israel: An Essay," in *Ah,*

nant of 34:10-28 defines and seals this divine commitment. It does so in part by renewing Israel's mandate to observe the fundamental stipulations of the Decalogue (34:1-4, 28; cf. 31:18; 32:15-19) and, of no less import, by augmenting them with provisions designed to guard Israel against further entrapment in idolatry and to promote communal holiness compatible with God's efficacious indwelling (34:11-26).[71]

Third, the renewed and augmented covenant in 34:10-28 is "Mosaic" in a substantive as well as consequential sense. This covenant — like the one granted to renew terrestrial life in Noah's time — acknowledges a superlative individual performance of work that God has delegated (33:12-13, 17; cf. Deut. 34:10-12).[72] Even more pointedly, though, this covenant is chiefly enacted "with" Moses himself, both to exalt him as a paradigm of divine agency (cf. Exod. 7:1; 14:31) and to preserve the people of Israel who now subsist in him (34:10, 27; cf. 32:7-11; 33:15-16).[73] In immediate effect of this, a radiant Moses epitomizes the image of God in human form (34:29-35; cf. 7:1).[74]

In the broader context of the Priestly Sinaitic traditions especially, Moses' apotheosis is mirrored in Israel's communal ordination to a vocation of holiness. This is exemplified by the ethical regimen and sacral collocation of the tribes, encamped around the cultic center of the "tent of meeting" (*'ōhel mô'ēd*) where God tabernacles (Num. 1–2; cf. Exod. 29:43-

---

Assyria . . . : Studies in Assyrian History and Ancient Near Eastern Historiography Presented to Hayim Tadmor, ed. Mordechai Cogan and Israel Eph'al, Scripta Hierosolymitana 33 (Jerusalem: Magnes Press, Hebrew University, 1991), pp. 196-212.

71. For an analysis of these provisions and their parallels in other biblical corpora, see Franz-Elmar Wilms, *Das jahwistische Bundesbuch in Exodus 34*, Studien zum Alten und Neuen Testament 32 (München: Kösel-Verlag, 1973).

72. Cf. Rolf Rendtorff, "'Covenant' as a Structuring Concept in Genesis and Exodus," *JBL* 108 (1989): 389-90 (reprinted in *Canon and Theology* [n. 41], pp. 130-31).

73. Cf. *Jubilees* 1:5. There is a remarkable reciprocity between this outcome and the act of idolatry that caused the crisis in Exod. 32. I.e., the bovine iconography sought to replace Moses' leadership by representing the deity who acted through him; God now recognizes the people as God's own only to the extent that they are conjoined with Moses. See Coats, "The King's Loyal Opposition" (n. 68); and my comments in "Transcendent Authority: The Role of Moses in Old Testament Traditions," *Int* 44 (1990): 234-36.

74. It is difficult to resist the conclusion that "Moses has become in this story a kind of deity, or at least a semi-divine mortal" (Julian Morgenstern, "Moses with the Shining Face," *HUCA* 2 [1925]: 5). Brichto (*Biblical Poetics* [n. 68], p. 111) provides an apt as well as more cautious assessment: "The radiance emanating from the face of Moses is a visible token of the presence of YHWH, the Radiant Presence, in the person of the prophet."

46; 33:7-11; 40:34-38). Even more emblematic are prescriptions for observance of the Sabbath, which is both an "everlasting covenant" *(bĕrît ʿôlām)*
and a perdurable "sign" *(ʾôt)* of Israel's intimate bond of sacrality with
God who creates (Exod. 31:12-17).[75]

The Covenant of Peace with Phinehas

The heading in Numbers 3:1 identifies the lengthy final segment of the
pentateuchal narrative as an account of "the generations of Aaron and
Moses." According to the appended temporal note, the chronicle commences "on the day that Yahweh spoke with Moses on Mount Sinai,"
which apparently refers to the covenantal agreement reached in Exodus
33–34 and amplified throughout Leviticus (cf. Lev. 26:26; 27:34). This
retrospective beginning of the narrative, which will trace Israel's journey
from Sinai to the plains of Moab, brings into immediate focus the orga-
nization of Aaronid and Levitical clergy, as well as the inauguration of
the tabernacle cultus they are ordained to serve (Num. 3:2–10:10; cf. Lev.
8–10). Moreover, review of cultic preparations for the departure from Sinai introduces the familiar Aaronic benediction (Num. 6:22-27) as a pre-
lude to the subsequent history of Israel as a "sacerdotal dominion" that
bears the creator's name in witness to the world.[76] While notes of beatitude will again resound harmoniously in the Mosaic finale (Deut. 33),
interim episodes are scored with themes that are often somber, and
sometimes shrill or harshly discordant. Intramural politics of holiness,
more so than conflicts with external foes (though these are important
too), pose the vexing issues addressed in this second major movement of
Israel's transformational odyssey.

The tribal procession that departs from Sinai is supposed to be a disciplined army on the move, confident that the God who accompanies it

75. Compare Exod. 20:8-11; 35:2-3; Deut. 5:12-15; cf. *Jubilees* 2:18-33. On the Sinaitic
covenant in P, see esp. Cross, *Canaanite Myth* (n. 1), pp. 297-98, 318-20; and, recently, Samuel E. Balentine, *The Torah's Vision of Worship*, OBT (Minneapolis: Fortress, 1999), esp. pp.
119-47.

76. Compare Lev. 9:22-23; Deut. 10:8; Pss. 67; 115. See Michael Fishbane, "Form and
Reformulation of the Biblical Priestly Blessing," *JAOS* 103 (1983): 115-21; and Patrick D.
Miller, *They Cried to the Lord: The Form and Theology of Biblical Prayer* (Minneapolis: For-
tress, 1994), pp. 281-303.

will prevail in the war to conquer the national homeland promised to the ancestors (Num. 10:11-36).[77] Both the initial campaign, which falters and fails due primarily to internal dissension (Num. 11–20; cf. 33:16-39; Deut. 1:19–2:1), and the renewed march, which scores an impressive series of military victories before it reaches the final encampment east of the Jordan in the plains of Moab (Num. 21–24; cf. 33:40-49; Deut. 2:2–3:17), demonstrate the primacy of Moses in the chain of command between God and people. Moses alone is entrusted with administration of God's entire "household" (Num. 12:6-8; cf. Deut. 34:10-12). As executive officer of the tabernacle cultus, Aaron occupies a subordinate but nonetheless indispensable position in the hierarchy of institutionalized leadership (Num. 16–18). Thus, in accord with divine instructions at the time of Aaron's death, Moses installs Aaron's son Eleazar to replace him (20:23-29; cf. Exod. 29:4-9; 40:12-15; Deut. 10:6). But the preeminence and permanent succession of this Aaronid lineage in priestly office is secured only later, through covenantal decree to Phinehas, Eleazar's son, in the context of yet another paradigmatic crisis in the nascent career of Israel as a communal medium of divine presence.

The golden calf and Baʻl Peʻor episodes are counterparts, exhibiting very similar thematic profiles.[78] In each case, the community is compromised by egregious sacrilege that provokes Yahweh's retributive wrath, which becomes manifest in a severe plague (Exod. 32:4-6, 10, 35; Num. 25:1-3, 9); destruction of the entire populace is averted when punitive ac-

---

77. The parallel version, in the Mosaic memoirs of Deut. 1:6–3:29, connects the departure even more closely with the recommissioning of Moses in Exod. 33–34; compare esp. the oracular commands of Deut. 1:7-8, 20-21 with Exod. 33:1; 34:11. On the procession from Sinai as a military campaign, see Thomas W. Mann, *The Book of the Torah: The Narrative Integrity of the Pentateuch* (Atlanta: John Knox, 1988), pp. 125-28; also *Divine Presence* (n. 70), pp. 164-95; and Cross, *Canaanite Myth* (n. 1), pp. 99-105.

78. Although each of these accounts includes material that seems to be archaic (i.e., embedded in JE or "Epic" traditions), in their received forms the narratives exhibit an unevenness indicative of literary conflation and redaction. Exod. 32:7-14 favors Deuteronomic or proto-Deuteronomic editing of the first episode (cf. Brevard S. Childs, *The Book of Exodus: A Critical, Theological Commentary,* OTL [Philadelphia: Westminster, 1974], pp. 557-62); Num. 25 has been shaped by Priestly tradents (or, according to Knohl's analysis [*Sanctuary of Silence* (n. 9), pp. 96-97], by their successors in the "Holiness School"). Cross (*Canaanite Myth* [n. 1], pp. 198-206) has identified the polemical features of the episodes, as representing the competitive interests of Mosaic-Levitical (or Mushite) and Aaronid priestly groups respectively.

tion is taken against the chief culprits (Exod. 32:25-28; Num. 25:4-8).[79] Although both of these accounts acknowledge Moses' role in prosecution of apostasy (with Levites as his principal agents in Exod. 32:15-29, and Israel's "judges" in Num. 25:4-5), the first episode draws attention to the redemptive outcome of Mosaic intercession, while the second features the implacable zeal of Phinehas. The latter's quick, efficient use of deadly force against an offending couple is declared to be a public exhibition of defensive "vehemence" *(qin'â)* that is the equal of God's own (25:7-11).[80] Moreover, this action is deemed expiatory, apparently because it restored the sanctity of the "tent of meeting" and allayed God's fierce anger before Israel was consumed (Num. 25:6, 13; cf. Lev. 10; Num. 18:1-7). As a consequence, God rewards Phinehas and his lineage with an elite vocational endowment (Num. 25:12b-13a):

> I grant him my covenant of peace [*bĕrîtî šālôm*].[81] It shall be a covenant of everlasting priesthood [*bĕrît kĕhunnat 'ôlām*] for him and his descendants after him. . . .

While the oracular formulation is somewhat cryptic or elliptical here, other witnesses attest to the enormous institutional significance of this fourth pentateuchal covenant: it confers on Phinehas the "high" or,

---

79. On the character of the cult of Ba'l Pe'or and the significance of the action attributed to Phinehas, see S. C. Reif, "What Enraged Phinehas? — A Study of Numbers 25:8," *JBL* 90 (1971): 200-206; George E. Mendenhall, *The Tenth Generation: The Origins of the Biblical Tradition* (Baltimore and London: Johns Hopkins University Press, 1973), pp. 105-21; and Marvin H. Pope, *Song of Songs,* AB 7C (Garden City: Doubleday, 1977), pp. 210-29.

80. I.e., the redemptive work of Moses in Exod. 32–34 emphasizes the divine propensity to forgive, based on the revelation of Yahweh as *'ēl raḥûm* (cf. Exod. 33:19; 34:6; Deut. 4:31). The action of Phinehas, on the other hand, implements God's identity as *'ēl qannā'* (cf. Exod. 20:5; 34:14; Deut. 4:24). Even so, the salvific character of Phinehas's initiative is identified as intercession *(wayya'ămōd pînḥās wayĕpallēl)* in Ps. 106:28-31.

81. Here and elsewhere (Isa. 54:10; Ezek. 34:25[-31]; 37:26; cf. Mal. 2:4-7) God's "covenant of peace" affirms and promotes reconciliation — providing assurance of divine favor and well-being, appropriately implemented through blessing (as in the concluding segment of the Aaronic benediction, Num. 6:26); cf. Bernard F. Batto, "The Covenant of Peace: A Neglected Ancient Near Eastern Motif," *CBQ* 49 (1987): 187-211. In Num. 25:12, the covenant apparently conveys special empowerment for the sacerdotal work of Phinehas and his line, which the Hebrew text of Sir. 45:24 describes as the capacity "to sustain the sanctuary" *(lĕkalkēl miqdāš)* and the Greek text elaborates as "to exercise authority over the sanctuary and his people" *(prostatein hagiōn kai laou autou).*

more literally, "great priesthood" *(kĕhunnâ gĕdōlâ)* as an inalienable hereditary prerogative.[82] Just as the covenant of Exodus 34:10-28 exalts Moses and conjoins God's people to him, this one refurbishes Aaron's elevated status as iconic figurehead of the sacral corporation of Israel.[83] Aaronid authority and the cultic instrumentality of divine blessing, already professionalized (Num. 6:22-27), are made more potent by concentrating them in a hierarchical office and discrete lineage.[84]

The "covenant of peace" with Phinehas thus ratifies a particular theocratic position: even though imitation of God's holiness is supposed to define the life of the whole community of Israel (e.g., Lev. 19:2), some Israelites — namely those who officiate before God's mediate presence in the sanctuary — are necessarily entitled and empowered to become holier than others (cf. Num. 16:3-5; 17). Deuteronomy, which concludes the pentateuchal narrative of "the generations of Aaron and Moses," expounds another and considerably more egalitarian view of Israel's theocratic holiness.[85]

The Covenant Enacted in the Land of Moab

Deuteronomy is an integral part of the Pentateuch. No mere homiletical appendix or pedagogical supplement, it brings to completion the extended theopolitical drama that we have been tracing.[86] The recommissioning of

82. So Sir. 45:24 (Hebrew text); similarly Josephus, *Ant* 5.159. Cf. Lev. 21:10; Num. 35:25, 28; and compare Exod. 6:16-25 (which anticipates the import of Phinehas); Josh. 22:13-34; Judg. 20:27-28. See also the data assembled by Kugel, *Traditions* (n. 19), pp. 715-17, 810-13.

83. On the tarnishing of Aaron's image, see Num. 12 and 20:12, 24; as well as Exod. 32:1-5, 25; cf. Lev. 10:1-3. The ostensible theopolitical significance of Num. 25:1-13 is to invest oversight of the tabernacle cultus in one of the two principal Aaronid lineages, i.e., bypassing or subordinating the priestly descendants of Ithamar (compare Lev. 10:6; Num. 4:16-33; 1 Chron. 24:1-6; Ezra 7:1-6; 1 Macc. 2:26). On this, see esp. Josephus, *Ant.* 5.361-62; 7.110; 8.10-12; cf. Aelred Cody, *A History of Old Testament Priesthood*, AnBib 35 (Rome: Pontifical Biblical Institute, 1969), pp. 175-92.

84. See Sirach's paeans to Aaron (45:6-22) and to the high priest Simon, son of Onias (50:1-21). On the taxonomy of priestly blessings, see also Mishnah, *Tamid* 3.8; 7.2 and *Sotah* 7.6-7.

85. See Moshe Weinfeld, *Deuteronomy and the Deuteronomic School* (Oxford: Clarendon Press, 1972), pp. 225-32; also Balentine, *Worship* (n. 75), pp. 148-211.

86. A critical view should be able to acknowledge the structural and functional co-

Moses in Exodus 32–34 — to administer the second half of the divine initiative announced in 3:8, 16-17 (cf. Deut. 10:10-11) — reaches its denouement here, as those who comprise a new, tested generation of Israel not only begin to possess a national homeland but inherit the covenantal vision, discipline, and blessing that Moses himself received in trust for them at Sinai-Horeb. In even longer view, the deuteronomic promulgation of Moses' legacy is a fifth and climactic implementation of the creator's cosmological agenda sketched in the protocol of Genesis 1:1–2:3.

Deuteronomy consists in the main of a four-part testament, drafted in the first-person words of Moses and addressed to an Israelite plenary assembled east of the Jordan, in a valley immediately north of Mount Nebo and west of Beth-peor in Moab (Deut. 1:5; 3:29; 34:1; cf. Num. 36:13). An editorial framework articulates the four major parts and links them into the Pentateuch's genealogical narrative; the narrative concludes with a brief account of Moses' death and an epitaph that memorializes his incomparable achievements as a sufficient and enduring measure of authentic Yahwism (Deut. 34:1-12).[87] Each part of the testament contributes to the idealized portraits of Moses as the human voice of God and of Israel as a people set apart in covenant with God, commissioned to lead a faithful and abundant life of witness among the world's nations.

---

herence of the Pentateuch in its received form without ignoring the distinctiveness of its component traditions and the signs of a complex history of composition (which may well have involved the books of Joshua through Kings). On the final stages of pentateuchal construction, see my sketch "Biblical Literature in Its Historical Context: The Old Testament," in *Harper's Bible Commentary,* ed. James L. Mays et al. (San Francisco: Harper & Row, 1988), pp. 22-24; Joseph Blenkinsopp, *The Pentateuch: An Introduction to the First Five Books of the Bible,* ABRL (New York: Doubleday, 1992), pp. 229-43; and Frank Crüsemann, *The Torah: Theology and Social History of Old Testament Law,* tr. Allan W. Mahnke (Minneapolis: Fortress, 1996), pp. 329-67.

87. Editorial integration of Deuteronomy into the Priestly pentateuchal narrative is effected in part by using segments of a brief obituary notice to frame his four-part address to Israel: compare Deut. 1:3 (which dates Moses' testament according to the chronological scheme of P) and 34:7 (his age at death) with Aaron's obituary in Num. 33:38-39. A more conspicuous link is formed by the resumptive paraphrase of Num. 27:12-14 in Deut. 32:48-52; see Blenkinsopp, *Pentateuch* (n. 86), pp. 229-31. On the hermeneutical import of the concluding epitaph, see Jeffrey H. Tigay, "The Significance of the End of Deuteronomy (Deuteronomy 34:10-12)," in *Texts, Temples, and Traditions: A Tribute to Menahem Haran,* ed. Michael V. Fox et al. (Winona Lake, IN: Eisenbrauns, 1996), pp. 137-43; and idem, *Deuteronomy,* JPS Torah Commentary (Philadelphia and Jerusalem: Jewish Publication Society, 1996), pp. 339-40.

The testament begins with Moses' valedictory address in 1:6–4:40, which includes a review of Israel's prolonged but ultimately victorious journey from Horeb to the plains of Moab (1:6–3:29) and a peroration that draws some pertinent, far-reaching theological conclusions (4:1-40). The three chief lessons are inexorable and interrelated: the community of Israel as an organized whole, and not only its elite leadership, is accountable before God and bears responsibility for the nation's varied political fortunes, the failures and the successes alike (1:9-18, 34-40); Israel's corporate existence will always depend upon its fidelity to the sole cosmic sovereign who created it (4:25-39); what God will continue to do for Israel, and to expect of it in return, is authoritatively revealed through Moses (4:1-8, 40).[88]

A second editorial preface in 4:44-49 introduces the lengthiest and most remarkable part of the Mosaic testament, namely the "polity" *(tôrâ)* elaborated in 5:1–28:68 (cf. 1:5).[89] This systematic national charter first reviews the foundational stipulations of the Decalogue and basic principles of Israel's covenantal identity (5:1–11:30); it then legislates a comprehensive constitution (11:31–26:15), and it closes with an overview of attendant rites of ratification, including sanctions of blessing and curse (26:16–28:68). It is important to observe that this part of the testament is not supposed to establish either a new or renewed covenant; instead, the polity set forth here amplifies and completes the covenantal bond forged with Moses

---

88. On the chief themes of Deut. 1–4, see the following essays: Norbert Lohfink, "Darstellungskunst und Theologie in Dtn 1,6–3,29," *Biblica* 41 (1960): 105-34 (reprinted in idem, *Studien zum Deuteronomium und zur deuteronomistischen Literatur I*, Stuttgarter Biblische Aufsatzbände 8 [Stuttgart: Katholisches Bibelwerk, 1990], pp. 15-44); idem, "The Problem of the Individual and Community in Deuteronomy 1:6–3:29," in *Theology of the Pentateuch: Themes of the Priestly Narrative and Deuteronomy*, tr. Linda M. Maloney (Minneapolis: Fortress, 1994), pp. 227-33 (originally "Wie stelt sich das Problem Individuum — Gemeinschaft in Deuteronomium 1,6–3,29?" *Scholastik* 35 [1960]: 403-7; reprinted in *Studien I*, pp. 45-51); William L. Moran, "The End of the Unholy War and the Anti-Exodus," *Biblica* 44 (1963): 333-42 (reprinted in *A Song of Power and the Power of Song: Essays in the Book of Deuteronomy*, ed. Duane L. Christensen, Sources for Biblical and Theological Study 3 [Winona Lake, IN: Eisenbrauns, 1993], pp. 147-55); and Patrick D. Miller Jr., "'Moses My Servant': The Deuteronomic Portrait of Moses," *Int* 41 (1987): 245-55 (reprinted in *Song of Power* [above], pp. 301-12).

89. On the jurisprudential character and structure of Deut. 4:44–28:68, see my treatment in "Polity of the Covenant People: The Book of Deuteronomy," *Int* 41 (1987): 229-44 (reprinted in *Song of Power* [n. 88], pp. 62-77); and Crüsemann, *Torah* (n. 86), pp. 201-75.

on Israel's behalf at Horeb (Exod. 34:10-28; cf. Deut. 1:3-4; 4:13-14; 5:2-3).[90] Sacral time and geography have been telescoped: the reciprocal oath-taking by God and a sanctified Israel "today" (Deut. 26:16-19) seals the formal relationship initially proposed to and accepted by the people a full generation earlier (Exod. 19:3-8).

The superscription in 29:1 (28:69) announces that the testamentary depositions which follow define yet another covenant — "the covenant Yahweh charged Moses to enact with the Israelites in the land of Moab" — which is expressly distinguished from the now finalized covenant initiated at Horeb.[91] Although the literary components of the covenant in Moab are only loosely coordinated, the themes of communal solidarity and blessing that hold the several parts together are critical for an understanding of the Pentateuch's overall design and purpose. Here, in fulfillment of divine commitments to its ancestors, "all Israel" finally comes of age as God's new creation.[92] The Israelite families whom Moses has guarded and guided since the confrontation with Pharaoh in Egypt are formally invested with

90. The "Temple Scroll" from Qumran Cave 11 seems to offer a strong interpretative precedent for understanding the deuteronomic polity to be an amplification of the revelatory template in Exod. 34:10-28. Cf. Hartmut Stegemann, "The Literary Composition of the Temple Scroll and Its Status at Qumran," in *Temple Scroll Studies: Papers presented at the International Symposium on the Temple Scroll, Manchester, December 1987*, ed. George J. Brooke, Journal for the Study of the Pseudepigrapha Supplement Series 7 (Sheffield: JSOT Press, 1989), pp. 123-48.

91. Deut. 29:1 (28:69) is set off as a distinct *pārāšâ* in the traditional Hebrew text. Although the verse has sometimes been read as a subscription to the preceding covenantal traditions in 4:44–28:68 (e.g., Tigay, *Deuteronomy* [n. 87], p. 274), I agree with those who identify it as a heading, the third in the series of the book's four superscriptions. Formal elements of this ostensible "covenant in Moab" are most easily identified in Deut. 29–30: see Klaus Baltzer, *The Covenant Formulary in Old Testament, Jewish, and Early Christian Writings*, tr. David E. Green (Philadelphia: Fortress, 1971), pp. 34-36; and Alexander Rofé, "The Covenant in the Land of Moab (Deuteronomy 28:69–30:20): Historico-Literary, Comparative, and Form-critical Considerations," in *Das Deuteronomium: Entstehung, Gestalt und Botschaft*, ed. Norbert Lohfink, Bibliotheca ephemeridum theologicarum lovaniensium 68 (Louvain: Louvain University Press, 1985), pp. 310-20 [reprinted in *Song of Power* [n. 88], pp. 269-80]. Norbert Lohfink has made a persuasive case for also including Deut. 31–32 in the "matters" covered by this covenant in Moab ("Der Bundesschluss im Land Moab: Redaktionsgeschichtliches zu Dt 28,69–32,47," *BZ* n.f. 6 [1962]: 32-56; reprinted in *Studien I*, [n. 88], pp. 53-82; cf. also Dennis T. Olson, *Deuteronomy and the Death of Moses*, OBT (Minneapolis: Fortress, 1994), pp. 126-58.

92. Cf. Och, "Creation and Redemption" (n. 37), p. 234.

strategies for their survival without his mediating leadership. In effect, Israel's generations receive Moses' vocational empowerment, becoming his successors as well as the ordained and accountable people of God.[93]

This theme of succession with ethical accountability is rhetorically developed in 29:2[1]–30:20, a discourse which exhibits elements of a loyalty oath.[94] Especially in 29:2-15[1-14], there is a striking overlap between the roles of God and Moses in relationship to a broadly inclusive, multigenerational Israel: Moses acts and speaks in God's stead, administering the "sworn covenant" (*'et-habbĕrît hazzō't wĕ'et-hā'ālâ hazzō't,* literally "this covenant and this oath") not only directly to both the leadership and the rank and file of the people assembled in Moab but also proleptically to their heirs. So too in 29:16[15]–30:20, Moses assures Israel's future generations that, come what will in accord with the covenantal paradigm of blessing and curse, God's life-affirming providence is both clear and accessible, and as constant as the witness of heaven and earth (30:20; cf. 31:28; 32:1, 43; Jer. 31:31-37). In Deuteronomy 31–32, the narrative frame brings Moses' imminent death strongly to the fore as he bestows a varied and invaluable legacy upon his successors. He bequeaths: conviction that God's presence will continue to accompany them, securing them victory through the agency of Joshua as well as by means of their own loyal and courageous action; the authoritative polity in written form, to facilitate their life together in a national homeland; and the perspicacious witness in song to the sometimes painful centrality of God's servant people in God's continuing exercise of cosmic sovereignty.

The key themes of Israel's solidarity, rooted in its observance of *tôrâ,* and of God's providence are echoed climactically in Moses' testamentary benedictions on the tribes (33:1-29). Like the creator's work at the end of

93. Deut. 29:13[12]; the reference here immediately recalls the ancestral covenant of Gen. 17. But Israel's increase and prosperity (Deut. 30:5, 9, 16, 19-20) will also implicitly fulfill God's offer to make Moses' heirs into a "great nation" *(gôy gādôl);* compare Gen. 12:2 and Exod. 32:18 (cf. Num. 14:12).

94. On the structure and thematic coherence of Deut. 29–30, see esp. Patrick D. Miller, *Deuteronomy,* IntBC (Louisville: John Knox, 1990), pp. 199-216. Some of the key diplomatic features are treated by Weinfeld, *Deuteronomy* (n. 85), pp. 100-116. For a broader view of relevant comparative data and their significance, see esp. Hayim Tadmor, "Treaty and Oath in the Ancient Near East: A Historian's Approach," in *Humanizing America's Iconic Book: Society of Biblical Literature Centennial Addresses 1980,* ed. Gene M. Tucker and Douglas A. Knight, Society of Biblical Literature Biblical Scholarship in North America 6 (Chico: Scholars Press, 1982), pp. 127-52.

the sixth day, Moses' service is now complete but not yet completed; his faithful successors will do that, when they bear witness to God's reign, walk in God's ways, enjoy God's bounty, and share God's Sabbath rest (cf. 33:5, 8-10, 26-29; 34:9; Isa. 58:13-14).

IV. Conclusion

Genesis 1:1–2:3 articulates the protocol for God's creational work, chronicling a beginning that will extend into the history of the world and its creatures. When viewed through the lens of this protocol, the genealogical narrative of the Pentateuch resembles a cosmogonic drama in which a series of five covenants secures the creator's primal benedictory commission, empowering humankind to serve as an iconic medium of divine presence. The central covenant, enacted with Moses, and the last two which implement it are designed to transform the people Israel into a "sacerdotal dominion and holy nation," a role that refocuses but does not negate the earlier and more expansive covenants made with Noah and Abram.

The comprehensive view of the received Pentateuch defended here has tradition-historical and theological implications whose treatment is well beyond the scope of the present essay.[95] However, it may be observed in conclusion that the larger corpora of Jewish and Christian scriptures understand the Pentateuch's cosmogonic drama, like the created order itself, to remain both foundational and open-ended. God who created continues to create — not abandoning the primal cosmic design revealed in tôrâ but renewing, adjusting, and amplifying it (e.g., Isa. 34–35; 40–45; Ezek. 34:25-31; Rom. 1–11; Rev. 21–22; cf. Sir. 24). If this is so, then biblical faith rooted in the pentateuchal witness — no less than religions of the ancient Near Eastern world with which this witness has often been contrasted — has a vital interest in the rational integration of created order and human history, of nature and society, of physics and ethics.[96] Philo of

95. Some of these implications have been cogently identified by Patrick D. Miller, "Creation and Covenant," in *Biblical Theology: Problems and Perspectives, In Honor of J. Christiaan Beker*, ed. Steven J. Kraftchick, Charles D. Myers Jr., and Ben C. Ollenburger (Nashville: Abingdon, 1995), pp. 155-68, 313-16.

96. Note the subtitle of Henri Frankfort's classic study, which specifically excluded serious consideration of biblical traditions: *Kingship and the Gods: A Study of Ancient Near Eastern Religion as the Integration of Society and Nature* (Chicago: University of Chicago Press, 1948).

Alexandria, whose cogent analysis of the cosmos as God's temple we noted earlier, reflected on this larger matter when he described the structure and purpose of the Pentateuch:

> We must now give the reason why he [Moses] began his law-book with the history, and put the commands and prohibitions in the second place. He did not, like any historian, make it his business to leave behind for posterity records of ancient deeds for the pleasant but unimproving entertainment which they give; but, in relating the history of early times, and going for its beginning right to the creation of the universe, he wished to shew two most essential things: first that the Father and Maker of the world was in the truest sense also its Lawgiver, secondly that he who would observe the laws will accept gladly the duty of following nature and live in accordance with the ordering of the universe, so that his deeds are attuned to harmony with his words and his words with his deeds.[97]

Philo's second point is, of course, a reflex of the first. Perfect harmony of words and deeds is what the protocol of Genesis 1:1–2:3 ascribes to God who creates. The chief business of humankind, created in God's image and sustained by God's covenants, is to live accordingly, celebrating and sharing God's lavish benefactions with the rest of creation.

---

97. *De Vita Mosis* 2.48 (tr. F. H. Colson, *Philo*, LCL [London: William Heinemann; Cambridge: Harvard University Press, 1935], 6:471-73). No one of my acquaintance better exemplifies the Philonic harmony of words and deeds than my friend and colleague of more than thirty-five years, W. Sibley Towner.

Human Creation in Canonical Context: Genesis 1:26-31 and Beyond

Marsha M. Wilfong

The story of creation in Genesis 1 makes a significant claim about who God is: God, the God of Israel, is the creator of the world. It also makes a significant claim about who we are as human beings. In regard to the creation and purpose of humankind, the emphasis is on relationships: with God, within human community, and with the rest of creation. The description of human creation in 1:26-31 points to this threefold relational purpose and sets human creatures in a unique and pivotal place in the story as a whole. Despite differences in focus and perspective, the second creation story in Genesis 2–3 echoes and confirms this relational purpose of human creation.

The mystery and wonder of humankind lies precisely in this set of relationships. Human beings are both like God (made in God's image) and different from God (creature, not creator). Human beings are both like one another (all are *'ādām,* humankind) and different from each other (male and female, among other things). Human beings are both like animals, fish, and birds (all are "living creatures," blessed with the gift of procreation) and different from other living creatures (charged with the task of dominion over them).

I. Humankind in Relationship with God

According to Genesis 1, human beings are the only creatures created in the image and likeness of God (vv. 26-27). They are also the only creatures addressed directly by God (vv. 28-30). This suggests a unique relatedness of human creatures to their Creator. But what is the nature of that relationship?

Much has been made of the creation of humankind in God's image as the necessary basis for the task of dominion over other living creatures. This aspect will be discussed below. However, the exercise of dominion is not the only consequence of human creation in God's image. It also suggests a correspondence to God that is distinct among the rest of creation. Genesis 1:26 begins: "Then God said, 'Let us make humankind in our image, according to our likeness *(běṣalmēnû kidmûtēnû).*'" The only other place in the Old Testament where these two terms "image" *(ṣelem)* and "likeness" *(děmût)* occur together is in 5:3: "When Adam had lived one hundred thirty years, he became the father of a son in his likeness, according to his image *(bidmûtô kěṣalmô),* and named him Seth." The word order is reversed, but the reference to 1:26 is unmistakable. Genesis 5 lists the descendants of Adam through Noah. It begins in vv. 1-2 by recalling the creation of Adam, using other vocabulary that echoes the creation story in Genesis 1: "When God created humankind, he made them in the likeness *(bidmût)* of God. Male and female he created them, and he blessed them and named them 'Humankind' when they were created."

The description in 5:3 that Seth bore the "likeness/image" of his father Adam implies that the promise and vocation of humankind at creation continues from generation to generation. Yet the suggestion also lingers that human beings are not only creatures among the rest of creation, but are also in some sense related to God as children to a parent in a way that the rest of creation is not. The familial relationship between God and human creatures, later expressed explicitly in relation to God's covenant people (e.g., Exod. 4:22-23; Jer. 31:9; Isa. 64:8; Hos. 11:1-4), is already implied in the fact that humans are created in God's image.

A more intimate and immediate relationship between God and human creatures is also suggested by God's direct address to them. In direct discourse, God bestows blessing and vocation to the human creatures (Gen. 1:28; cf. 1:22), as well as provides food for them (1:29). Genesis 2–3 suggests not only address, but also conversation and interaction between

God and the human creatures. In 2:16-17, God addresses the human creature about what food he may and may not eat. In addition, 3:8-13 suggests the possibility of regular interaction (during garden walks) and presents a conversation between God and the human creatures.

According to Genesis 2–3, the intimate relationship between God and human beings did not work out because of human disobedience. Consequently, being "like God" is viewed negatively in 3:22. Nevertheless, both creation stories affirm that God's intention at creation was that humankind would stand in an immediate, ongoing, and perhaps even familial relationship with God their creator.

II. Relationship within Human Community

In Genesis 1:26-27, human creation implies human community. Here *'ādām* is used as a collective noun: "humankind." This is obvious in v. 27: "So God created humankind *('ādām)* in his image, . . . male and female he created them *('ōtām)*." The image of God resides not simply in the individual human being but in the community of humankind.

The gender distinction, "male" *(zākār)* and "female" *(nĕqēbâ)*, is related to the blessing of procreation (v. 28). The same gender terminology is also used elsewhere in the Old Testament to refer to animals, most notably in the flood story in Genesis 6–7. There God commands Noah to bring onto the ark male and female pairs of animals and birds (6:19; 7:3, 9, 16) in order that the blessing of procreation might continue after the flood (9:1, 7; cf. 1:22, 28). But the fact that a gender distinction is mentioned only in relation to the human creatures in Genesis 1 suggests something more: the necessity for human community.

This necessity is confirmed by the second creation story in Genesis 2. There only one human being *('ādām)* is created initially (2:7). But God concluded that the aloneness of the human being was "not good" (2:18a) — in contrast to God's assessment of creation as "good" in Genesis 1 (vv. 4, 12, 18, 21, 25, 31). The solution to the predicament of aloneness was the creation of a second human being (2:21-22). Thus, Genesis 2 makes explicit what 1:26-27 already implies: human creation is complete only when human beings exist in community, in relationship with one another, distinct from their relationship with God and with the rest of creation.

III. Relationship with the Rest of Creation

The creation of "living creatures" (*nepeš ḥayyâ,* vv. 20, 21, 24) begins on Day 5 with the creation of water creatures and birds of the air (1:20-23). It continues on Day 6. The land animals are the first act of creation on Day 6 (1:24-25), followed by the creation of humankind (1:26-31). Humankind is both similar to and distinct from other "living creatures."

The similarities are threefold. (1) As in Genesis 1:1, the verb "create" *(bārā')* is used to describe God's act of creation: in v. 21 in relation to water creatures and birds, and in v. 27 in relation to humankind. (2) God's blessing of procreation is given only to these "living creatures": in v. 22 to water creatures and birds, and in v. 28 to humankind. The obvious assumption is that the land animals are also included in this blessing (cf. Gen. 8:17; 9:1, 7). The verbs of the blessing are the same in vv. 22 and 28: "Be fruitful *(prh)* and multiply *(rbh)* and fill *(ml')*." (3) God provides vegetation for food to both humankind and land animals (including birds) (vv. 29-30).

The second creation story in Genesis 2 also suggests similarities between human creatures and land animals and birds. (Water creatures are not at issue in the second creation story.) Both the first human creature and the animals and birds are formed from the ground (2:7, 19; 3:23). The relationship between the human creature and other land creatures is even more striking in Genesis 2. Animals and birds are created in an effort to resolve the aloneness of the human creature, though without success (2:18-20).

The distinctions between humankind and other "living creatures" also signify a relationship between them. In addition to being created in God's image, humankind is charged with the task of "dominion" *(rdh)* over other living creatures (1:26, 28). Verse 28 supplements the task of "dominion" over living creatures with the charge to "subdue" *(kbš)* the earth.

In exercising "dominion" over the rest of creation, human beings act as God's representatives or stewards. Created in God's image, humankind stands in the place of God in relation to the rest of creation. Like earthy rulers who set up statues of themselves to assert their sovereignty in places where they were not present, so humankind is set upon the earth to assert and to carry out God's sovereign rule over all of creation.

But if humankind is to carry out the task of dominion as God's representatives on the earth, then the exercise of human dominion should imitate God's own dominion over creation, and should have as its goal the fulfillment of God's good purpose for creation. Exploitation of animals or the earth is not appropriate. Autonomous dominion that ignores or seeks to overthrow God's ultimate dominion over creation is not appropriate. Humankind is called to serve God in the exercise of dominion, and so to serve God's creation by maintaining its goodness and order on God's behalf.

The second creation story in Genesis 2–3 confirms the human task of dominion. The human creature is placed in the Garden of Eden in order "to till it and keep it" (2:15). As the animals and birds are created, the human creature is charged with naming them (2:19-20). Yet this second creation story also recognizes the danger inherent in this task of dominion. The human creatures transgress the limits set by God by eating of the tree of the knowledge of good and evil (2:16-17; 3:1-7). They become like God, "knowing good and evil" (3:22). Here, then, is the shadowy side of creation in God's image: the temptation not to serve faithfully as God's representatives but to take the place of God in the world and in their own lives.

The biblical witness is clear that when humankind gives in to that temptation, God leaves them to their own devices, casting them out of the Garden of Eden (3:14-24) and withdrawing God's own continuing oversight of the good and orderly creation (e.g., Gen. 6–8; Amos 5:18-20; Jer. 4:23-26).

IV. Humankind as the Lynchpin of Creation

That human beings are unique in their creation for relationship with God, one another, and the rest of creation suggests that humankind is, in fact, the lynchpin that holds creation together. Humankind serves as an ongoing link between God and the rest of creation. It is humankind that enables God's purpose for creation to be fulfilled, keeping chaos at bay by faithfully carrying out the task of dominion in God's image. Perhaps that is why God's assessment at the end of Day 6 (Gen. 1:31) refers not simply to the creation of land creatures, including humankind, but to the whole of creation, and why that assessment is not simply "good" (as before), but "very good" *(tôb mě'ōd)*. Perhaps that is also why God, having finished the work of creation, can then rest (2:1-3)!

V. Vision and Reality

Genesis 1 offers us a vision of creation as God intended it. At the heart of that vision is humankind and its threefold relational purpose. Genesis 2–3 confirms that relational purpose but also juxtaposes the harsh reality of human existence alongside the vision of God's intentions. The reality proclaimed is this: human beings were unfaithful in their relationship with God the Creator by transgressing the limits set by the creator. They yielded to the temptation to "be like God" (Gen. 3:4, 22) by attempting to take God's place rather than exercising their likeness to God as God's faithful representatives on earth. As a consequence of their sin, their relationships to one another and with the rest of creation became distorted (3:14-19), disrupting the order and goodness of creation as God intended it.

The connection between human sin and the disruption of creation is perhaps most obvious where the description of God's judgment negates God's work of creation. The introductory statement in 1:1-2 reads: "In the beginning when God created the heavens and the earth, the earth was a formless void *(tōhû wābōhû)* and darkness *(hōšek)* covered the face of the deep *(tĕhôm)*, while a wind from God swept over the face of the waters." In the process of creation, God creates light to counter the darkness (1:3-5, 14-19), sets barriers to protect the dry land from the deep, chaotic waters (1:6-8, 9-10), and populates and orders the "formless void" of the earth (1:11-13, 20-31). Yet the menacing description in v. 2 lingers, suggesting that the "deep," the "darkness," and the "formless void" continue to exist as threats to the order and goodness of God's creation.

This imagery recurs in the Old Testament in descriptions of God's judgment upon human disobedience. The threat from the "deep" was realized in the flood of Noah's day: "[O]n that day all the fountains of the great deep *(tĕhôm)* burst forth, and the windows of the heavens were opened" (7:11). Amos describes the day of the Lord as "darkness *(hōšek)*, not light" (Amos 5:18). Jeremiah envisions the consequence of God's judgment against Judah as a reversal of creation (Jer. 4:23-26):

> I looked on the earth, and lo, it was waste and void *(tōhû wābōhû)*;
> and to the heavens, and they had no light.
> I looked on the mountains, and lo, they were quaking,
> and all the hills moved to and fro.
> I looked, and lo, there was no one at all *('ēn hā'ādām),*

and all the birds of the air had fled.
I looked, and lo, the fruitful land was a desert,
    and all its cities were laid in ruins
    before the Lord, before his fierce anger. (NRSV)

These echoes of the chaotic imagery of Genesis 1:2 suggest that the order and goodness of creation cannot be taken for granted and must be maintained. When humankind is unfaithful in its relationships, all of creation suffers.

The whole of Scripture tells of God's persistent efforts to restore the intended order and goodness of creation despite the persistent failures of humankind to live faithfully in relationship with God, one another, and creation, to live faithfully as creatures made in God's image. According to the witness of Scripture, the bottom line of human sin is always faithlessness in relationship with God. Furthermore, the distortion of humankind's relationship with God is reflected in humankind's distorted relationships with one another and with the rest of creation. Cain murders his brother Abel because God accepted Abel's offering and not his (4:1-16). In consequence, Cain was isolated from human community and could no longer produce an abundant harvest from the ground (v. 12). The builders of the tower of Babel sought to make a name for themselves and consequently were scattered, no longer able to communicate in the same language (11:1-9).

God's covenant people were not exempt from faithlessness in their relationship with God. Abraham and Sarah did not trust God's protection and promise and attempted to ensure its fulfillment on their own. Twice they lied about their marriage. The chaotic consequences fell not on them but on the victims of their lies: plagues came upon Pharaoh's house (12:10-20) and barrenness upon Abimelech's (20:1-18). They also sought to secure the child of God's promise through Sarah's maid Hagar (16:1-6), causing enmity between Sarah and Hagar (v. 6) and leading to the banishment of Hagar and Ishmael (21:8-21).

The Israelites, impatient with Moses' lengthy stay on Mt. Sinai, persuaded Aaron to "make gods" for them to lead them out of the wilderness in Moses' place — and God's (Exod. 32). As a consequence of the construction and worship of the golden calf, three thousand Israelites were killed at the hand of the Levites (vv. 25-28), and a plague was sent upon the rest (v. 35).

Israel's entire history as a nation was characterized by repeated episodes of forsaking God. Once they settled in the land of Canaan, the worship of Baal was a constant temptation, to which they repeatedly succumbed. Their desire for a king like the other nations was, in fact, a rejection of God's kingship over them (1 Sam. 8:7). But Israel's reliance on its own political wit and on paying homage to other gods did not result in security and prosperity. Rather, the consequences were internal strife and injustice, wars with neighboring peoples, and the ultimate destruction of nation and land.

Again and again, the biblical witness declares that the relationships of humankind with God, with one another, and with the rest of creation are inseparably intertwined. Distortions in one relationship have consequences in the other arenas. Yet distortion in any of these relationships is viewed as faithlessness in relationship with God. The law given to Israel reflects the intertwining of these three areas of relationship and their grounding in the relationship with God. In particular, the sabbath commandment reveals the connections. The Exodus version grounds sabbath keeping in God's own rest on the seventh day after the work of creation (Exod. 20:8-11). In Deuteronomy 5:12-15, keeping the sabbath is to serve as a reminder of Israel's slavery in Egypt and of God's deliverance. Both versions include a sabbath rest for *all* persons, including children, slaves, and resident aliens, as well as for domestic work animals. In Leviticus, the sabbath rest is extended to the land itself every seventh year (Lev. 25:1-7; cf. vv. 18-22) and to the ownership of land every fiftieth year, when the land was to revert to its original owners (25:8-55). These various aspects of sabbath keeping are a reminder that to God all things belong — human beings, other living creatures, and the land itself. The people of Israel do not own anything. They are tenants on God's land (25:23). They are God's servants, not the property of other people (25:42, 55). Their relationships with one another and with the rest of creation, as expressions of their faithfulness in relationship with God, are to be governed by God's gracious intentions.

VI. Jesus Christ: The Image of God

According to the New Testament, in Jesus Christ God shows us once again what it means to be human, created in the image of God and charged with the task of dominion. This is the example Christ offers, the witness he brings, and the deliverance he provides. Jesus Christ is the culmination of God's attempts to overcome human sinfulness and to restore creation to its intended order and goodness.

The author of Hebrews points to this connection:

> Long ago God spoke to our ancestors in many and various ways by the prophets, but in these last days he has spoken to us by a Son, whom he appointed heir of all things, through whom he also created the worlds. He is the reflection of God's glory and the exact imprint of God's very being, and he sustains all things by his powerful word. (Heb. 1:1-3a, NRSV)

Colossians 1:15-16 also speaks of Christ as the "image" of God (cf. 2 Cor. 4:4) and of his participation in creation (cf. John 1:1-3):

> He is the image of the invisible God, the firstborn of all creation; for in him all things in heaven and on earth were created, things visible and invisible, whether thrones or dominions or rulers or powers — all things have been created through him and for him. (NRSV)

Not only did Christ, "the image of God," participate in creation, he was also given the task of dominion through his death and resurrection:

> For he must reign until he has put all his enemies under his feet. The last enemy to be destroyed is death. For "God has put all things in subjection under his feet." But when it says, "All things are put in subjection," it is plain that this does not include the one who put all things in subjection under him. When all things are subjected to him, then the Son himself will also be subjected to the one who put all things in subjection under him, so that God may be all in all. (1 Cor. 15:25-28, NRSV; cf. Eph. 1:20-23; Heb. 2:5-9)

The ultimate goal is not the reign of Christ but that "God may be all in all," that all things will again be ordered according to God's good and gracious intentions (cf. 1 Cor. 15:24; Eph. 1:9-10).

But between the beginning (creation) and the goal (God being all in all) lies the incarnation, the means by which Christ is to carry out his task. The Christ hymn in Philippians 2:5-11 suggests that, unlike God's human creatures, Christ took the path of faithfulness. "[T]hough he was in the form of God, [he] did not regard equality with God as something to be exploited, but emptied himself, taking the form of a slave, being born in human likeness." And being found in human form, he humbled himself, and became obedient to the point of death — even death on a cross" (Phil. 2:6-8). Humankind, created in God's image, exploited that image again and again, grasping at equality with God (cf. Gen. 2:22). Jesus Christ, the image and form of God, did not exploit his equality with God but, in humility and obedience, took on human likeness in God's service.

This then is the example that God's human creatures are to follow. Paul urged the Philippians: "Let the same mind be in you that was in Christ Jesus" (Phil. 2:5). For in Christ lies the possibility of a new beginning: "So if anyone is in Christ, there is a new creation: everything old has passed away; see, everything has become new!" (2 Cor. 5:17). By conformity to the image of Christ (Rom. 8:29; cf. 2 Cor. 3:18), the image of God in humankind — long distorted by human sinfulness — can be renewed (Col. 3:9-10).

The purpose of this new creation in Christ is the same as the original intention of human creation. It consists in and makes possible faithful relationships with God within human community and with the rest of creation. First and foremost is the restoration of the relationship with God. Those who are in Christ have been reconciled to God and, moreover, have been given "the ministry of reconciliation" (2 Cor. 5:18). This ministry extends the offer of reconciliation with God to all humankind (2 Cor. 5:19-20), indeed, to the whole of creation (Col. 1:19-20). When this reconciliation is complete, creation itself will be freed from the consequences of human sinfulness (Rom. 8:18-23). The goodness and order of creation will be restored.

The restoration of relationships within the human community begins within the community of faith. Those who are in Christ are called to "love one another" (John 15:12), with the goal that "they may all be one" (John 17:21a). Those who are in Christ are members of one body, the body of Christ (1 Cor. 12:12). In Christ, distinctions and divisions among human beings no longer apply: "There is no longer Jew or Greek, there is no longer slave or free, there is no longer male and female; for all of you are one in Christ Jesus" (Gal. 3:28; cf. Rom. 10:12; 1 Cor. 12:12-13; Col. 3:11). Unity with God in Christ results in, and is expressed by, unity among believers, which in turn makes possible their faithful witness to the world: "As you, Father, are in me and I am in you, may they also be in us, so that the world may believe that you have sent me" (John 17:21b). By their life together, believers proclaim who God is and what God's intentions are for all humankind.

VII. The Beginning and the End

Genesis 1 stands at the beginning of Scripture and offers a vision of God's intentions for creation — in particular, for human creation. Jesus Christ incarnates that vision as the true image of God — God's own Son and the new Adam (cf. Rom. 5:12-21), the "firstborn within a large family" (Rom. 8:29). Christ shows us what it means to be human, the purpose and vocation for which we were created. Through his death and resurrection, Christ makes possible our new creation here and now. As risen and exalted Lord, Christ seals the promise that God's good intentions will ultimately prevail. Sin, evil, and even death will be overcome, and God will be all in all. "And the one who was seated on the throne said, 'See, I am making all things new'" (Rev. 21:5).

The Gates of Dawn:
Reflections on Genesis 1:1-10; 2:1-4a

E. Carson Brisson

Two companions, by nature more given to breaking bread than to embarking on adventure, a mole and a rat, learn that a young friend is missing. Impelled by concern, the mole and the rat set out on an improbable quest to find and, if need be, rescue their lost friend. They take their journey by night and by river, a time and a means neither would have chosen were the need not so urgent.

After many fruitless hours of searching amid the silence and risk of both sides of the river, their hearts aching from the absence of their friend, the mole and the rat find themselves greeted by the subtle hues of a distant dawn. As the light slowly deepens around and before them, they hear, far down the river, the sweet call of pipes. They become enthralled.

Despite the loss under which they toil, the inexplicable melodies of the pipes gradually become for these companions the river's truest current, and the trembling creatures are lured forward by the beauty of what they are hearing. In time, the river's waters give way to the dry land of a small island, and the mole and the rat are drawn into the verdant clearing from which the music has originated. There they are afforded and overcome by a glimpse of the Being whose care for them, for their lost friend, and for all things living is beyond comprehension. To use Kenneth Grahame's inspired phrase, the mole and the rat catch a momentary and holy vision of the "piper at the gates of dawn":

Then suddenly the Mole felt a great Awe fall upon him, an Awe that turned his muscles to water, bowed his head, and rooted his feet to the ground. It was no panic terror — indeed he felt wonderfully at peace and happy — but it was an awe that smote and held him and, without seeing, he knew it could only mean that some August Presence was very, very near. With difficulty, he turned to look for his friend, and saw him at his side, cowed, stricken, and trembling violently. . . . "Rat!" he found breath to whisper, shaking, "Are you afraid?" "Afraid?" murmured the Rat, his eyes shining with unutterable love. "Afraid!" . . . "O, never, never! And yet — and yet — O, Mole, I am afraid!" Then the two animals, crouching to the earth, bowed their heads and did worship.[1]

Mole and Rat, in their vulnerability, in their courageous search, in their awe, and finally in their worship, may serve as reliable guides into the meaning and beauty of the Hebrew creation narrative of Genesis 1:1–2:4a. Driven by the loss of that which is familiar and precious, they find, through darkness and in the early dawn, their lives lifted by and included in a long arch of purposes whose author and ends are more beautiful than they ever dreamed, had they never been driven from home. Their need and their search become ordered by a grace that will give them the means to remember and practice the wholeness for which they were formed. They are — river, night, missing friend, confusion, fatigue, and long journey from home notwithstanding — shown the way, received, encouraged, blessed, accepted, and invited into the joy of their calling. In the midst of their loss, in the midst of their journey into another's need, they are found.

Genesis 1–9 frames within the greater destiny of all creation the particular history by which the Hebrew community came to know and remember its God. This location offers the worshiping community resources that enable it to continue hoping in its God even when catastrophic events challenge the place of that God in its life. The text means to claim that the God of Israel, and none other, reigns even when circumstances suggest otherwise. The account rises before the community as a cascading bid for service, worship, and, finally, sabbath peace and witness amid the mingled and rushing promise and danger of the many waters of personal and national history.

Genesis 1 begins by announcing that the God of Israel is the source

1. Kenneth Grahame, *The Wind in the Willows* (London: Methuen & Co. Ltd., 1951), pp. 165-67.

54

and Lord of existence, the first and current cause, directly or through mediation, of all creation. The world itself, and not solely the history by which Israel has discovered itself chosen, is the theater within which the drama of the divine self-giving of Israel's Lord will express itself and make possible faithful response. This is signaled by the text's use of *bārā'*, the Hebrew verb employed exclusively for God's creative activity, and by the inclusive object of that activity, "heaven and earth." The God who is already known through history as the One who sees the affliction, hears the cry, aches the aching, and redemptively enters the life of the community (Exod. 3) is the same God who wills the world into colors, shapes, seasons, and substance in anticipation of and preparation for that community.

Since all of life is created by Israel's God, there can be for the community of faith no place or time that falls beyond the creative reach of the divine heart. The God who creates all, rather than being reduced to a particular topography, climate, or national boundary, reigns within the Hebrew community and continues to define that community even during circumstances of extreme loss and wandering. The covenant promises of the God who creates "heaven and earth" may be trusted, this God may be worshiped, and the ethical will of this God, codified in the liturgies and patterns of life of the community, may be followed even when the smoke rising from the temple is from the flames of the temple itself. In its final form, Genesis 1 expresses the conviction that proper worship is essential to the preservation and mission of the community even in exile. Indeed, the text will provide guidance for worship and conduct when the familiar ballads of Jerusalem have given way to the confusing and tempting songs of Babylon and other points east of Eden.

The covenant-shaping presence of this God and the response of the worshiping community are realized in Genesis 1 against a backdrop of creation's ancient adversary — a chaos of unlimited darkness and unfathomable deep. This agent of uncreation has visited havoc upon the creative efforts of lesser gods. Its waters and darkness are familiar and vicious opponents of life among cultures who know too well how fragile existence upon the lips of great river systems and their flood plains can be. The desire of this chaos is to contest order and life. Indeed, the very sounds of the Hebrew words for the chief agents of this nemesis convey a menacing purpose to those listening to the text.

Yet however real they may be, the malevolent forces opposed to creation will be shorn of their authority before the creative will of Israel's

God. The dragons, confusions, and tragedies that would oppose this God have barely been identified when we feel the shadow of the creative intentions of the Lord of heaven and earth (v. 2), depicted in a feminine participle, already hovering, coursing, and swooping back and forth across the world-ocean in a mood of determination, expectancy, and hope:

> But the earth was under the dominion of the Chaos, and where it was not darkness it was measureless deep; yet, even then the Presence of God, determined, hopeful, expectant, calm, swooped back and forth, back and forth, drawing ever closer to what would surely be.[2]

The abyss of uncreation is real. To live with irreparable loss is to know this. But real as it is, it is not final. Israel's God alone is final. This God does not wrestle chaos for the world. Nor does this God take chaos as partner. This God, in eloquent testimony to the sovereignty of the life-giving intentions of the divine heart, will, through a series of eight fiats (1:3-26a) "speak" the world into being. By the sheer authority of the divine will, with complete and immediate correspondence between the desire of that will and the architecture of the world that unfolds, the Lord of the worshiping community will order and establish creation. There will be no scuffle. There will be the sure and measured pace of the result of centuries of theological reflection on how to be sustained as the faithful community in the midst of shifting circumstances. All will be done. All will be done in its time and season. By this pattern the community will remember and realize its vocation, its witness, before the One God of heaven and earth, between whose word and the object of that word, so unlike even the best of human words, there is no difference.

The majestic style and pace of this creation account grounds the community in the reality of its God in a liturgical cadence greater than the sum of its parts. Over and over again, with surety, this God will begin by intending, realize that divine intention, value what results, and establish the reality of those results over against anything that might scheme to undo it.

The creative will (or word) of Israel's God will first quell and delimit undifferentiated night. Darkness will be assigned its limits, circumscribed by the brilliance of God's first creative act, the speaking of light into the world. The light will forever be less than God, yet at the very moment it appears, it is already more than the darkness can ever be.

2. Author's paraphrase.

God "sees" that the light is "good." That is, the light corresponds to its purpose. It is what its Lord has created it to be. It is *true;* it embraces its divinely appointed mission *never* to become what the darkness is. Darkness still exists, but it may never again govern. The light may indeed be bruised, and the arch of its final and full dawn may seem tragically and inexplicably delayed, but the believing community bears witness that even when the darkness is more present, the light is more real.

The unfathomable and formless deep is subdued as well. It is drained and assigned its place by means of a vault and dry land around, over, and under the breathing space for life God has willed into being. The deep is still a menace, but no longer one without end. It is now held in check by the sovereign Lord of Israel. It will soon be filled with new meaning and not a few fish (v. 27), and while it may for God's purpose still be ruptured, it will never again rule (Gen. 7–9).

With chaos now leashed, now given its limits and purpose, creation begins its formal move toward the sabbath purpose for which it is brought into existence. In expanding circles of meaning and complexity, glad to harvest from but careful not to become confused by other sagas of world genesis, the creation account delineates an ever-burgeoning and increasingly purpose-filled earth-home in which all of life is assigned its meaning and value according to the personal will of God. The earth, with no fecundity natively its own, is given permission to robe itself with a seeding, fructifying verdancy. The astral sphere, defined by impressive lamps but completely vacant of gods, will neither own nor cause liturgical or agricultural seasons but will in absolute obedience to the command of its creator accept the assignment to begin marking time, to signal what is supposed to be happening, in anticipation of a creature whose vocation is to know what time is. The seas and the heavens below the firmament, wondrous realms where one might hardly imagine life could be sustained, will be directed to spill out with creatures whose wonderful mobility seems to be an advance over the plants. All animal creatures, from the exotic, intriguing, and threatening who dwell in the margins of dreams, journeys, and misfortunes, to the commonplace whose smells and sounds are often too near, will be willed to life and given value and purpose. Even the blind, groping creatures of the deeps, who had so much trouble making the good list in other creation accounts, will have their value, place, purpose, and time.

Creation is now a breath away from completion. That completion will occur "in sabbath." Sabbath will be what time it is. Sabbath is the *telos* of creation. As such, it exists by the sovereign will of God. Sabbath is the repose in God offered to creation by the parts and sum of the reigning will of Israel's Lord. This sabbath, this rest, the willed destiny of the created order from fleas to Philistines, will constitute the relationship offered in providential and splendid freedom by the divine heart of the covenant and creator God to all that grows and creeps and flutters and trots and snores and simply waits. God, as has been the case with all of creation, is alone the cause and author of sabbath. Creation, very good though it may be, cannot conjure or produce this relationship. It may only receive it, enter it. Indeed, were the entire created order to embrace sabbath, the world would in that moment become a hymn (Ps. 148:7-8).

But in this account there is one more moment before the sabbath rest of God will be offered. One more creature will be added to the goodness of creation. That creature will be the human. This creature is created in a relative flurry of language. The cohortative mood of consultation appears (v. 26). The creature will be in some unique (but not exclusive) way precious to the creator. It will be accountable for itself, and for the creepers and flyers and floppers. It is given vocation. It is to be mutually she and he. It will be blessed. Particular care is given to its feeding. The exclusive verb for God's creative activity will be employed three times before the creature is fashioned just right for its purposes before God.

Will this creature, given life just before the cool and shade of the sabbath is established, come to embrace sabbath rest along with all creation? Will this creature accept as its true vocation the life-giving relationship with God and with all others, however *other* they might be, for which the sabbath was created and for which it is offered?

It has been said that out of the first silence prayer arose, that out of that prayer faith emerged, that out of that faith love grew, that out of that love service was done, and that out of that service the sabbath peace of God was born.[3] Heaven and nature noticed first and began to sing. It may even be that the darkness, somewhere within the gates of dawn, will find its true voice. Blessed be the name of the Lord.

3. Author's paraphrase of words attributed to Mother Teresa.

Remembrances of "Historical Criticism": Speiser's Genesis Commentary and Its History of Reception

James Barr

Many of the new trends in biblical studies today identify themselves over and against "historical criticism." Thus — to pick out one of a thousand similar statements — Brevard Childs wrote of German Old Testament scholarship between the two world wars:

> The period was one of intense debate in search for a new theological model for Old Testament studies which was highly critical of the scientific, historical-critical approach which ironically owed much of its origin and success to German scholarship and which now dominated the entire discipline.[1]

Unfortunately, as this period of "domination" by "historical criticism" moves further into the past, there are fewer and fewer people who remember what it was really like. Naturally, by means of careful historical investigation one could find out. But much of what is said about this earlier period of scholarship does not depend on such investigation. Its basis lies

---

1. Brevard S. Childs, "Old Testament in Germany 1920-1940. The Search for a New Paradigm," in *Altes Testament — Forschung und Wirkung*, ed. Peter Mommer and Winfried Thiel (Frankfurt: Lang, 1994), p. 233.

rather in the zeal of the more "modern" or "postmodern" trends to identify and advertise themselves.

Historical criticism never did much to state its own theory or to explain its own philosophical basis. It worked rather on an empirical basis of trial and error: suppose this piece of text (e.g., Gen. 1) did not belong with the text next to it (Gen. 2–3), but did belong better with one a page or two later (Gen. 5), would this not help us in our understanding? Most people came to accept that such a supposition would indeed help, and historical criticism came in the end to have quite wide acceptance. For this reason, most of its results continue to have broad acceptance today, even among those who want to build a much different approach.[2] In spite of very substantial results, historical criticism by the time of its retreat in the twentieth century had still produced no proper theoretical justification of itself. This contrasts strikingly with the various recent trends, which produce ample theory but no substantial and widely accepted results. It thus comes about that most of the theoretical statements about historical criticism current today were produced by its enemies. What they tell us is not what historical criticism in its heyday was like, but in what way it is useful for the ideology of newer movements that the past should be depicted.

I.

A good example of this is to be found in the attractively written *Narrative in the Hebrew Bible* by David M. Gunn and Danna N. Fewell (1993). They begin their book with a survey of various possible approaches. The "Varieties of Interpretation" are illustrated from the story of Cain in Genesis 4, and among these, naturally, they include the "historical-critical." Thus they write (p. 21):

2. Compare Brevard S. Childs, *Exodus* (London: SCM, 1974), which continues to present us with a minute analysis of, for example, the plagues narrative (pp. 130-42), distinguishing J, E, and P down to quarter-verses. It is ironic if this commentary, certainly written in order to help us get away from historical criticism, ends up actually demonstrating the *strength* of that approach. See, for example, the comments of Alastair G. Hunter in *Dictionary of Biblical Interpretation* (London: SCM, 1990), who writes that "what is most effective" in this commentary is "detail of a traditional historical critical kind" (p. 107) and also that "it would be hard to improve on his treatment of [the historical critical] aspect of the text" (p. 106).

Coming now to the latter part of the twentieth century, we take up the Jewish American scholar E. A. Speiser's commentary on Genesis (1964), the first in the Anchor Bible series, possibly the most widely sold "critical" commentary series of the century. Its scholarly tradition is mainstream "historical critical." Speiser characterizes the meaning of the text in his very first sentences. "The story of early man is now carried a step further, embracing the conflict between the pastoral and the agricultural way of life. The conflict is depicted in terms of the impact on the given individuals." So much for that. Next he turns to some matters of more burning interest. On the translation of verse 1, he argues that "know" is "inadequate" and "had experience of" is better. The stem of the Hebrew word in question, *yd'*, is applied "not only to normal marital situations . . . but also to clandestine conduct . . . and even homosexuality." Use of the term is "thus not a matter of delicate usage, as is sometimes alleged." And to make his point stick he delivers his *coup de grâce,* the datum drawn from comparative philology. Akkadian "extends [the term] to dogs."

After reviewing two additional comments by Speiser based on comparative Akkadian evidence, Gunn and Fewell conclude:

> Speiser's, then, is an interpretation perhaps more interesting for what it fails to say than what it says. Comparative philology offers a useful strategy for constructing a reading that says nothing about possible theological issues or themes (e.g. theodicy, sin, and judgement), nothing about the individual characters and their intentions or emotions, nothing even about Speiser's own claim that the story really depicts a social rather than individual conflict. Still, we do learn that in Akkadian dogs "have experience of" other dogs.[3]

The first sentence of the next paragraph goes on to say that "Speiser's commentary in many respects epitomizes a major and prevalent vein of twentieth-century scholarship." Speiser, it alleges, is "typical" (p. 23).

What Gunn and Fewell say about Speiser's work, however, is a massive misunderstanding and misrepresentation. For one thing, their depiction makes much of the very limited amount of comment Speiser provided. His comment, as they say, contemptuously though not wrongly, is "a little thin."

---

3. David M. Gunn and Danna N. Fewell, *Narrative in the Hebrew Bible* (Oxford: Oxford University Press, 1993), pp. 21-22.

The fact is that Speiser expressly avoided setting out to provide anything like a complete commentary on the text. His preface began by acknowledging Genesis to be "one of the most intensively cultivated books of the Bible."[4] "Accordingly," he continued, "the present work devotes only as much space to matters that have already been covered elsewhere as is necessary for clarity and continuity." He here refers to a "minimal bibliography of the excellent works that are available." Then he goes on, "By the same token, greater emphasis has been placed on questions about which there is as yet no definite consensus, and on points which remain to be adduced."

In other words, Speiser had no intention of providing a complete commentary on Genesis. What he provided was a *translation* accompanied by *sparse and occasional notes* on those particular points *at which he thought he had something original to contribute.* This is exactly what the dust jacket of the book says: "Genesis, translated with an introduction and notes by E. A. Speiser." A glance at an important text like Genesis 1:1–2:4 shows how this works out. There is the translation, followed by a little less than three pages of "Notes" (pp. 5-8) — and most of them are either references to recent information (Harry M. Orlinsky on v. 2, Ugaritic evidence and William F. Albright on v. 4, David Noel Freedman on v. 9), or explanations to justify or clarify features of his own translation, or observations from his own very substantial knowledge of Semitic languages. With few exceptions they coincide exactly with Speiser's expressed intentions for his work. The section on "Comment" (pp. 8-13) contains a short, general discussion of the relationship between Genesis and Mesopotamian materials, including some guidance about the relation of the story to modern scientific knowledge and the significant hermeneutical principle that one has to ask what it meant "from the vantage point of another age." Finally, a discussion of the syntax of the first line of the Bible, Genesis 1:1, is provided: "When God set about to create heaven and earth."

The point is: much is not commented upon (e.g., what is meant by the "image" or "likeness" of God). Speiser comments on the singular "I" and "my" of his translation ("I will make man in my image, after my likeness") but says nothing about any of the various other problems of these terms. We are hardly to suppose that his interpretative method as a "historical critical" scholar made him unaware of such problems (*contra* Gunn

---

4. Ephraim A. Speiser, *Genesis: Introduction, Translation, and Notes*, AB 1 (Garden City, NY: Doubleday, 1964), p. v.

and Fewell). Of course he knew about them. But, as he clearly stated, if he felt that others had sufficiently dealt with a problem, he would pass it by without comment.

Speiser, as we noticed, made it his policy to comment specially "on points which remain to be adduced." Many such points came from Akkadian, not surprisingly, for he was on the whole known as an Assyriologist more than he was as a biblical scholar. In fact, a more appropriate criticism of Speiser's commentary would be to say that he not only quoted the similar Akkadian terms but too often assumed that the Hebrew cognates had the same meaning: thus for *ṣābā'* in Genesis 2:1, usually "army, host" in Hebrew, Speiser tells us that the Akkadian cognate means not only "soldier" but "member of a work gang, laborer," and hence that "the basic sense of the stem is to be engaged in group service."[5] This may be quite true, but it is not necessarily the right explanation for the Hebrew at this point. Again, at Genesis 2:2, translating "On the seventh day God brought to a close the work that he had been doing," Speiser introduces the Akkadian verb *šuteṣbû* "in the sense of 'inspect and approve'" and explains the Hebrew text accordingly.[6]

To sum up, a primary interest of Speiser's work lay in putting before his readers aspects of words, locutions, situations, new or old, known from Akkadian. His use of Akkadian information is quite sensible and balanced, for he does not imply that every piece of such information is a vitally important comment in itself. It was part of Speiser's policy to introduce new information that he considered helpful but not necessarily definitive. If the book had aspired to be a full-fledged commentary, then many of Gunn and Fewell's criticisms would hold, such as the charge of concluding "categorically" the matter of the missing text ("Let us go outside") in Genesis 4:8. But this first volume of the Anchor Bible was intended to be only an annotation to a translation.

Gunn and Fewell are grossly unfair to Speiser's work. I am not concerned to defend Speiser's volume or to suggest that it was a great work; surely nobody, even in the "historical critical" time, thought that it was. But they have not troubled to consider the circumstances and intentions of his work. They not only have taken advantage of its deliberately intended limitations in order to make historical criticism look foolish, but they also

5. Speiser, *Genesis*, p. 7.
6. Speiser, *Genesis*, pp. 7-8.

then say that they do not wish "to denigrate historical criticism."[7] They recognize that important values have been achieved — for example, it was "instrumental (following the spirit of the Renaissance) in opening the Bible to scrutiny as a document of human literature" — and that Speiser's work is in that sense a "profoundly literary study." Historical criticism has a future, they continue, "in a major reconstruction of its program in terms of social world studies, with its positivistic ('objective') notion of 'history' radically reconceived." It is a pity, however, that the example they use gives no indication of what its value may be. Of the varieties of interpretation that Gunn and Fewell discuss, none is treated so contemptuously or made to look so foolish as the "historical critical" (as they suppose Speiser's work to be), in spite of the value that they attach to this "powerful movement" and Speiser's "profoundly literary study."

II.

Gunn and Fewell spoke not only of Speiser as an individual scholar but also of the Anchor Bible series as "possibly the most widely sold 'critical' commentary series of the century."[8] Its scholarly tradition, they inform us, "is mainstream 'historical critical.'" To me this is quite doubtful. Apart from the most basic aspects of format, the style and interpretative character of the various volumes are quite disparate. (I leave aside the more recent *Anchor Bible Dictionary*.) A reader would not be wrong to say that the authors of the various volumes were given a free hand to follow whatever interpretive guide or principle they chose. Many of the volumes, particularly the earlier ones, have been more or less translations with a brief scattering of notes — exactly the style that Speiser followed.

It is dubious therefore whether the series in its beginning was intended to be a "critical commentary" or indeed a "commentary" at all. The title "Anchor Bible" itself suggests something different: it was a fresh *translation* of the Bible with a selection of notes and comments, often such as might explain or justify the translation. In this it is, or then was, more like the annotated editions of newer Bible versions, which come out from time to time. Later Anchor Bible volumes have often been much fuller and more

7. Gunn and Fewell, *Narrative*, p. 11.
8. Gunn and Fewell, *Narrative*, p. 21.

consistent, but they have still followed the author's particular bent. Thus the fine volumes on Samuel by P. Kyle McCarter are particularly strong in detailed textual criticism. However, the three volumes on the Psalms by the late Mitchell Dahood have little contact with textual criticism and even less with historical criticism. They are wholly dedicated to proving that Hebrew and Ugaritic are virtually identical and that the Psalms can be fully understood on this basis. Dahood had little historical sense; as most reviewers and critics have observed, he attributed to the texts religious ideas that, by criteria of historical criticism, could not have existed at the periods to which he ascribed the writing of the texts.

If one were to identify any feature of the Anchor Bible commentary series as characteristic (at least in the earlier stages and leaving aside the New Testament volumes), one would not be far wrong in saying that it was the series' association or identification with the Albrightian school. There are exceptions, but few, I think, would question this characterization. And there is nothing wrong with this, for the Albrightian tradition is a learned and influential one. But to say that it is "mainstream historical critical," or indeed "historical critical" at all, is rather questionable. To generalize about this important tradition is of course dangerous. Nevertheless, looking at it broadly, I would say it was more "historical" than "historical critical," and in some of its stages and manifestations it was more "anticritical." Unquestionably much of William F. Albright's enormous reputation, on a public as well as scholarly plane, was built upon his strongly conservative positions, at least as they appeared at the time. He spoke strongly against evolution and evolutionary ideas; he repeatedly claimed to have hard evidence that proved the customary "critical results" to be wrong; he insisted that the basic characteristics of Israelite religion were there from the earliest times; and he often joined in repeating the attacks on Julius Wellhausen and his supposed ideological biases that many others were making.

There were, of course, other sides to this. Even where he refuted customary critical opinion, Albright often replaced it with opinions of his own that were just as far from the traditional as were those of the customary historical criticism. Far from being an enemy of evolutionism, he was himself a complete evolutionist, as anyone could see from the title of his major work *From the Stone Age to Christianity: Monotheism and the Historical Process.*[9]

---

9. William F. Albright, *From the Stone Age to Christianity*, 2nd ed. (Baltimore: Johns Hopkins University Press, 1957).

George Ernest Wright, one of his most influential pupils, also took a strong "anticritical" line on one of the most important questions: Hebrew religion, he argued, could not have developed out of the environing religions. Indeed, there was no such development; the essential characteristics of the religion were there from the beginning. (Wright nevertheless, as it later emerged, was actually an evolutionist too). The two general editors of the Anchor Bible, Albright and David Noel Freedman, have certainly been linguistic and historical scholars, but on the whole they have struck out an individual line on matters of biblical criticism and, though certainly not rejecting "mainstream" historical criticism, have stood distinctly apart from it.

Thus the work of Albright, and of at least some of his followers, was often "historical anticritical" or "philological anticritical." Or, one might say, the main characteristic of the Albrightian tradition was a logic of *discovery* (in true archaeological style) rather than a logic of *criticism*. New facts, new discoveries, and new inscriptions were so very often offered as realities that would solve problems; and Albright's pupils were very well trained in knowing about these new entities. Their attitude of discovery is reflected in some volumes of the Anchor Bible, including Speiser's; their approach was not "mainstream historical critical."

Although Speiser did accept some traditional critical positions, such as the source analysis of the Pentateuch into J, E, and P, a glance at his commentary shows that these positions were not central for him. A perception of J, E, and P does not make one into an advanced historical-critical thinker. Though Speiser recognized source analysis, it played little part in his actual commentary.

The original elements in his scholarship worked in the opposite direction, as was widely recognized at the time, especially in his treatment of the wife-sister stories concerning Abraham and Isaac. Critical scholarship had often suggested that there is no historical reality to these tales since scholars could not imagine how such events could have taken place. Speiser's triumph was that he claimed to show from actual Akkadian evidence that something of this sort had been actual social practice. This, it was understood, upset the older critical calculations, and it certainly pleased the conservative, anticritical, religious constituency. Later, Speiser's use of Akkadian evidence on this matter came under severe criticism.[10]

10. See Thomas L. Thompson, *Historicity of the Patriarchal Narratives*, BZAW 133 (Berlin: de Gruyter, 1974).

In sum, Speiser's *Genesis,* like much of the Anchor Bible Old Testament as a whole, belongs only marginally to historical criticism, and not at all to its "mainstream." In fact, *not a single one* of the points adduced from his work by Gunn and Fewell is characteristic of historical criticism! All the points commented on by him belong either to textual criticism or to comparative philology. Both of these approaches, although combinable with historical criticism, are quite different from it and are equally compatible with the rejection of historical criticism. Indeed, when historical criticism is rejected, these features become particularly conspicuous. *None* of the characteristic historical-critical operations, such as the identification of different sources, or the identification of "what really happened," or the "privileging" of the "original," are to be found in the passages Gunn and Fewell quote from Speiser.[11] Thus, even by their own criteria Speiser's comments fail to illustrate the case they argue.

III.

Gunn and Fewell add another remark to their presentation of "historical criticism." It was, they tell us, "the dominant method of biblical interpretation in the universities of Europe and America."[12] Both of them, they tell us, were "taught that it was the only responsible method for biblical scholars." This idea, held by their professors and apparently accepted by them as representing what was thought at the time, is a common assumption among the opponents of historical criticism. They have to see it not just as an influential movement or tradition that has contributed much to the understanding of the Bible, but as a devouring monster seeking domination. Thus, Jon D. Levenson sees it as something that is "awarded a monopoly in the interpretive process" — something disproved by the existence of the same biblical theology against which he protests so vehemently.[13] In the same vein Gunn and Fewell present their account of historical criticism and its "disadvantages."[14] Whether this was what was "taught" them, or

11. Gunn and Fewell, *Narrative,* p. 8.
12. Gunn and Fewell, *Narrative,* p. 11.
13. See Jon D. Levenson, *The Hebrew Bible, the Old Testament and Historical Criticism* (Louisville: Westminster/John Knox, 1993) and my review in *JTS* 47 (1996): 555-60; citation from p. 559 of the latter.
14. Gunn and Fewell, *Narrative,* pp. 7-8.

whether they worked it out for themselves, they do not say. For the moment we leave aside their actual presentation of it. Our focus is rather on their assertion that they were "taught" that this was the "only responsible method."

Considering how ready they are with their criticisms of the long "dominant" historical critical approach, one would expect them to be equally critical toward the views they were "taught" and to question whether these views correspond to the reality of scholarly thinking. That they do not question their own views only shows how narrow their basis of experience was.

None of the professors with whom I studied, except perhaps one, thought that historical criticism was the only responsible method of interpreting the Bible; even those who taught us traditional historical-critical views did not think or say this. We were certainly given a good and clear account of such things as the source criticism of the Pentateuch, the various strata of the book of Isaiah, and likewise the document Q and the various sources of the Gospels. But even those who taught us these interpretations did not suppose that they were absolutes, as depicted by Gunn and Fewell. On the contrary, anyone who said that this method "established some kind of absolute truth"[15] would have been laughed to scorn. Much interest and consideration went toward trends and methods that seemed to rival and — potentially — displace historical criticism. Such approaches included form criticism, the Scandinavian emphasis on tradition, the Martin Noth–Gerhard von Rad tradition approach, and the entire looming edifice of biblical theology. For most of us, these latter approaches, though compatible with historical criticism, were closer to being "dominant" than historical criticism was. Very few scholars assigned to historical criticism the absolutely dominating role envisaged by Gunn and Fewell.

The dominant thing in scholarship, in fact, lay in the control of the languages. And it is here above anywhere else that the falsity of Gunn and Fewell's notion that historical criticism was considered the only responsible method for biblical scholars is proved. They have not taken into account the Hebraists. The Hebraists, the lexicographers, the language teachers, and the grammarians remained relatively untouched by historical criticism, even when they themselves accepted its methods and results in a general way. D. Winton Thomas, for example, Regius Professor of Hebrew

15. Gunn and Fewell, *Narrative*, p. 7.

at Cambridge, published a lecture entitled *Understanding the Old Testament* in which there is no mention of historical criticism at all. For G. R. Driver, one of the most eminent Hebraists and Semitic philologists of his generation, historical criticism played a negligible role, though he was not against it. Distinguished Hebraists like these, leading persons in university and society, would never have considered their work nonacademic or irresponsible because it was not historical critical.

Moreover, Orientalists on the whole were not very welcoming to historical criticism as practiced on the Bible. In fields like Arabic, for instance, historical criticism comparable with what was done in the Bible was rarely practiced. But no Orientalist ever for a moment admitted that his work was not academic or not responsible. Up to the present day many of the grammars and dictionaries of Hebrew show only limited awareness of historical-critical methods and results. Among the dictionaries, Brown, Driver, and Briggs was something of an exception, giving indications of J, E, D, and P at suitable points and sometimes trying to order the structure of entries in a historical sequence. And, when they did this, it was not always welcomed. (I remember quite often how this aspect of *BDB* was regarded as "unscholarly," resting on "theories" rather than on "facts," and some people on these grounds preferred to use some other dictionary, even though that meant abandoning any historical presentation of data.[16]) We must acknowledge, moreover, that the world of biblical language is an area that critical scholarship and conservative anticritical scholarship share in common. Much valuable linguistic work came from scholars who in other respects were close to fundamentalism, if this term is taken to mean radical opposition to historical criticism.

IV.

According to Gunn and Fewell, there are "three major and (usually) crippling disadvantages" to historical criticism.[17] First, there is circularity of argument, "a fundamental problem for a method that claimed to be establishing some kind of absolute truth." Second, the analysis of sources was

---

16. It was this *anti*-historical critical tendency that was "positivistic," *contra* Gunn and Fewell, *Narrative*, p. 11.

17. Gunn and Fewell, *Narrative*, pp. 7-8.

"basically dependent on aesthetic premises which were often arbitrary and rarely acknowledged." Underlying most source criticism has been an "aesthetic preference for a rationalistic, literal reading of literature." Third, privilege was accorded the notion of the "original," and this is "devastating" to the understanding of the final, canonical text, which is the text people read. To these are added the concentration of biblical interpretation in the hands of scholars, the assumption that texts have only a single right meaning, and the conviction that historical criticism is *the* correct method. "Historical criticism, indeed, was the summit of the interpretational pyramid."[18] The arrogance of this position "is, of course, breathtaking, but recognizably Western."

Essentially restating the common current position against historical criticism, many of these points have little that is original about them. Within the setting of Gunn and Fewell's book, however, which concludes with a warm appreciation of the variety of *ideologies* to be found in the Bible, I cannot see this *depiction* of historical criticism as anything other than an obvious ideology. There may be some truth in some of the points made: circularity of argument, maybe (although it is not so clear that such argumentation is necessarily wrong); too much emphasis on the "original," yes (I have said that myself); but a "devastating" effect on the final text is wild and unsubstantiated exaggeration. Good final-form exegesis is another part of historical criticism that was mistakenly neglected by Gunn and Fewell.

"Objectivity," the "aesthetic preference for rationalistic, literal reading," "establishing some kind of absolute truth," the inability to perceive irony in a text or contradiction within a single work, the idea that historical criticism was *the* one right method and the "summit of the interpretational pyramid" — all this is pure ideology. Such language comes not from the thinking of historical critics or their writings but from those who are busily inventing categories to discredit them and to justify their own different approach. Phrases like "absolute truth" and "summit of the pyramid" reveal how little the authors understood historical criticism when it was "dominant."

Particularly untrue is their claim that it was an "assumption" that historical criticism expounded "if not the correct meaning of the text, at least a step towards the correct meaning."[19] Although "a step towards the

18. Gunn and Fewell, *Narrative*, p. 8.
19. Gunn and Fewell, *Narrative*, p. 8.

correct meaning" may be justified, the rest is remote from reality. People did not think as Gunn and Fewell imagine them to have thought. In particular, historical criticism was not thought of as a mode for *determining meaning*. I do not remember anyone in the relevant epoch saying this. What *was* frequently said and uttered as a complaint against historical criticism, and even admitted by its practitioners, was the very opposite: that it did not even *try* to determine meaning. It stopped short of doing that. This characterization has some validity to it. Indeed, it fits to some extent with what Gunn and Fewell say about Speiser himself, but it is quite the reverse of their generalizations about historical criticism.

Naturally, some of what I say depends on what exactly is meant by "historical criticism." When this term is used, people mostly mean either (1) the detection of different sources within the text and the attempt to detect the real events and entities referred to there, or (2) *all* the operations referred to as "critical," like form criticism, tradition criticism, and so forth. I think the latter is a mistake. I am not sure that these operations, though "critical," are necessarily "historical." Form criticism, as applied in the Old Testament, surely was not. Maybe in the Gospels it was — by detecting the *Gattung* of a story one could perhaps tell how far it belonged to the historical teaching of Jesus — but in the Old Testament it worked the other way. Form criticism recognized types of text and their sort of setting, but it did not reveal anything about their date or origin.[20] The Psalms are the outstanding example. After Hermann Gunkel and S. Mowinckel, practically no one supposed that the Psalms could be dated or that the events they referred to were identifiable. Moses Buttenwieser's commentary, which tried to supply some of these facts, was already regarded as far out of date at the time of its publication.[21] In other words, form criticism, extremely influential from the twenties on, was not "historical criticism." If there was no "historical criticism" in the Psalms, how can one think that it was "dominant" in Old Testament studies? A fresh analysis of the way in which these factors interacted is obviously necessary.

20. This is rightly recognized by Mark G. Brett, *Biblical Criticism in Crisis? The Impact of the Canonical Approach on Old Testament Studies* (Cambridge: Cambridge University Press, 1991), p. 77: "In spite of the characteristic stress in form criticism on a text's locus in life *(Sitz im Leben)*, it seems that this stress often simply amounted to positing a highly generalized social or cultic location, e.g., 'legal contexts,' 'the New Year festival,' and so on."

21. Moses Buttenwieser, *The Psalms, Chronologically Treated* (Chicago: University of Chicago Press, 1938).

The trouble with all this is that the book of Gunn and Fewell is a well-written, attractive, and interesting one designed for students and lay persons. It is unfortunate that it will spread among them a picture of the past that is essentially ideological. The authors can, I think, scarcely object to this term, for, though many feel it to be pejorative, it seems to be for them a term of high praise: the Bible itself, they tell us in their conclusion, sets before us a variety of ideologies that "can transform us."[22] Truth other than ideology seems hardly to exist for them, as their treatment of Speiser illustrates.

Our authors tell us, grandiosely, that "we find ourselves participants in a major epistemological shift which is, in the larger picture, but a phase in a long-standing Western debate, stretching back to Aristotle and beyond."[23] Really? As they themselves say, "the arrogance of this position is, of course, breathtaking, but recognizably Western."

22. Gunn and Fewell, *Narrative*, p. 205.
23. Gunn and Fewell, *Narrative*, p. 10.

PSALMS AND JOB

"Maker of Heaven and Earth": Creation in the Psalms

James L. Mays

I.

In order to investigate the various ways creation is featured in the Psalter, it is necessary to identify at the outset the following items of consideration.

(1) "Creation" in the sense frequently used today is not a notion that appears in the Psalms. The term has come to mean no more than the natural world in the vocabulary of New Age religion, nature romanticism, environmental enthusiasm, artistic aestheticism, and even in unselfconscious traditional religion and liberal piety. There is no term or text in the Psalms, indeed in the entire Bible, for creation in this sense.

(2) The term "creation" can refer to an activity and to the outcome of the activity. It means, roughly, creating and what has been created. In the psalmic world of thought both verbal and nominal senses are always and specifically theological. The actor who creates is always Yahweh, the God of Israel. What there is in creation is the Lord's making.

(3) The topic of "creation," of making and of what has been made, is never an independent topic in the Psalms, that is, it is never itself the subject of an entire psalm. It is rather a subtheme that is combined with other themes in the composition of Psalms. There is nothing like what is found in Genesis 1–2, which is unique in this respect in the Bible. Psalm 104 comes closest, but its interest is more in providence than in creation.

(4) The vocabulary of creation is quite simple and is largely shared

with Old Testament literature in general. The following examples of words and phrases are illustrative.[1]

(a) **verbs**

establish *(kwn)*	8:3; 24:1; 93:1
make *('śh)*	33:6; 95:5
found *(ysd)*	24:1; 89:11
form *(yṣr)*	95:5
create *(br')*	104:30, the only instance

(b) **nouns**

earth/world *('ereṣ/tēbēl)*	19:4; 24:1
heavens/earth *(šāmayim/'ereṣ)*	8:1; 57:5, 11
work(s) *(ma'ăśeh)*	104:24
creatures *(qinyān)*	104:24

(5) The famous phrase "Yahweh, maker of heaven and earth" belongs to the provenance of psalmic literature (115:15; 121:2; 124:8; 134:3; 146:5, 6). Outside the Psalter it appears in the liturgical sentences in Genesis 14:5, 6. The phrase is confessional in function. The contexts in which the phrase appears show that its purpose is to identify Yahweh as the deity who *can* help and bless the people of the Lord because of Yahweh's power as creator of all that is. The creator's identity is firmly connected with the work of saving and blessing the congregation.

(6) In the Psalms the making-activity of Yahweh is spoken of as an exercise of sovereignty. This active dominion is portrayed by several metaphors and poetic images, such as those of cosmic artisan (e.g., Yahweh's hands formed the dry land [95:5]) and cosmic monarch (e.g., Yahweh spoke and it came to be [33:6]). The most important portrayal, the one that furnishes a semantic and imaginative source for the others, is the conflict scenario in which Yahweh is victor over opposition (often the chaotic waters) and establishes the world as manifestation of divine rule — for example, Yahweh rules the raging of the sea, scatters enemies, and founds heaven and earth as revelation of divine dominion (89:5-18; 104:1-9).

(7) It is important to note that the scenario and vocabulary used to speak of Yahweh's making of heaven and earth are also employed in a col-

---

1. Verses are numbered according to the English text.

lateral way to speak of Yahweh's exercise of sovereignty in the affairs of nations and human beings. Note the use of the conflict scenario in Psalms 68, 74, and 77. Some texts place the cosmic and historical spheres in synonymously parallel positions (65:7; 96:10). The vocabulary of making is used to describe the creation of both the world and the people of God (95:5-7). Some psalms represent the activity of making the world and making the history of the people of God as linear (136, 146, 147). The sovereignty that made the world is at work in the judging and saving of the world.

These seven considerations summarize the primary features of the way "creation" is conceived and spoken about in the Psalms. But it is not through such ordered reviews that the topic engages the thinking, feeling, imagination, and reflection of those who read and sing the Psalms as Scripture and liturgy. Rather the topic is met in individual psalms where it is combined with other topics in a larger whole that furnishes a specific literary context. These specific contexts integrate the topic in a composition that has its own plan and purpose. The perspective shifts from psalm to psalm, each adding to the range and depth of the ways in which faith is instructed to view what is.

It is helpful, then, to look at specific psalms in order to inquire after their perspective. The general topic "creation" is so comprehensive and complex that it seems best to sharpen selectively the subject and focus on "world" or "earth." The topic will be identified not just by the occurrence of the word pair "world/earth," but by significant reference in the text to "world" and its constituents. The psalms explored in the following discussion are illustrative and certainly do not exhaust the possibilities. They provide examples of the ways in which "world" can be rendered in individual psalms. Particular attention will be given to literary features crafted into the composition, which will serve as guides to understanding the perspective on "world" that informs the psalm being read.

II.

Psalm 8 is the first in the Psalter in which world is a significant theme. Here "world" is envisioned as the manifestation of Yahweh's majesty.

(1) The subject of the psalm is stated in the choral line that opens and closes it as a defining inclusion: "O Lord, our sovereign, how majestic is your name in all the earth." The sovereign to whom the worshipers sing this hymn

has a royal identity throughout the earth! The vocabulary of royalty permeates the entire text: sovereign, majestic, glory, founded a bulwark (established power), crowned, glory and honor, and dominion. The psalm sees the whole earth bearing the signature of Yahweh. Its vision is like that of the seraphic song: "the whole earth is full of his glory" (Isa. 6:3). To be in the world is to be confronted with the reign and the ruling of the Lord.

(2) The repetition of the second person pronoun in the body of the hymn ("your," "you") ties everything mentioned to Yahweh's name and majesty. In its exuberance the psalm views all in the heavens and on earth as radiant with the royalty of its creator. The psalm speaks of the world in direct address to Yahweh. Hence, the world is incorporated in the I/Thou idiom of praise.

(3) The surprise in the psalm lies in the contrast between vv. 1b-4 and 5-8. In the first section the majesty of Yahweh would seem to belong to the realm above the earth. The splendor of Yahweh is visible in the heavens. The sight of the night sky with its moon and stars overwhelms the psalmist in his human finitude. But the second section goes on to say that this humble human has been crowned with glory and honor, constituted with a royal domain. Notice the pairing of "work of your fingers" and "works of your hands" to refer respectively to the solar sphere and to the animal realm. Over the latter the human rules in analogy with Yahweh's cosmic rule as a vassal establishment. There is a special perspective on "world" here. The world is the place where the human species knows its insignificance in the cosmos and is given its significance in the earth. "The heavens are the Lord's heavens, but the earth he has given to human beings," says Psalm 115:16. The human being is given dominion by the divine realm, and that means accountability for as well as power over. The vision is admittedly anthropocentric and hierarchical. But not only is such a vision theologically inescapable, it is closer to reality and more pregnant with promise. In any case, according to the psalm's view it is in this human royal rule that the majesty of Yahweh is present in all the earth. The hierarchies of the earth are a clue to the meaning of "world."

III.

Psalm 24 views the "world" as a place of accountability and expectation. It begins with a simple memorable couplet that states the essential and central declaration of the psalmic view of the world: "The earth is the Lord's and all that is in it, the world and those who live in it; for he has founded it on the seas and established it on the rivers."

(1) What makes Psalm 24 remarkable in its treatment of the world is what follows the introductory declaration of vv. 1-2. Two more sections complete the psalm (vv. 3-6, 7-10). All three sections are so different in topic and style as to seem incoherent; yet their literary continuity with the opening declaration makes them serve as exposition to vv. 1-2. In the context of the composition they assume the opening theme, which gives their content special significance.

(2) The second section (vv. 3-6) reveals that the Lord, to whom the world and its inhabitants belong, has a special place in the world before which its inhabitants are accountable for their character and conduct. The world is not undifferentiated space. It is particularized by the Lord's relation to it, and the Lord's relation to persons is individualized by the particularizing of space into place. The world in the mode of "mountain of the Lord/holy place" translates the declaration about the Lord's sovereign universal relation to all into a question about the living of each person. The world, because it is the Lord's, is searchingly particular as well as inclusively universal.

(3) The third section (vv. 7-10) declares that the world is where its sovereign wants to come, and is coming. This owner of the world not only is above and beyond the world but wants to be in the world. It is the Lord's purpose to come as the "king of glory" who has won the battle over seas and rivers to found the world. Until the victor appears, it is not evident what the meaning of "world" is. Cosmic gates and sacred doors must open so that the sovereign who owns the world may enter and be present in the world. The liturgy of advent in vv. 7-10 intones the meaning and destiny of the world. The world is where the kingdom of God is coming. "Lo, he stands at the door and knocks" (cf. Rev. 3:20).

IV.

Psalm 29 envisions "world" as the theater of the glory of God. Although the word pair "earth/world" does not appear in the psalm, there is a compelling description of something happening in the world that bespeaks the truth about the world.

(1) This psalm is in many ways a counterpart of and companion to Psalm 24. In Psalm 24 Yahweh is called "king of glory," and a liturgy of entrance celebrates the king's coming as the victor who is strong and mighty in battle. In Psalm 29 Yahweh is called "God of glory." The psalm describes an epiphany that is proleptic of Yahweh's coming in the world. The unmistakable theme is "glory," established by its repetition in vv. 1, 2, 3, and 9.

(2) Glory is the visible appearance of power (vv. 1, 4). The compositional strategy of the psalmist is to employ a poetic description of a thunderstorm to portray power and evoke the experience of power (vv. 3-4). In the cultural world of the psalms the thunderstorm was virtually a classic medium for describing the divine victor whose victory over the counter forces of chaos brings about the world and manifests the reign of the deity. As often is the case in the tradition, the adversary is the primeval ocean, the mighty waters (vv. 3, 10). Here the poet has used the bending, flashing, shaking, reverberating, stripping effect of a thunderstorm's onset to evoke the direct experience of power, a power that surpasses the natural elements. This display of power is celebrated as a theologumenon of "the voice of the Lord," a motif repeated seven times, unifying the sequence of lines in vv. 3-9. The imagery of the thunderstorm is used to visualize a power in the world that symbolizes the power that sustains the world.

(3) Two significant notions concerning the world are presented by the use of the thunderstorm to represent the "voice of the Lord." Indeed, both are spoken in the concluding verses. Verse 10 proclaims, "The Lord is enthroned over the flood . . . as king forever." This poetic metaphorical declaration means that the powers of the physical world that coalesce and cohere to render the world extant and continuous are ordered by one supreme transcendent power. To behold the powers operative in the world is to behold refractions of the power that constitutes the universe. And the psalm knows its name (v. 2)! Verse 11 claims that this cosmic "king" whose name is the Lord is the source of strength and peace for his people. The people of the Lord have a cosmic connection. The very power that informs the universe with existence offers the people of God the coherence and constancy of *shalom*. The very strength that flows through the universe can flow through them to maintain order and future in the face of the floods of human history.

V.

Psalm 65 portrays the world as the farm of God. It evokes a fertility so abundant that the very earth and its produce transform themselves into a music of joy.

(1) This theo-agricultural vision of earth does not appear in the psalm until v. 9. It occupies the final stanza of the hymn (vv. 9-13). It is preceded by two stanzas, each with its own topic. The first stanza comprises vv. 1-4 and addresses God as God of the temple in Zion. The second consists of vv. 5-8 and addresses God as God of the cosmos. These first two stanzas each open with a vocative of identification, "God in Zion" in the first and "God of our salvation" in the second. The third stanza contains no vocative at its beginning; it simply speaks to God directly. In the composition as a whole the identifications of the first two stanzas serve to say who the God is that is addressed in the third. In Israel it was theologically crucial that the God of the sanctuary and cosmos be the same as the God of fertility. Of course, the first two divine identities themselves have an inner connection with "world" in psalmic thought and form, an important context for thinking about the world as the medium of divine goodness through fertility.

(2) In the first stanza God engages the world through a place where divine presence is available. The focus is on Zion, courts, house, and temple. God is one to whom mortals may come. The availability is inclusive and universal: "all flesh" may approach. God's presence in his place means that God is there to answer prayer and forgive transgressions. There is a goodness in this ministry to human finitude and fallibility that is the prime and first satisfaction of mortal neediness. By putting this stanza first, the psalm argues that the first joy in God is the nearness of the presence available in a special place in the world.

(3) In the second stanza God is praised as the one whose strength is manifest in the existence of the world and what happens in the world. The two domains that God rules as sovereign are both in view here and are interwoven in the composition of the stanza. The double dimension of God's relation to the world is specifically evident in v. 7: "You silence the roaring of the seas *and* the tumult of the peoples." The delivering events of salvation history and the cosmic signs of the world's stability and continuity are both reasons for hope and joy from one end of the earth to the other. This stanza places the joy in the knowledge of God as creator and savior alongside the joy in the presence of God in preparation for the final stanza.

81

(4) Because of what has been said in the first two stanzas, God can be simply and directly addressed in the third as "you." In the opening thematic verse, the watering and enriching of the earth, by which grain is provided for its people, is acknowledged as the visitation of God. The rest of the stanza tells how God's visitation is at work from spring rains until abundant harvest takes on the appearance of joyous praise. The world is envisioned as the medium of God's satisfying goodness and personified as participant in God's praise.

(5) Psalm 65 is a hymn of thanksgiving and has been used in liturgical tradition for harvest festivals and in services of thanksgiving. As such it puts the world in a significant perspective. The poetic vision of the psalm centers attention on God rather than on any assumed natural good fortune of the congregation and insists on keeping every thanksgiving a liturgical occasion. It puts God's saving response to our neediness and sin first on the agenda and keeps the worshiper from slipping into self-satisfaction and self-congratulation over current well-being. The psalm shows that thanksgiving must take place in a universal setting; its reasons and possibilities belong even to those who live at earth's farthest bounds, thus correcting any proclivity to confine thanksgiving to the limits of a national identity. Finally, the psalm provides, especially for urban people, language to celebrate the goodness of the fertile earth and to view its provisions less in commercial and technical ways and more in relation to water, fields, and animals, the realia of world.

VI.

Psalm 98 casts the world in the role of orchestra and choir to celebrate the coming of the Lord. In prophetic praise this hymn anticipates a time when the whole heart will resound with joy at the presence and rule of its rightful king.

(1) The psalm is composed along the lines of the traditional formula for the imperative hymn: summons to praise and content or reason for praise. It begins with a brief summons (v. 1a) followed by the basis of the summons (vv. 1b-3); then calls to praise resume (vv. 4-8), to be concluded by a final statement of praise. The second and long series of imperatives that call to praise is divided into two stanzas by an inclusion ("Make a joyful noise before the Lord"), which marks off vv. 4-6 as a separate stanza to

create a hymn of three stanzas. A progressive line of thought runs through the whole. A new song must be sung to the Lord because God has done marvelous things; the marvelous things are the victory by which God is vindicated through Israel's salvation, a victory seen by the whole earth. The whole earth, therefore, should orchestrate praise before the Lord, whose right to be king has been vindicated in victory; even sea and earth are expected to join in the praise of the one who comes to rule the world with righteousness. The psalm is a hymn of praise to the One whose faithfulness to Israel is a revelation to the world of the sovereignty that is the destiny of the world.

(2) When the synonyms earth and world are tracked through the lines of the hymn, certain perspectives on the world become apparent. Appearing in each of the three stanzas, one or both of the synonyms play a crucial role in the progression of thought. First, earth as the comprehensive place where the nations live is witness to the saving victory of the Lord; earth as the place where human history unfolds is the field on which the righteousness of Israel's God is revealed. Second, earth/world makes up the constituency of praise. Praise is no longer limited to Israel; it belongs to the world. Third, by the personified topography of the world, even the voiceless oceans and mountains are included in praise as a way of making the world's praise exhaustively inclusive. Fourth, the destiny of the earth is to be the realm of a righteous and equitable rule.

(3) By its inclusion of the physical world of seas and hills in the performance of joyous praise, the psalm reflects a transformation in the way the earth's components are affected by the coming and action of the Lord. The pattern in the classic description of theophanies is a portrayal of the devastating impact of the appearance of God on the earth. Earth and its components melt, shake, are shattered, and so forth (e.g., 97:4-5). The shift from the reaction of awe and terror to the response of joyous acclamation shows that the coming of the kingship of the Lord into the world as savior transforms the very relation between God and created order. "For the whole creation awaits with eager longing for the revealing of the children of God" (Rom. 8:19).

VII.

Psalm 104 is a hymn whose theme is the "works of the Lord." Its poetry offers us eyes to behold the world as wisdom.

(1) More than any other psalm, the Psalm 104 is occupied with the topic of creation in general and the world in particular. It is composed of two major sections, each beginning with a vocative address to the Lord and a summary statement of praise (v. 1b introducing vv. 2-23 and v. 24a introducing vv. 24-35). The first section opens with yet another portrayal of the Lord as cosmic monarch who has gained dominion in the heavens by the power manifest in the thunderstorm (vv. 1-4) and has established the earth by driving the waters off its surface and containing them in their appointed places (vv. 5-9). From these contained waters, the Lord makes springs and streams to flow so that "the earth is satisfied with the result of your works" (vv. 10-13). The first section concludes with an extended recitation of the features of life in the earth, which serves as an exposition of the satisfactoriness of the works of the Lord, who has provided food, habitat, and times for living things (vv. 14-23). The second section begins with an exclamation over the variety of the Lord's works and an illustration of that variety (vv. 24-26). Then the psalmist reflects on the dependence of all these creatures on the providence of the Lord (vv. 27-30) and concludes with a wish-prayer that the Lord may rejoice in creation as the psalmist rejoices in the Lord (vv. 31-35).

(2) The psalm looks at the world as the work of the Lord's wisdom. "Wisdom" is the combination of knowledge, understanding, and capacity that makes one competent for the task at hand. "World," as the sum of the "works" of the Lord, is a display of such wisdom (v. 24). Note how the term "your works" is used at strategic points for the world and all that is in it (vv. 13, 24, 31). Note also that the description of the cosmic victor includes the motif of building (v. 3) and ordering things to their appointed place (vv. 8-9). In the poetic portrait of the world in vv. 10-23, everything has its provender, its place, and its time. Everything coheres. All are interrelated in the great web of the works of the Lord. To watch the wild animals, to enjoy a glass of wine, to see birds building nests, or to observe the rhythm of the passing of day and night is to sense and wonder and revel at the wisdom of it all. This dimension of the psalm comes quite close to the environmental ecological sensibility of modern times that knows from observation and accumulated experience how ex-

quisitely interrelated the world is. Only the secular mind misses the transcendent power informing it all.

(3) The psalm discloses the continuity between creation and providence, between the making of creatures and provision for their existence. The earth that the Lord has set on its foundations is depicted as a vast habitat. The Lord's creative activity continues through the shaping of the cosmos and the bringing forth of the earth from the primeval waters into the watering, feeding, and situating that make it possible for creatures to live. It is not too much to say that life itself is in the view of the psalm the crowning purpose of creation. The total dependence of life on the works of the Lord, described by the psalm in its best-known section (vv. 27-30), points finally to the integration of every life form into the great process of making and supporting. Life and death, death and life, together witness that creation continues in the world.

(4) In the way that it speaks of the human species (Heb. '*ādām*, NRSV "people") the psalm puts us in our place, so to say. "Adam" is arranged along with cattle and other animals in dependence on the great process of providence; humanity's activities are set in conformity to the calendars of the world (vv. 14-15, 20-23). The human species is simply one more of the creatures, with and among them, in contrast to its position at the apex of the created hierarchy in Psalm 8. All our similarities to the animals indicate how much we are part of the world. The human position of authority and responsibility does not promote us above the ranks of creature. Knowing the world is knowing self and knowing self is knowing the world. Our living and dying are knit together in the Lord's way with the world.

(5) Verse 35 must not be overlooked. It says that in the world known as the works of the Lord wickedness is a shocking and unacceptable incongruence. Wickedness, whether in others or in self, is a jarring, discordant note in the praise that alone is an adequate response to the world as the work of the Lord. So the psalm will not end without raising the question for the reader about accountability for what distorts the great system of life from its purpose of reflecting on the wisdom of God and responding with prayer and conduct, "Bless the Lord, O my soul."

VIII.

There are, of course, other psalms in which one may discover perspectives in which world is viewed. Psalm 19, with its opening declaration that the heavens are revealing the glory of their creator, is a well-known example. Like Psalm 24, Psalm 19 is composed of three quite different parts, which together point to the incompleteness of the revelation of God's glory in the heavens. While the glory is visible in the created world, the salvific word is heard only through the torah of the Lord, which calls humans to self-knowledge and reliance on the divine. The glory beheld by the eye supports the word heard by the ear and drives the heart to prayer. Psalm 148 uses the word pair "heavens/earth" as a compositional device: the first half calls for everything in the heavens to praise the Lord; the second half calls for everything on the earth to praise the Lord. Praise *in* the world is united with praise *above* the world so that the name of the Lord is declared as the truth about all reality. In such ways the topic "world" is incorporated into psalmic poetry that the Spirit can use to open the eyes of our spirit to see what otherwise we could not. There is more to this world through whose places and times we blunder than ever our unaided imaginations would surmise. There are, however, good reasons to believe that the one to whom this paper is written to honor and thank is more likely than most to discern the world in psalmic vision.

The Poetry of Creation: Psalm 104

Patrick D. Miller Jr.

Theological interpretation of creation has taken its biblical cues primarily from the first chapters of Genesis, recognizing that there are other places where God's creative activity is also spoken of or alluded to (e.g., Isa. 40–55 and Job 38–41). The Psalms also include various expressions of praise of the creator (e.g., Pss. 8, 19, and 33). In each of those instances, the praise of God's creative power is a feature of a larger whole that encompasses other concerns, so that the focus on creation and what God did and does in the act of creation and its maintenance is only a particular and not very large part of the whole. There is one psalm, however, that not only speaks wholly about God's creation of the world but does so extensively, namely, Psalm 104. As the most extended explication of God's work of creation outside of Genesis, it deserves a central place in any attempt to think about God as creator and about the doctrine of creation.[1]

I. The Structure and Movement of Psalm 104

The psalm begins and ends in praise, thus presenting itself to us as a hymn that is meant to exalt the Lord of Israel and evoke the praises of the people of God. The repeated participles describing the Lord's creative activities

---

1. There are clear reasons for seeing connections between this psalm and the hymn of Amenhotep IV to Aten, but such comparative analysis is not the aim of this essay.

(e.g., vv. 2-4 et al.) further serve to define the genre of the psalm as a hymn of descriptive praise.[2] The movement of the psalm is not straightforward. As poetry, the psalm reflects the kind of freedom to repeat, return, and move in different directions, even if such freedom is exercised under tight controls in the mind and imagination of the poet. This poem betrays just such a mixture of freedom and control. The psalm stakes out certain areas of the creative work of God and develops them, but it does so in a way that echoes earlier parts, repeats critical language, and marks pauses of exuberance and astonishment. What follows is a proposal about that movement.

Beginning with God and the creation of heaven (vv. 1-4)

After the opening self-command of the psalmist — "Bless the Lord, O my soul," a call to thanksgiving that forms an *inclusio* around the psalm and ties it to the preceding psalm — God is addressed in two formulations: "You are very great" and "You clothe yourself with honor and majesty." Here the praise of God begins by focusing directly upon the object, or better, the subject of praise with language that points the hearers of the psalm to the grandeur and greatness of God. No reference is made to God's activity or work. Only the sovereign and majestic "Lord my God" is in view. Praise begins with its eyes focused solely and fully on God known in greatness and majesty, characteristics whose implications are immediately laid out in the rest of the psalm.[3]

The second of these two formulations leads into a series of doxological participles that are characteristic of the descriptive praise of God: "the one clothing self with light like a garment" (v. 2a). This clause clearly parallels the preceding one, "you clothe yourself with honor and majesty," and so continues the exaltation of God as great and majestic. But

---

2. On this genre, see among others, Claus Westermann, *Praise and Lament in the Psalms* (Atlanta: John Knox, 1981), pp. 81-151; Patrick D. Miller, *Interpreting the Psalms* (Philadelphia: Fortress, 1986), pp. 64-78; and Frank Crüsemann, *Studien zur Formgeschichte von Hymnus und Danklied in Israel*, WMANT 32 (Neukirchen-Vluyn: Neukirchener Verlag, 1969), pp. 81-154.

3. Readers of the Psalter may hear in these words echoes of Psalm 8, where the creative works of God are also in view and where the definition of the human creature as "a little less than God" is found in the Lord's crowning humankind with "glory and honor," thus reflecting the honor and majesty of God.

in form and content, v. 2a is also parallel to the clause that follows and begins to speak of God as the creator. The function of this descriptive clause as a hinge between the exaltation of the deity and the enumeration of God's creative acts is evident in the following *identification of God with light* and the *light as the first creation of God.*

The equation of God with light is familiar in Scripture in several ways. There are texts that explicitly identify God and light, as, for example, Isaiah 60:19: "Your Lord will be your everlasting light, and your God will be your glory." In the New Testament, the equation is carried further as "God is light" becomes a part of the church's proclamation on a par with "God is love" in 1 John (1:5; cf. 4:8) and as the final visions of the Revelation to John reveal a time when there will be no darkness and no need of sun or light because "the glory of God is its light" (Rev. 21:23) and "the Lord God will be their light" (22:5). The equation of "light" and "glory" is appropriate in that the *kābôd,* which in the priestly tradition and elsewhere is a symbol of God's presence, is itself an image of light and radiance. Thus, this first participial phrase in Psalm 104 continues the description of the deity — great and shrouded with honor, majesty, and light.

But light is also the first of God's creations in Genesis 1. The one wrapping self in light is also the creator of the light. Light refers both to the beginning of creation and to the wondrous and mysterious nature of God. Note that the initial creative act is not the creation of light and darkness. It is only light, which is part of the very being of God. Darkness comes much later as part of the provisioning work of God and for a particular purpose (see below). There is something significant in seeing the first creative work of God as also characteristic of the being and nature of God. God and the world begin in light, and the light is both God and God's creation.

A series of five participial clauses in vv. 2b-4 sets out the first of three major movements in the poetry of creation (cf. Ps. 146:6): the creation of heaven. As in Genesis 1, heaven is the first creative work after light. It is no small moment that heaven is created. There is a vital tension in viewing heaven as both God's creation and God's abode. From heaven come the decrees that determine all that happens on earth. But heaven is not something other than earth at the point that they are both parts of the created order of God. Solomon attests to the paradox of heaven as the divine locus and creation when he prays to God in heaven and says, "Even heaven and the highest heaven cannot contain you . . ." (1 Kings 8:27). The priority of heaven over earth is hinted at in the ordering of creation here and in Genesis 1, but it is not a different order than that of earth. Heaven and earth are linked by a common maker.

II. The Creation of Earth (vv. 5-23)

Creation of earth and water (vv. 5-9)

The creation of heaven is followed by the creation of earth, but the poetry does not seek to set the sequencing of the acts of creation as a matter of any consequence. The fundamental fact about the earth is its stability.[4] Just as the one who keeps *tôrâ* and is kept by the Lord is not shaken (e.g., Ps. 15:5; 16:8; 17:5), so the earth created by the Lord does not shake or totter. An intimation of chaos is found in the reference to the watery deep *(tĕhôm)* that represents the pre-creation chaotic waters of Genesis 1 and even of the Babylonian creation epic. That "deep," however, is here demythologized and turned into a piece of clothing. Its potential for enveloping the earth and thus turning back the creation is hinted at in the description of the deep as a garment with which the Lord covered the earth. But the deep is not preexistent. Its presence is not mysterious in any way.

The focus on water in creation does, however, point to God's ordering and control of what might potentially be chaos. While the covering of the earth with water is the Lord's doing, it is not God's final intention for the ordering and stability of earth. That comes when the Lord's rebuke, in the form of thunder, sends the waters scurrying like animals to their ap-

---

4. The MT begins this section with a third person verb: "he set the earth on its foundations." While that may be the more difficult reading, it makes little sense in the context. More likely is the participial form *(yōsēd)*, that is, "the one setting the earth on its foundations." Most of the acts of creation here begin with participial expressions and then move to finite verbal forms, as in the case of these verses. In this instance, the finite verbal forms are especially appropriate as a way of referring to creation as a past act. The perfect and imperfect tenses that dominate this section of the psalm are probably all to be understood as referring to past events in creation. The parallelism of *qtl* and *yqtl* forms in v. 6 and the return to the *qtl* at the end of this section in v. 9 suggest a past tense translation of the *yqtl* verbs, *contra* NRSV. There is a tendency to use *yqtl* verbs to speak of the activity of the creatures and participles and perfect tenses to speak of God's activity.

The participial form of *yāsad* is reflected in some of the Greek witnesses as well as in one of the Psalms manuscripts from Cave 4 at Qumran. For the latter, see Peter W. Flint, *The Dead Sea Psalms Scrolls and the Book of Psalms*, STDJ 17 (Leiden: Brill, 1997), p. 97.

propriate place, the place that the Lord has set for them.[5] The creation of earth thus occurs in two stages, both of which are the Lord's doing: the covering of earth with the deep and the movement of these waters to places where they may function in a constructive way (see vv. 10-13). Reference to "earth" (*'ereṣ*) forms an *inclusio* around the section (vv. 5, 9).

Provision of water for fertility and life (vv. 10-13)

Again the section opens with a descriptive participle: "the one sending springs in the valleys." It closes with a summary statement that joins two key verbs of the passage: "The earth is *satisfied (śāba')* with the fruit of your *works (ma'ăśēkā)*." The creation of water as a flood control, which was the subject of the preceding section, shifts now to God's provision of water as a source of sustenance. Verse 13 is clearly transitional: the first half looks back to the preceding verses about watering the earth (cf. v. 3); the second half looks forward to the following verses about providing what is necessary to satisfy the needs of God's creatures.[6] The whole is a marvelous picture of springs and rivers and animals drinking from them. But the rivers are also there as the place where trees grow so that birds have a place to nest and sing. As in the preceding section, the passage concludes with a reference to the chief subject of these verses, earth (*'ereṣ*). The focus of vv. 5-23 is on the earth as the landmass on which the animals and human beings live. The poet turns to the sea later.

Provision of food and home (vv. 14-18)

The passage moves further into God's provisioning for life. As in the previous sections, a doxological participle begins this section and describes the

---

5. Some would see in this poetic rendition of creation mythological or mythopoeic antecedents having to do with the victory of the high god and the establishment of his palace after the victory is won. That reading seems to assume a great deal that is not explicit in the text and so does not commend itself as a governing metaphor. But the reference to the rebuke of the deep waters by the Lord is an explicit motif reflecting the activity of the warrior or storm god. It recurs in the New Testament when Jesus "rebukes" the wind and sea in the midst of a storm (Matt. 8:26 par.).

6. On this transitional technique, see H. Van Dyke Parunak, "Transitional Techniques in the Bible," *JBL* 102 (1983): 525-48.

basic creative act that characterizes it: "the one making the grass to sprout for the cattle and plants for the service of humankind." This is followed by an explicit series of purpose constructions with two infinitives (*lĕhôṣî'* and *lĕhaṣhîl*). The first two verses clearly have to do with the provision of food: plants for animals, bread and wine for human beings. The last two verses, however, building on the reference to the trees of the Lord, describe the provision of place or home for the creatures of earth: the trees as the place for birds (cf. v. 12) and the hills for the animals.

Provision of time for the creatures (vv. 19-23)

Paralleling the description of appropriate food and place, the exaltation of God's creative work moves now to speak of the provision of appropriate times for the different creatures to work for their food, that is, to satisfy their basic needs. This section probably also begins with a doxological participle (*'ōśeh* instead of *'āśâ*). The sun and moon and the darkness and light are not simply part of a sequence of creative acts. They are created for a purpose, to provide time for animals to hunt (darkness and night) and for people to do their labors (day). This function of the heavenly elements to provide time is underscored as the section closes with the words "and to their labor *until evening*" (v. 23).

Interlude (v. 24)

The poet's movement through the creative and providing work of God is interrupted by a burst of praise and a summary affirmation in v. 24. The whole point of the psalm is expressed in the first colon of the verse: "How marvelous are your works, O Lord!" The rest of the verse continues that exultant praise in a way that brings to conclusion and summarizes the creative work of God. The "all of them you have made" rounds off the extended description. The focus on earth and its creatures is reiterated in the final colon: "The earth is full of your creatures." The pronominal suffix "your" is not surprising here but important because the text has not really spoken about the creation of the creatures. It is all about providing the context for the creatures. Here the point is made explicitly that "all of them" — sensate and insensate things — are "your creatures."

III. The Creation of Sea (vv. 25-26)

The focus of the psalmist's praise hitherto has been entirely upon God's marvelous creation of the earth, of the landmasses, and of the waters that fertilize the land. Even where the "deep" appears in the preceding verses, it is as a garment, a skirt for the earth *(hā'āreṣ)*. Now the poet turns to the great waters, the seas, and makes two observations about them, each introduced by a directive "there" *(šām):*

1. The sea is the container for another whole group of creatures, the creeping or gliding things of the ocean. Like the earth, the sea was created as a habitat, specifically as the appropriate place for the manifold sea creatures, of whom Leviathan is the greatest of all.
2. The sea is a means of transportation. As with *hā'āreṣ,* the earth, the sea is a place for both animals and human beings.

IV. A Concluding Coda (vv. 27-35)

A series of mostly two-line strophes brings things to a close in different ways, wrapping up the account of God's creation and echoing earlier sounds of the poem.

The providing hand of God (vv. 27-28)

The whole of the poem is pulled together in terms of God's provision of what is good and needful for life. The concluding and summary character of these lines is suggested immediately by the *kullām* ("these all") at the beginning and by the "filled with good things" at the end (cf. v. 13).

The creation of life (vv. 29-30)

While the creation of sensate creatures comes at the end of this description of God's creative work — as also in Genesis 1 — this poetic rendition of the creation has already dealt extensively with the living creatures. The key to these verses is the order: death and then life and renewal. The creation of living beings is not reported as another step, or series of steps, in the creation. Like many other aspects of creation, the breath of life is part of the providence of God, the provision of continuity, so that each new birth is an act of creation, renewing the earth. Death is on the way to renewal.

A doxological benediction (vv. 31-32)

Now the psalm comes to its end in praise. The qualitative judgment that God makes in Genesis 1 that the creation is good is here turned into a wish for the Lord's joyful celebration over "his works." The use of the term "works" triggers a final creation doxology, consisting of participial clauses that have appeared before to refer to the creative acts of God, including now the creation of earthquakes and volcanoes.

Ascription of praise (vv. 33-34)

The psalmist who sought the Lord's rejoicing and celebration *(śāmaḥ)* in all "his works" now declares that he or she will rejoice and celebrate *(śāmaḥ)* in the Lord.

The fate of the wicked (v. 35a)

While this note seems an intrusion in the context of the praise of the creator, one who has read the Psalter from the beginning should not be surprised that a reference is made to the sinners and the wicked. The first psalm introduces the Psalter as an account of the ways of the righteous and the wicked. That the psalmist has turned in praise for God's great creative power and imagination does not mean that the reality of the wicked and their presence in this created order are forgotten. The psalmist calls for what Psalm 1 says will happen: the disappearance of the way of the wicked.

The inclusio-conclusion (v. 35b)

The psalm returns to its beginning with the framing self-command: "Bless the Lord, O my soul." This concluding note of praise is reinforced by the

94

hallelujah at the end, though this expression is fluid in the tradition, being set at the beginning of Psalm 105 in the Septuagint.[7]

V. Theological Reflections on Psalm 104

The richness of this psalm cannot be fully developed in any single study. Several observations may be made to suggest something of the contribution of the psalm to our understanding of theology, anthropology, and creation.

(1) To begin, Psalm 104 offers itself to the community of faith as *one of the most powerful interpretations of the first article of the Apostles' Creed:* "I believe in God the Father Almighty, Maker of heaven and earth." While that formulation is not exhausted by Psalm 104, it elaborates a picture of the "maker of heaven and earth" in detail. The wholeness of heaven and earth as the created works of God and, conversely, the testimony of heaven and earth to the imagination and power of God are the subject of this psalm from beginning to end. Psalm 104 fleshes out the making in a way that is reminiscent of Genesis 1 while in various respects more fully developed and in other respects more spartan (e.g., the distinctiveness of male and female).

(2) The two words that stand out in the psalm are "work(s)/made" (*ma'ăśeh/'āśâ;* vv. 13, 19, 24, 31) and "satisfy/fill" (*śāba';* vv. 13, 16, 28, and 11 in the Syriac). This is no accident, for they suggest that the psalm's chief subject matter is *the "works" or creation of God and God's "satisfying" or providing for the creation.* That is what this psalm talks about, and, when those are subjects in theological discussion, Psalm 104 is a primary text for our engagement.

(3) Psalm 104 makes us aware how much *poetry is the proper language of creation.* The poetic images of the psalm are many and rich. For example:

- The heavens are a great tent over us all and shelter the earth. What if it gets holes in it? The earth is like a giant oil-rig set up in the midst of the oceans, which, like the doer of *tôrâ*, is not "shaken."
- Clouds are chariots, the Lord's "dune-buggy" on which the Almighty God rides through the skies.

7. See Bruce Waltke, "Superscripts, Postscripts, or Both," *JBL* 110 (1991): 577-82.

- Thunder scares off the waters, so that they scurry away to their proper homes like frightened animals.
- The deep waters are locked up and held back like a dam.
- The ocean is a giant playpen for sea animals.
- Earth quakes when the deity looks and volcanoes erupt at the touch of God's finger.
- The Lord is architect, contractor, and breathing machine.

Surely no text of Scripture speaks more directly and in detail about the creation and about what God did and does in creation and in the sustaining of creation than does this psalm. But here we are not in the genealogical and liturgical style of Genesis 1 or the narrative account of Genesis 2, both of which have been constantly misinterpreted by the community of faith, who are unable to resist literality, technicality, scientific interpretation, and oversimplification. The beauty of Psalm 104 is that it is all about creation as God's act, an act that is complex and beautiful, whose manifestation in the created order is such that difference, complexity, and mutual interdependence are constantly evident.

Here, however, there is no external report vulnerable to literal and scientific analysis. One cannot analyze Psalm 104 that way. It is poetry, and we know not to interpret poetry literally. It stirs our imaginations and speaks about God's creative work in the only language that can really incorporate the reality of God in the creative process, thus enabling us to speak of "creation" and not simply "cosmos" or "nature." Psalm 104 is not an account, scientific or mythological; it is praise to the "Lord my God." God's creation may indeed be studied, but in the Scriptures it is the cause for grand praise. Theologians, therefore, and the community of faith may well be instructed to turn to this text as much as to Genesis 1 and 2, if for no other reason than to avoid misreading what the Bible tells us about creation and the creative work of God.

(4) Perhaps more than any other formulation, Psalm 104 conveys the *centrality of order and purpose in creation*. From the sending of the waters to their appropriate locales to the setting of night and day for animals and human beings, the *orderliness* of God's creation is underscored. The notion of harnessing the forces of nature is familiar to us as a human activity, from building dams to the splitting of the atom. Here such harnessing characterizes divine activity. The picture of the chaotic waters bounded and turned into useable water corresponds to the image of dam building.

That feat of engineering is often done precisely for flood control, as in vv. 5-9, or as a way of harnessing the power of the water for electricity. And there is surely nothing more devastating or evocative of the return to chaos than the power of a flood of water unleashed when a dam breaks.

In this text, however, it is especially the *purposefulness* of God's creative acts that is underscored. Thus, for example, the darkness is created to give time for animals to hunt their prey, and the springs of water come forth to provide water for them. Moreover, water is provided to make the trees grow so that the birds can nest and sing! A whole sequence of creative acts has bird songs as its goal!

The purposefulness of all that God did and does in creation is implicit in the celebration of the creation of sea. It is there to enable ships to sail and sea animals to play. This sense of the purpose of creation is quite explicit, however, in many other places. The high mountains are "for" the wild goats and the rocks are created as a refuge "for" the coneys. The Lord causes grass to grow "for" cattle and plants "for" the use of human beings. Especially in the provision of bread and wine, the purposive character of the divine creative activity is underscored with two infinitives: "to bring forth food . . . to make the face shine" (vv. 14-15).

Thus creation is to be understood as not simply occurring. It is a process of past and present. Indeed, the poetry does not set neat distinctions between these temporal dimensions or between creation and providence. The creative process is also complex and filled with significant interactions among its various elements or facets. This portrayal of an orderly and purposeful creation may be related to the psalmist's exclamation in v. 24: "*In wisdom* you have made them all." Although the text never raises the question of "why" creation, it makes clear that creation reflects the wisdom of God. There is a sensibility to the creation, an intelligibility that can only come from divine wisdom. This psalm joins with such passages as Proverbs 8:22-31 and Job 38–41 to make explicit connection between theological reflection on the creation and the wisdom of the sages. But while Job 38–41 *argues* for the wisdom of God, Psalm 104 discovers it in a *burst of praise*. It all makes such sense that one cannot but extol the amazing wisdom that has worked it all out.

(5) The order and purpose of creation also uncovers its *beauty* and the *pleasure* it brings. The order of creation is a part of its aesthetics, the beautifully crafted universe of heaven, earth, and sea brought into complex and pleasurable shape by the artistry of God. The praise of v. 24 is like the

exclamation a viewer makes before a magnificent painting. There is also a sense of playfulness, joy, and pleasure in this world God made. The word *śāmah*, "joy," "celebrate," "take pleasure in," is one of the most common words of the psalm. This is not an austere portrait of the "works" of God. There is delight in the world God made and in contemplating it. As a specific instance of the pleasure of creation, wine is to make the heart happy *(śāmah)*. But the psalmist makes this judgment more generally about the creation with the blessing-wish, "May the Lord take pleasure in *(śāmah)* his works" (v. 31), and follows that with the personal declaration, "I take pleasure in *(śāmah)* the Lord" (v. 34b). The goal of creation, in its details and in its whole, is to provide pleasure and delight.

There are two specific ways in which the creation as a place of pleasure is signaled. One is in the repeated identification of the trees as the locale for birds. Indeed, the ultimate purpose of fresh water is to nurture the birds so that they may sing! The singing of birds is one of the more obvious pleasures of the created order available to all and irresistible to the human senses. One of the answers to the why of creation is so that birds can sing and, by inference, that other creatures can enjoy their song.

A second way in which this point is made is in the portrayal of Leviathan as God's rubber duck in the great ocean bathtub, as it were.[8] Elsewhere, Leviathan is a terrible, fierce, and intimidating sea creature (e.g., Job 41). But the world God made, whether earth or sea, is not Jurassic Park. It is a place where birds can sing and monsters can play in the great sea. With all that water, God needed something to enjoy it, literally to "play" *(śāhaq)* in it. The text conjures up in our minds an image of Loch Ness, which everyone hopes really does contain a Leviathan playing in its depths!

One cannot romanticize this picture of a playful world, however. Nature is also there, red in tooth and claw. Indeed, the psalm understands the "preying" of the lion as a kind of "praying" (v. 21). The lions' roar for their prey is paralleled by a line that speaks of their seeking food from God. The lion's kill is an answer to prayer in this portrayal of God's created order. The chain of nature, dependent upon other animals for their food, is assumed. God's provision of food is extended throughout the natural world,

---

8. I am indebted to Jon D. Levenson for this marvelous contemporary translation of the picture of Leviathan sporting in the ocean. See his *Creation and the Persistence of Evil* (San Francisco: Harper & Row, 1988), p. 17.

but it incorporates the understanding of a food chain that pits animal against animal (cf. Job 38:39-41).

(6) The natural world is to be understood as *a home for the sensate beings God created,* creatures who *share the world together. Adam,* human being, is referred to in the midst of the other animals. There is a clear distinction between humankind and the different animals, but they are talked about in parallel ways as creatures of the world God has made. Humankind assumes not a central or special place but an integral part of the whole. Human and beast are paralleled in God's provision of sustenance (v. 14). God's creating of light and darkness, sun and moon, provides times for the animals to prowl for food (night) and for human beings to work for theirs (day). Even in vv. 27-30, there is an inclusiveness to the created order that transcends the distinctions and joins all the sensate beings in a shared experience. *"All"* (human and beast) look to God for their food (v. 27). That "all" is the plural subject of every verb that follows. All are dismayed when God's face is hidden. All return to dust. All are created by the spirit of God.

There is thus no language of domination, no *imago dei* that sets human beings apart from or puts them in rule over the other beasts. This rich, beautiful, and orderly world includes both kinds of living beings. They belong together and their provision is God's work, which is as fully there for the one category as for the other. Further, one is conscious of the plants, mountains, and rivers as necessary habitats for sensate beings. They have their place, their purpose in God's order precisely to provide homes for God's creatures. While bypassing all the complex issues of the interrelationships among these "creatures," the psalm assumes a world in which they are all present, all in their place, all doing their work, and all provided for by God's goodness.

(7) The text begs for some reflection on *bread and wine.* It understands both elements as provisions of God in the creation, bread for our strength and our life and wine for our joy and our relaxation. Here and elsewhere wine and beer are considered God's good gifts for our enjoyment of life. Noah is identified as the one who brought us "relief from our work and from the toil of our hands" (Gen. 5:21). How did he do that? Genesis 9:20 states he was the first to plant a vineyard and so provided wine that "gladdens the heart." Noah then gets drunk in the very next verse, and we have the messy little story of his son's disrespect. The Bible knows about this outcome of beer and wine and warns about the way in which God's good gifts can create havoc in their misuse (e.g., Prov. 31:4-5).

This text, therefore, reminds us of something very fundamental about God's provision of both our *sustenance* and our *enjoyment*. It is surely no accident that bread and wine, which are the elements of life in this text, are also the "elements" of the church in its sacramental life.

(8) Finally, one must recognize that if there are significant resonances and differences between this psalm and Genesis 1–2, it seems that Genesis 3 is also lurking in the background as the psalm comes to a close with the prayer: "Let sinners be consumed from the earth, and let the wicked be no more" (v. 35a).

We know now that what Genesis 3 speaks about is real, and one cannot speak about creation without a realization that there is a blemish on this wonderful world God has made. It has nothing to do with the way God created it. It has everything to do with the way the human creature responds to it. The "sinners" and the "wicked" can be any who sin, who disobey the divine commands. The context, however, makes us think of any who violate the creation, who take human life, who interfere with God's good provision for each creature, who tear down the trees in which the birds sing, who destroy Leviathan playing in the ocean, who poke holes in the heavenly tent, who let loose the forces of nature that God has brought under control in the very creation of a world. None of that is explicit in this brief concluding imprecation, but the total character of the psalm cautions us against defining the categories of "sinner" and "wicked" too narrowly when we confine ourselves to their apparent reference in the laments of the Psalter.

VI. The Psalm in Its Literary and Theological Context

One should not conclude an examination of Psalm 104 without some attention to its context. There are explicit indicators that this psalm is to be read in direct connection to the psalms that surround it. The most obvious of these is the *inclusio* "Bless the Lord, O my soul," which occurs not only at the beginning and ending of Psalm 104 but also in identical positions in Psalm 103. Such a duplication of beginning and conclusion can hardly be accidental or insignificant. That point is underscored, however, when one realizes that this sentence appears nowhere in Scripture except as a bracket around each of these psalms. The strong tie of Psalm 104 to the psalm that precedes it is further suggested by the presence of a superscription *lĕdāwîd*, "for David," at the beginning of Psalm 103 and by the lack of a superscription at the beginning of Psalm 104 to separate it from the preceding psalm.[9] Furthermore, Psalm 103 incorporates the thematic note of Psalm 104 ("who satisfies you with good as long as you live," v. 5; cf. 104:28 and other verses) and concludes with a call to "all his works" to bless the Lord, "works" whose detailed description then follows in Psalm 104.[10]

The intertextual connections extend to the psalms that follow Psalm 104. The "hallelujah" at the end of Psalm 104 serves to link it with the psalms that follow, which either begin or end with the same word, at least through Psalm 107. The absence of any superscription between Psalm 104 and the ones that follow through Psalm 107 further links these psalms. The conclusion to Book IV obviously creates a kind of break between Psalms 106 and 107, but it has often been noted that the connections between these two psalms are strong enough to bridge the separation effected by the benediction.[11]

There are also quite specific vocabulary links between the conclusion of Psalm 104 and Psalm 105.[12] At the end of Psalm 104, the psalmist says, "May my *meditation (śîḥî)* be pleasing to him" (v. 34). Then, at the beginning of Psalm 105, the psalmist calls for the community to "meditate on *(śîḥû)* all his wonderful works" (v. 2). The act referred to probably involves speaking out loud. I would suggest that the meditation of which Psalm 104 speaks is the poem itself, the praise of God that is sung in the psalm. So

9. In the Psalms Scroll from Qumran Cave 11, fragment E has the beginning of Psalm 104 and, like the LXX, includes a superscription *ldwd*. Among other fragments containing the beginning of Psalm 104, one seems to have this superscription while another does not. The tradition, therefore, is not unanimous on the continuous reading of Psalms 103 and 104. See Flint, *The Dead Sea Psalms Scrolls*, p. 96.

10. For further discussion of some of the linguistic connections between Psalms 103 and 104, see Norbert Lohfink and Erich Zenger, *Der Gott Israels und die Völker: Untersuchungen zum Jesajabuch und zu den Psalmen*, SB 154 (Stuttgart: Verlag Katholisches Bibelwerk, 1994), pp. 172-73. They note, for example, that only near the end of Psalm 103 and near the beginning of Psalm 104 do we have the expression "his ministers" *(měšārětāw)*.

11. That is particularly suggested by the way Psalm 107 begins with the same formulaic sentence as Psalm 106, part of which also begins Psalm 105: "O give thanks to the Lord for he is good; for his steadfast love endures forever." But the next two verses of Psalm 107 (vv. 2-3) also serve to answer the cry that concludes Psalm 106 (v. 47). The cry to the Lord to save and gather the people from among the nations is responded to in Psalm 107 by reference to those who have been redeemed and gathered from the lands.

12. For a detailed analysis of possible structural and linguistic connections between Psalms 104 and 105, see Pierre Auffret, *Essai sur la Structure Littéraire du Psaume 105*, Biblische Notizen Beihefte 3 (Munich: Manfred Görg, 1985), pp. 109-27.

also the meditation of Psalm 105 is the praise of God's wonderful works. The term "wonderful works" *(niplā'ôt)* looks backward and forward, backward into God's wonderful works of creation in Psalm 104 and forward into the wonderful works and acts for Israel in Psalm 105. Further, at the end of Psalm 104, there is the sequence of verbs "sing" *(šîr)*, "sing praise" *(zāmar)*, "meditate" or "tell" *(śîḥ)*, and "rejoice" *(śāmaḥ)* to express the psalmist's intention to praise (vv. 33-34). The verbs then follow the same sequence in Psalm 105:2-3 with the verb *hithallēl* inserted before the last one. This is the only place in the Psalter or anywhere in the Bible where this combination appears.

What then is the meaning of these associations? They are several. Most importantly, Psalms 103 and 104 are to be read together as "twin psalms." The poetic praise of God as creator and sustainer of the world, consequently, must be read and heard with the preceding thanksgiving to God for compassion, mercy, and forgiveness. If the works of God are celebrated in Psalm 104, it is the steadfast love of the Lord that is celebrated in Psalm 103. One cannot be sung without the other. Similarly, in Psalm 145 praise of God for and by "your works" (vv. 4, 10) is joined with thanksgiving that "the Lord is gracious and merciful, slow to anger and abounding in steadfast love" (v. 8; cf. 103:8). Moreover, the declaration that the Lord is "good to all" (v. 9; cf. 104:28) is set alongside the claim that "his *compassion* is over all *his works*" (v. 9; cf. 103:4, 8, 13; 104:13, 24, 31). In similar fashion, Psalm 33:4-7 joins the creative works of the Lord with the works of righteousness and justice. As "the earth is full of your creatures" (Ps. 104:24), so also "the earth is full of the steadfast love of the Lord" (Ps. 33:5).

In each of these instances, the community praises the Lord for the works of creation and the works of redemption, for satisfying the earth with good and filling it with steadfast love. The "works" of the Lord are manifold and complex: creating, sustaining, providing, redeeming, forgiving, righteous, and just. One may not escape in any kind of retreat to a cosmic praise removed from the realia of individual and communal history, from the hurts and wounds, the sins and injustices of this life. But the one who redeems and heals the sufferer, whether one or many, is also the one who stretched out the heavens and provides the continuities of the universe's existence. This joining of creation and history, of the universal and the particular, in God's "works" is then underscored as Psalm 104 leads on into the "national" hymns of Psalms 105 and 106. The wonderful works of the Lord that fill the earth with its creatures also bring salvation to and judgment on the chosen community of Israel. Psalm 104 in its literary context evokes a sustained "meditation" upon the God who is all in all, whose works encompass all of history and creation, and whose care of the wounds of the faithful is comparable to God's care of the animals of earth and sea. Such meditation can only end in praise: "Bless the Lord, O my soul! Hallelujah!"

"More than an 11 A.M. Savior": A Homily on Psalm 8

Dusty Kenyon Fiedler

Do you know about "the 11 A.M. Savior"? Some who are critics of the church and of Christians — perhaps because they have not seen us put into action often enough the forgiving, transforming, powerful love that we profess — suggest that we Christians acknowledge Jesus Christ only at 11 A.M. worship each Sunday. There we sing praises to him and promise to follow him, but in reality, they say, we leave Jesus behind in the church sanctuary and go our merry way. We pay him little attention until we meet him again in church at 11 A.M. the next Sunday. This is what some critics and cynics say.

Of course, our critics speak some truth, for we are all guilty of leaving Jesus behind. We leave him out of our decision making; we rely too stubbornly on our own strength, even when we know that his strength is far more powerful; and we pridefully want to stay in control rather than submitting to his gracious providential care. Yet the truth is that even if we in our willfulness *do* choose to relate only to "the 11 A.M. Sunday Savior," even if we choose to have nothing to do with God, that's not enough for God. No matter what we choose for our life, God our loving creator does not give up on us.

Perhaps what our critics do not understand is that — no matter how fickle or hypocritical we are — God remains faithful still. Trusting in God's goodness, we can declare there is no such thing as an 11 A.M. Savior, one who is just tangential to our lives or unimportant, on the periphery. God

104

has created us in his own image, according to the biblical story, and God is intimately related with every moment of our lives, whether we accept God's love or not. The idea of a limited 11 A.M. Savior fails to recognize the "wideness of God's mercy" toward us. The idea of an 11 A.M. Savior is too stingy, too wasteful, and too tightfisted for the gracious God whom we worship, the God "who so loved the world that he gave his only Son" (John 3:16).

The author of Psalm 8 knows our God, who is so much more than an 11 A.M. Savior. The psalmist sees a God whose intricate handiwork in creation shows loving care for all things. The psalmist is overwhelmed with awe and praise in the face of such tender love. "When I look at your heavens, the work of your fingers, the moon and the stars that you have established" and "set in their places" (TEV), then I see how awesome is God's concern for each of us, the psalmist says. If, as is sometimes suggested, this psalm of praise was written by David himself, one can imagine the shepherd boy looking up at all the twinkling, starry host while tending his father's sheep, feeling a little less alone and knowing that God's closeness and care are for real, so that he is moved to sing this song of thanksgiving to the One who has designed such a great and magnificent world.

Or, if you are not much of a stargazer, there are so many other places to see and be moved by what the psalmist calls "the work of God's fingers" (v. 3) — like double rainbows, the glorious painted hues of sunrise and sunset, waterfalls, newborn babies, and the red and orange and yellow carpet of autumn leaves. Just revel in their beauty! Who can escape the closeness of God's presence when standing at the ocean's edge and listening to the pounding waves rolling in? And who does not marvel at the goodness of a creator God when seeing shimmering blue salamanders sunning themselves on a wall, or bright yellow finches arriving at the feeder to announce dark winter's end, or floppy stingrays saluting us at the water's edge? Annie Dillard's nearby Tinker Creek certainly became a vista for admiring God's handiwork, and Robert Frost's "swinger of birches," bending left and right, comes closer to heaven as he swings. Just look around you, the psalmist encourages, look at this magnificent world and you'll see God's tender love! You'll see how God cares intimately about all creation. Thank goodness, our God is so much more than an 11 A.M. Savior!

But the vastness of God's creative gifts makes the psalmist aware of the distance that separates creature from creator. When the psalmist looks up at the wide expanse of the night sky, he feels so insignificant. The psalmist recognizes his own finiteness in the face of God's infinite ways. He sees how fleeting is his own transient life in comparison to God's eternity. As he looks at the heavens, the psalmist sees how orderly, steady, and dependable are God's ways in comparison to his own perpetual capriciousness and instability. No doubt the psalmist also remembers his own sinfulness — how he has let others down while God remains faithful still; how he gets petty with his hurtful gossip and mean words while God is pure and kind. Looking up at the magnificent sky, the psalmist sees the great, holy distance that separates us from our creator God.

"Yet" — that little word is chock full of grace — "Yet you have made [human beings] a little lower than God, and crowned them with glory and honor" (v. 5). The following paraphrase expresses the psalmist's utter amazement that God is so gracious: "Yet you have made me in your image. . . . I am dumbfounded that you should care personally about me."[1] That little conjunction "yet" is a declaration of God's gracious willingness to reach across the vast distance that separates us as creatures from our creator. This little word "yet" is the forerunner of the truth we come to know in Jesus Christ. "Yet" declares that *nothing* "will be able to separate us from the love of God in Christ Jesus our Lord" (Rom. 8:39).

The psalmist declares that God is "mindful" (v. 4) of us, fully aware of each one of us. That's such a wonderful image! With the psalmist, can you make that leap of faith to imagine God thinking about you? In your mind's eye, or as your heart sees, can you envision that the great Lord God Almighty, the very One who brought order out of chaos and now continues to bring light into our darkest days, knows when you are bone-weary but still have so much to do. This God knows where you are ticklish and what mellow thoughts prompt you to whistle in the shower. God is so "mindful" of you as to know your daydreams and why you cry yourself to sleep at night. God knows "when you sit down and when you rise up" and is "acquainted with all your ways," says the author of Psalm 139 (vv. 2, 3); and God knows "your going out and your coming in," a declaration of faith from the beloved Psalm 121 (v. 8).

Even if we choose to remember God in Christ Jesus only at 11 A.M. on Sundays, that does not change the truth that God is always "mindful" of each of us in all seasons. We are so precious in God's sight! That's Good News indeed!

---

1. Leslie F. Brandt, *Psalms Now* (St. Louis: Concordia Publishing House, 1973), p. 17.

Creatio Corporis and the Rhetoric of Defense in Job 10 and Psalm 139

William P. Brown

Among the numerous recent studies devoted to the topic of creation in the Bible, the subject of the human being's genesis *in utero* has been largely overlooked.[1] Most treatments have focused upon biblical texts that depict the *cosmic* contours of creation,[2] and understandably so. Today's interpreter lives in an exciting age in which the frontiers of knowledge about the universe are expanded almost daily. Consequently, those texts that refer to the more "mundane" creation of the individual, of *creatio corporis*, have

---

1. Richard J. Clifford's survey of the ancient Near Eastern accounts of creation misses this dimension entirely, a lack most notable in his treatment of Psalms and Job (*Creation Accounts in the Ancient Near East and in the Bible*, CBQMS 26 [Washington, D.C.: Catholic Biblical Association, 1994], pp. 151-63, 185-97; idem, "Creation in the Psalms," in *Creation in the Biblical Traditions*, ed. Richard J. Clifford and John J. Collins, CBQMS 24 [Washington, D.C.: Catholic Biblical Association, 1992], pp. 57-69). Any discussion of the theological import of the individual's creation is also lacking in William P. Brown, *The Ethos of the Cosmos: The Genesis of Moral Imagination in the Bible* (Grand Rapids: Eerdmans, 1999); Bernard W. Anderson, *From Creation to New Creation*, OBT (Minneapolis: Fortress, 1994), pp. 209, 245; Jon D. Levenson, *Creation and the Persistence of Evil* (San Francisco: Harper & Row, 1988). See, however, Ronald A. Simkins's cursory survey, which makes no distinction between birth metaphors that describe the genesis of corporate Israel and those that describe the creation of an individual (*Creator & Creation* [Peabody, MA: Hendrickson, 1994], pp. 91-99).

2. For example, Gen. 1:1–2:3; Pss. 8, 19, 33, 136, 104; Prov. 8:22-31; Job 38–41; Isa. 40–55.

been neglected in most discussions of creation theology.[3] Observing that many recent collaborative studies on cosmology and theology are far too abstruse, Janet Martin Soskice rightly complains, "Why do our collections of essays always have that swirling galaxy on the cover, or a piece of electron-microscopal photography, and never a baby's foot, or a woman drawing water at a well . . . ?"[4] To be sure, absent in Scripture is any sustained reflection upon the genesis of the individual comparable to the extensive accounts of cosmic creation. Moreover, in a world seemingly on the brink of overpopulation and in a culture poisoned by the politics of abortion, the ever-repeating mystery of creation in the womb has lost its power to stir our imagination and to propel us to reflect upon God's purpose for *all* of life. For a few biblical poets, however, the concrete events of conception and gestation were no less evocative of the mystery of divine providence than God's primal act of cosmic creation.[5] Like the accounts of cosmic creation, biblical descriptions of personal genesis are fraught with much background.

This essay examines two accounts of personal genesis that share a common rhetorical aim, namely, that of effecting vindication from God in a situation of dire conflict. While Psalm 139 and Job 10 bear comparable terminology, they are strikingly dissimilar in tone and tenor. Both illustrate in dramatically different ways how the language of creation is employed to address moral crises. Together, these two divergent texts form a rhetorical bridge between genesis and moral character, indeed, between creation and covenant.

I. Psalm 139

This much beloved psalm begins in much the same way as it ends (vv. 1, 23).[6] It opens with an intensely personal pronouncement that will prove to be

---

3. The exception is the account of the first man and woman (Gen. 2:4-25), which, however, depicts the genesis of humankind, a one-time event.

4. Janet Martin Soskice, "Creation and Relation," *Theology* 94 (1991): 32.

5. For example, Num. 11:11-12; Jer. 1:5; Isa. 49:1, 5; Job 10:8-11, 18-19; Ps. 22:9-11; 139:13-18; Prov. 8:22-25; Eccles. 11:5; 2 Macc. 7:22-23, 27.

6. The genre of the psalm is that of individual complaint (see vv. 19-24), more precisely a defense of innocence against an undefined false accusation. See the survey in Leslie C. Allen, *Psalms 101–150*, WBC 21 (Waco, TX: Word, 1983), pp. 254-60.

broadly retrospective in scope: "YHWH, you have searched me and known me." Cast in exhortative form, the penultimate verse transforms the initial pronouncement into an appeal, while the last verse specifies this appeal. The movement from pronouncement to petition characterizes the development of the psalm as a whole. The psalmist's claim in v. 1, along with vv. 2-18, lays the groundwork for the psalmist's appeal in vv. 19-24. The temperature of the rhetoric rises dramatically in this latter section, suggesting a situation of grave conflict between the psalmist and his enemies.

It is often claimed that for all of its sublime language this psalm was originally a prayer for vindication by one falsely accused of a crime.[7] Certainly, the polemical discharge in the latter section suggests something of the sort. Furthermore, the psalmist's offer to be tested by God at his enemies' expense indicates a situation in which the psalmist's integrity is vigorously questioned. The reason remains elusive, although the key may very well lie in the interpretation of the last verse, in which the word commonly translated as "wicked" (*'ōṣeb*) refers also to idolatry.[8] In any case, the rhetoric of vindication is unmistakably present. Beneath the poetic elegance lies an urgent, if not defiant, appeal to YHWH to test the psalmist's moral mettle.[9]

Unlike other psalmic appeals for vindication or deliverance from unnamed enemies, this psalm refrains from reveling in the rhetoric of bitter lament or accusation.[10] In addition, the psalm lacks a litany of righteous deeds, as in Psalm 26. God is never the object of bitter complaint, although

---

7. See Robert Coote's socio-liberationist treatment, "Psalm 139," in *The Bible and the Politics of Exegesis: Essays in Honor of Norman K. Gottwald on His Sixty-Fifth Birthday*, ed. David Jobling, et al. (Cleveland: Pilgrim, 1991), pp. 33-38. Albert Anderson identifies the psalm as a "thanksgiving of an acquitted man," that is, a thanksgiving *after* the accused has been acquitted (Albert A. Anderson, *Psalms: Volume 2 [73–150]*, NCBC [London: Marshall Pickering / Grand Rapids: Eerdmans, 1972], pp. 904-5). However, the psalmist's moral status is still in question at the end of the psalm.

8. Much has been made of the particular nuance of *'ōṣeb*, which can denote either pain (1 Chron. 4:9; Isa. 14:3) or idolatry (Isa. 48:5). Hence, it is often suggested that the psalmist has been falsely accused of idol worship (so, e.g., Ernst Wurthwein, "Erwägungen zu Psalm 139," *VT* 7 [1957]: 165-82; Anderson, *Psalms: Volume 2*, p. 912; Allen, *Psalms 101–150*, pp. 250, 253).

9. In the last section (vv. 19-24), the psalmist makes the remarkable move from vindictively pronouncing the fate of his wicked enemies (vv. 19-21) to beseeching God to discern (and, thereby, expunge) any wicked way *within him*. Humility may not be the psalmist's virtue, but neither is blind self-righteousness his vice (cf. Ps. 7:8-9; 17:3).

10. Compare Pss. 10, 13, 22, 44, 89.

the Deity is urgently exhorted to act (v. 23; cf. v. 19). From beginning to end, YHWH is profiled as an enduring presence, the source of wonder and self-knowledge (vv. 2-5, 7-12, 13-18). Knowledge of God affirms and protects the human self, though its potential to convict and correct the self lies ever in the background. The psalmist's testimony to such knowledge even transports the language of military siege into the realm of divine beneficence (v. 5).[11]

YHWH's sustaining hand keeps the psalmist secure, but secure from what? Given the larger context, vv. 19-24 notwithstanding, the psalmist is concerned not so much with the specific threat of his enemies as with potential threat to his moral integrity. God's hand has kept him safe from moral turpitude; it holds him fast and leads him in the way (vv. 10, 24).[12] Yet that is not all. The term that most graphically evokes divine protection, ṣûr ("hemmed in") in v. 5, also adumbrates the psalmist's creation (see v. 16).[13] As will be shown, the psalmist's very genesis is inextricably bound up with the testimony of his unassailable integrity.[14]

Borne on the wings of his imagination, the psalmist traverses the height, depth, and breadth of the created order (vv. 7-10) and concludes with the nature and mystery of his own genesis (vv. 13-16). His travels to the farthest limits of the cosmos serve to demonstrate God's all-pervasive presence. By themselves, the rhetorical questions of vv. 7-9 might suggest the scenario of an individual attempting to escape the wrath of divine justice. The fact that the psalmist cannot escape from God's searching pres-

---

11. For the primary meaning of "besiege" (ṣûr), see, e.g., 2 Sam. 11:1; 1 Kings 15:27; Isa. 29:3 (cf. Ezek. 5:3; Cant. 8:9; Deut. 14:25).

12. Regardless of the particular nuance of ʿôlām in v. 24 ("everlasting" or "ancient"), the way (derek) is a common metaphor that denotes moral conduct and character (e.g., Ps. 5:9; 39:2; 49:14; 50:23; 119:5, 26, 59, 168; Prov. 4:26; 5:8, 21; 10:9; 14:2, 8, 12; 16:2, 7, 9, 17, 25; 19:3, 16; 21:2, 29).

13. See Exod. 32:4; 1 Kings 7:15; Jer. 1:5a (ketib). The example in Jeremiah finds peculiar resonance with the psalm: "Before I formed you (ʾeṣṣôrĕkā) in the womb, I knew you" (cf. Ps. 139:13-16). Furthermore, Old Greek, Peshitta, and Vulgate understood ṣûr in v. 5 to refer to the psalmist's creation rather than to his protective confinement. Compare the related verb yṣr in v. 16.

14. This can be discerned in part by its placement in the body of the psalm. Logically, vv. 13-16 would have been more appropriately placed after v. 6, given the constant reference to wonder (root plʾ) in vv. 6, 14. Instead, the section on the psalmist's genesis bears greater rhetorical weight in its position immediately preceding the final exhortative section (vv. 19-24).

ence is, however, no reason to lament.[15] It is, to the contrary, his source of comfort and basis of appeal. God's searching presence is not the outstretched hand of judgment poised to snatch the psalmist in flight (cf. Isa. 5:25; 9:12, 17), but the accompanying, guiding hand that has formed the psalmist's being and determined his moral direction (v. 10).[16]

Eschewing the language of lament, the psalmist is resolutely confident that he can rely upon God's help to safeguard him wherever he is, even at the point of death (vv. 11-12).[17] The images of darkness and light, along with their natural associations with death and life, respectively, have everything to do with what follows in the psalmist's account of his genesis. The psalmist makes the startling claim that darkness is like light in God's sight (v. 12), suggesting that death and life are paradoxically related (cf. v. 8). Since the threat of death is ever present in the act of birth, the confluence of such opposing images is not surprising (cf. Gen. 1:3-4). Indeed, the one domain that joins the separated domains of light and darkness is the warm womb, where life itself is generated, hidden from all except God's penetrating purview. To God the womb bears the radiant effulgence of new life, in contrast to Sheol, death's dark domain (v. 8). Only in the womb do these contrasting metaphors, light and darkness, share the same tenor, life.

From the spatial extremities of the cosmos the psalmist moves to the temporal extremities of his own life (vv. 13-18). Reaching back to his gestation, the psalmist extols the mystery of his genesis. This unit features a veritable catalogue of creation rhetoric: "create" (*qnh;* v. 13),[18] "knit" (*skk;* v. 13),[19] "make" (*'śh;* v. 15), "weave" (*rqm;* v. 15),[20] and "form" (*yṣr;* v. 16).

---

15. E. Baumann ("Der 139. Psalm — ein Bekenntnis der Metanoia," *EvT* 11 [1951]: 187-90) claims that vv. 7-12 indicate the psalmist's attempt, like Jonah, to flee from God's abusive control of his life (vv. 13-16). Such an interpretation introduces, however, an artificial break between vv. 7-12 and 13-18.

16. J. Holman ("Analysis of the Text of Ps. 139," *BZ* 14 [1970]: 302-7) rightly observes the central significance of v. 10 in the first half of the psalm.

17. Compare Job 3:3-10, 16, wherein the images of darkness are correlated with death.

18. The object of this verb can include all creation (Gen. 14:19, 22) as well as corporate Israel (Deut. 32:6) and individuals (Prov. 8:22; Gen. 4:1).

19. The term is attested elsewhere only in Job 10:11 and possibly Prov. 8:23 (emended *nĕsakkōtî*).

20. Only here is the verb used to denote conception, whereas the term is typically used, for example, to refer to the embroidery of the priestly vestments (Exod. 28:39; 36:37) and cloth hangings for the tabernacle (Exod. 26:36; 27:16; 38:18, 23; 39:29).

In addition, certain anatomical terms — "womb" (v. 13), skeletal "frame" (v. 15), and "embryo" (*gōlem*;[21] v. 16) — signify the particularity of personal genesis. The movement within this central section is subtle and systematic, as illustrated in the following outline.

A	Spatial beginning: "in the womb"	13
	B Praise of God: declaration of intent	14aα
	C Reason: self-wonder	14aβ
	B′ Praise of God: divine wonder	14aγ-b
A′	Spatial beginning: "in the depths of the earth"	15
A	Temporal beginning	16
	B Praise of God: incomparable thoughts	17-18a
A′	Temporal end	18b

Both subsections, distinguished by their respective references to the spatial and temporal dimensions of individual creation, are united in the language of direct address (vv. 13a, 18b). It is God who fashioned the psalmist's identity in the beginning, and at the end of life it is the same God to whom the psalmist casts his allegiance (*wĕˁôdî ˁimmāk;* v. 18b).[22] In both sections, praise of God plays an indispensable role, evidenced in the alternating placement of doxological pronouncements. Creation and praise are strategically related in the psalmist's appeal.

Also inseparable are the individual and the corporate, even cosmic, dimensions of creation. First and foremost, gestation in the womb indicates that the psalmist in particular is "fearfully and wonderfully made" (v. 14a). However, the psalmist is also moved to declare in the same breath that *all* of God's works are wonderful.[23] Moreover, a corporate understanding of personal creation is evident in the reference to "the depths of the earth" (v. 15b). Forming a literary envelope with v. 13 (*tĕsukkēnî bĕbeṭen ˁimmî*), this expression does more than repeat the psalmist's conception; it correlates his own genesis with the creation of *all* humanity. The maternal womb is now the chthonic womb. The womb and the earth's

21. Given its attestation in Talmudic Hebrew, this nuance is suggested in *BDB*, p. 166 (so also Anderson, *Psalms: Volume 2*, p. 910; Allen, *Psalms 101–150*, p. 252).

22. The expression is the reverse of Ps. 23:4 and Isa. 41:10, which stress God's presence with the speaker. In Ps. 139:18, it is the *psalmist's* solidarity with God that is stressed, which, in turn, defines the psalmist's integrity.

23. See Pss. 78:32; 86:10; 105:2; 107:8, 15, 21, 31; 136:4.

depths are, respectively, the microcosm and macrocosm of human creation.[24] The psalmist's creation in the womb replicates the genesis of humanity from the earth's "womb."[25] His "genesis of secrecy" is, consequently, made public. By collectivizing the private, unique moment of his conception, the psalmist invites the larger community to stand in solidarity with him, and therein lie the seeds of his vindication.

The concentric structure of the first section (vv. 13-16a) reflects an egocentric orientation. The psalmist likens himself to a miraculous wonder *(pl').* The passive verbal form (Nip'al) is juxtaposed with its pair *yr'*, which denotes fear (v. 14). Both terms stereotypically denote God's mighty acts in judgment and redemption.[26] In Psalm 106:22, for example, the niphal participles are set in parallel to describe the deeds of God in the "land of Ham" and at the "Red Sea." "Wondrous works" *(niplā'ôt)* and "awesome deeds" *(nôrā'ôt)* are stock descriptions of God's dealings with Israel in history. Through such deeds, God gains international renown (e.g., Ps. 111:4, 9) and elicits undivided reverence and praise from a covenant people (Ps. 96:4).

What is striking about Psalm 139:14 is that the typical attributes of divine activity are applied to the psalmist.[27] God's wondrous work in creation provokes self-wonder. Far from considering himself a "maggot" or "worm" (Ps. 22:7; Job 25:6), the psalmist finds a direct correspondence between God and himself. The chasm that divides the divine and the human is bridged in conception and supported by God's leading presence throughout life. The psalmist is a work of wonder as well as a work in progress. Through his testimony, the formation of the human self, physically and morally, is rendered comparable to the divine acts of deliverance, covenant, and conquest, those marvelous deeds that elicit corporate praise and covenantal obedience.

---

24. See Simkins, *Creator & Creation*, p. 95. In addition, the psalmist paradoxically utilizes imagery most normally associated with Sheol to refer to the birth of humankind (cf. Deut. 32:22; Ps. 86:13; Ezek. 31:14-18).

25. See Job 1:21; 2 Esd. 5:48; 10:9-14; Sir. 16:30; 40:1; Gen. 2:7; 3:19.

26. For *pl'*, see Exod. 3:20; Judg. 6:13; Jer. 21:1; Ps. 9:2; 26:7. For *yr'*, see Deut. 10:21; 2 Sam. 7:23; Isa. 64:2; Pss. 106:22; 145:6. Both terms are paired or interrelated in Exod. 34:10; Pss. 96:3-4; 106:22; 145:5-6.

27. This unusual case of self-reference evidently provoked the textual revision found in Old Greek, Targum, Peshitta, Vulgate, and 11QPs[a], which ascribe the psalmist's attributes to God. The masoretic *yod* cannot be explained by simple textual corruption. The MT is the *lectio difficilior.*

As a personal embodiment of divine action in history, the psalmist reshapes the Priestly notion of creation in God's image with the bold contours of doxology and self-wonder (cf. Gen. 1:26-27). Created and nurtured, the psalmist's very being reflects an awesome God (v. 14).[28] He is a living testament to God's marvelous ways. Any attack against the psalmist's personal integrity, thus, is tantamount to an affront against God (vv. 21-22). The language of gestation serves to establish lines of correspondence between the divine and himself, thereby driving deeper the wedge between the psalmist and his detractors. As the psalmist was fashioned "in secret" by the God from whom nothing is hidden (v. 15), so the psalmist's integrity, though publicly attacked, remains secretly intact.

The psalmist's reflections upon his own genesis constitute the cornerstone of his appeal to God (and neighbor). Every sinew and synapse is the wondrous result of God's uncompromising love and justice, for it is as judge and tester that God creates and sustains the human self.[29] Every physical thread woven in secret contains the moral fiber of the psalmist's being. In conception was established both the physical and moral constitution of a human being. In his unabashed preoccupation with the sheer wonder of the self, the psalmist's praise becomes his apologia. By persisting in praise and wonder over his very being, the psalmist holds fast to an inviolable integrity. He praises God for creating and comprehending every fiber of his being over and against a world that would deny him that right and privilege. Only the God who created the psalmist can comprehend the full and intimate measure of his integrity (v. 4).

Notably absent is any reference to the psalmist's righteous conduct, except as it is demonstrated in his display of righteous indignation against his enemies (vv. 19-24). The psalmist strategically sets the onus of his innocence upon God, his creator. As God created him with an inviolable integrity, so God continues to lead the psalmist throughout his life. His genesis in the womb is an "inward testimony" to the promise of a righteous life, publicly vindicated. The granting of life is, in turn, a granting of moral direction and triumph. The psalmist trusts that God will continue to justify

28. It is often noted that beginning with the 18th Dynasty, Pharaoh is called the "image of Re" as well as "beloved son" (see Hans Wildberger, "Das Abbild Gottes," *TZ* [1965]: 245-59, 481-501; Werner H. Schmidt, *Die Schöpfungsgeschichte der Priesterschrift* [Neukirchen-Vluyn: Neukirchener Verlag, 1964], pp. 136-42).

29. James L. Mays correctly notes the prevailing divine image of judge in the psalm (*Psalms*, Interpretation [Louisville: John Knox, 1994], pp. 426, 429).

him whenever his integrity is impugned (vv. 19-22). As the product of God's creation and the object of God's comprehension, the psalmist's integrity is God's bulwark against his foes.

II. Job 10

The language of individual creation plays an equally crucial role in Job's discourse. Chapter 10 marks the height of Job's acrimony, and, not accidentally, the language of gestation comes to the fore. As is often noted, the chapter is a mixture of accusation (vv. 2-7), lament (vv. 15-17), and appeal (vv. 20-22) set within a larger disputation or protest of innocence that seeks redress from God (9:2–10:22).[30] In contrast to the psalm, Job's discourse makes explicit at the very outset what is at stake, namely, a situation of moral conflict (cf. Ps. 139:19-24). For Job it is a crisis of such unprecedented proportions so as to precipitate a legal disputation (*rîb;* 10:2; cf. vv. 6, 14-15, 17a; 9:2-4, 12-16, 19b-20).[31] As in the psalm, Job's discourse is replete with the nomenclature of character and creation. Job speaks not only of condemnation and acquittal (vv. 2, 14), but also, like the psalmist, of God's probing presence. What is notably absent, however, is any reference to praise or wonder. Effusive praise is replaced by bitter complaint; self-wonder (Ps. 139:14) is overcome by self-loathing (Job 10:1).

The flow of Job's rhetoric is striking in its alternating arrangement of references to creation (vv. 3a, 8-12, 18a) and jurisprudence (vv. 3a, 3b, 6-7, 13-17). Whereas the psalmist's juridical concern frames the psalm as a whole, Job's discourse tightly interweaves matters of creation and courtroom throughout. Also in alternating sequence are Job's reflections on birth and death (vv. 8-9, 18-19). In these verses, Job moves fluidly from describing his genesis to accusing God of blatant duplicity: God created Job; now God seeks his destruction (vv. 8-9). The temporal distance between his pristine past and his present distress only heightens this inscrutable discrepancy in God's design. Had the womb become his tomb, Job wistfully asserts, the incongruity would have been relieved. Job's final plea is

---

30. See D. J. A. Clines, *Job 1–20*, WBC 17 (Waco, TX: Word, 1989), pp. 224-26, 244.

31. For further background, see J. J. M. Roberts, "Job's Summons to Yahweh: The Exploitation of a Legal Metaphor," *RestQ* 16 (1973): 159-65.

that he be left alone by God to seek his place where "light is like darkness," Sheol, the anti-womb (v. 22; cf. Ps. 139:11-12).

In the series of pointed questions in vv. 3-7, the language of creation first emerges in a general statement in v. 3a. Job asks, "Does it seem good to you . . . to despise *(m's)* the work *(yĕgîaʿ)* of your hands?" Job identifies himself as a unique creation that entails certain responsibilities on the part of the creator, such as comprehending and sustaining the creature. Such responsibilities are made quite clear in the series of rhetorical questions posed in vv. 4-5. Job reverses, in effect, a proverb found in the story of Samuel's anointing of David that attributes unqualified perceptive ability to God: "YHWH does not see as mortals see" (1 Sam. 16:7). For Job, God is no different from Job's shortsighted friends, who see only guilt in his suffering. As God sees, so God is, grossly finite and partial (Job 10:5). As in the psalm, the issue of God's comprehension is of critical import. Whereas the psalmist extols God's perceptive capacity, penetrating even the dark womb, Job accuses God of shortsightedness, of seeing only guilt in his misery. Nevertheless, in v. 7 Job stridently adjures that God knows his innocence;[32] the psalmist simply implies it (cf. Ps. 139:1-3, 19-24). In so doing, Job asserts that God's divine status is irreparably compromised. God stands accused of willful and gross negligence, of deliberately seeking out Job's iniquity when God fully *knows* it is not there. Although the psalmist and the sage affirm the presence of God's hand upon them both (Ps. 139:5, 10; Job 10:7), Job seeks deliverance from it while the psalmist appeals for continued support by it. Unwilling to move from knowledge to acknowledgment of his innocence, the God of Job is at cross purposes with creation and, so Job insinuates, with God's very self.

How does God know that Job is truly innocent, despite all appearances to the contrary? His answer is simple: God created him. The numerous metaphors that refer to Job's divinely fashioned existence in vv. 8-12 and 18-19 constitute the height and heart of his complaint. As conveyed in the psalm, creation involves intimate, affirming knowledge on the part of God; the integrity of Job's being is attested in his genesis. The thematic parallels in vv. 6-9 are suggestive. Here, two inseparable cross purposes are set side by side upon God's shoulders: seeking Job's iniquity while knowing his innocence (vv. 6-7) and seeking Job's death despite having created him

32. Divine knowledge of Job's innocence marks a new development in relation to Job's previous complaint (cf. 9:15, 20, 21).

(vv. 8-9). Their juxtaposition forges a correlation between Job's creation and his innocence. By the same token, Job's integrity is bound up with God's credibility as creator. The defamation of Job's character amounts to an unraveling of his moral and physical fiber, which God had carefully knit (*skk;* v. 11; cf. Ps. 139:13). Along with creation comes God's preserving favor (v. 12). As in the psalm, the continuum of God's sustaining and discerning care begins with creation; its culmination is reached in vindication, a certainty for the psalmist, a lost cause for Job.

In a fit of irony, Job twists the "genesis of secrecy" motif of Psalm 139:15. Perceived only by God, prenatal development remains hidden from all human eyes. Yet for the psalmist the secrecy of genesis attests to an intensely personal relationship with God for all the world to see and confirm. Job, however, accuses God of intentionally hiding his genesis with the aim of destroying him publicly (v. 13). Although his embryonic frame was not hidden from God, Job accuses God of concealing all evidence of his birth and, thus, his character and favor (vv. 12-13). Job's creation is his "exhibit A," but 'God refuses to allow such evidence in court. As Job's physical being deteriorates, all evidence of his moral constitution crumbles: with little left of his beleaguered character, Job cannot even lift his head, so burdened is he by misery and disgrace (v. 15).

Job ends in the same way he concludes his first discourse in chapter 3, with an appeal to God to grant him the respite of death. As Job's conception in the womb was wrought in secret, so Job wistfully desires his death hidden from view (v. 18). Without the womb as his tomb, Job opts simply to be left alone, abandoned, as he seeks his rest in Sheol.

III. Intertextual Relations

The respective rhetorical aims of Job and the psalmist are further set in relief with a comparison of similar vocabulary and themes. Comparable terminology and concepts suggest some level of intertextual dependence, specifically Job's use of the psalmist's rhetoric to further his case against God.[33] The following list correlates identical and synonymous terms.

---

33. Job's subversive use of Ps. 8:5-7 in Job 7:17-18 is widely acknowledged (e.g., Michael Fishbane, *Biblical Interpretation in Ancient Israel* [Oxford: Clarendon, 1985], pp. 285-86; Paul E. Dion, "Formulaic Language in the Book of Job: International Background and

Creation in the Womb

Psalm 139	Job 10

ACT (VERBS)

Psalm 139	Job 10
skk ("knit," v. 13)	*skk* ("knit," v. 11)[34]
ʿśh ("make," v. 15)	*ʿśh* ("make," vv. 8-9, 12)
rqm ("weave," v. 15)	*lbš* ("clothe," v. 11)
qnh ("form," v. 13)	*ʿṣb* ("fashion," v. 8)
ṣwr ("fashion," v. 16)	
	ntk ("pour," v. 10)
	qpʾ ("curdle," v. 10)

LOCATION: "WOMB"

Psalm 139	Job 10
beten (v. 13)	*beten* (v. 19)
	reḥem (v. 18)

ANATOMICAL STATE

Undifferentiated

Psalm 139	Job 10
gōlem ("embryo," v. 16)	*kaḥōmer* ("like clay," v. 9)
	kĕḥālāb ("like milk," v. 10)
	kaggĕbinnâ ("like cheese," v. 10)

Differentiated

Psalm 139	Job 10
ʿōṣem (v. 15)	*ʿăṣāmôt wĕgîdîm* (v. 11)
("skeletal frame")	("bones and sinews")
	ʿôr ûbāśār (v. 11)
	("skin and flesh")

Even a cursory glance reveals that Job's repertoire of creation terminology is more extensive than comparable language attested in Psalm 139. Regarding terms of location and state, there are at least two if not three words for

---

Ironical Distortions," *SR* 16 [1987]: 187-93). Yet an equally valid case of dependence can be argued for Job's deconstruction of Ps. 139. Although some have suggested some kind of relationship between Job and this psalm, it has been for the purpose of situating the psalm's *Sitz im Leben* within the wisdom environment (e.g., Helen Schüngel-Straumann, "Zur Gattung und Theologie des 139. Psalms," *BZ* 17 [1973]: 46-51; Jan L. Koole, "Quelques remarques sur Psaume 139," *Studia biblica et semitica T. C. Vriezen dedicata*, ed. W. C. van Unnik and A. S. van der Woude [Wageningen: H. Veenman en Zonen, 1966], pp. 176-80).

34. See n. 19.

every comparable term in the psalm. Much is synonymous and expanded in the Joban discourse. A distinctive use of the generic creation verb *'śh* is found in v. 12 to denote the granting of both life and "loyalty" (*ḥesed* [NRSV, "steadfast love"]), establishing a tight correspondence between *creatio in utero* and *creatio continua* with covenantal nuance. As in the psalm, creation for Job does not end with conception; it continues, undergirded by God's *ḥesed*, a testimony of covenantal favor.[35] Relative to the psalm, Job takes the language of personal creation one step further: Job laments his birth out of the womb into conflict and misery. Would that he had remained within to die! For both Job and the psalmist, the womb is the intimate vehicle of God's sustaining care. On the one hand, the psalmist in a sense never leaves the womb; he regards his life as one of seamlessly sustained favor established in the womb and continued throughout his life outside it. Severed from the womb, Job, on the other hand, is born to suffer shame and misery. Thus, Job can only hope to "return" to the womb's closest analogue, Sheol, for deliverance from the misery that comes from the presumption of guilt. Job's sentiments find a parallel in Qoheleth's despair over the man who is unable to enjoy life: "I say that a stillborn child is better off than he. For it comes into vanity and goes into darkness, and in darkness its name is covered" (Eccles. 6:3b-4).

Light and Darkness

Related to the language of gestation and birth are the images of light and darkness, as well as those that denote hiddenness. This series of terms highlights another set of similarities and contrasts between Job and the psalmist.

---

35. "You have fashioned *('śh)* life and loyalty on my behalf" (v. 12a). For a general investigation of the meaning of *ḥesed* as covenantally based loyalty, see Katharine D. Sakenfeld, *Faithfulness in Action*, OBT (Minneapolis: Fortress, 1985).

Psalm 139	Job 10

VISUAL PERCEPTION

rā'û 'ēneykā (v. 16)	*'ênê bāśār* (v. 4)
("your eyes beheld")	("eyes of flesh")
	kir'ôt 'ĕnôš tir'eh (v. 4)
	("you see as humans see")
	rĕ'ēh 'onyî (v. 15b)
	("look upon my misery")

HIDDENNESS

lō' nikḥad (v. 15)	*ṣāpantā* (v. 13)
("not hidden")	("you hid")
sēter ("secret," v. 15)	(cf. v. 18b)

DARKNESS

laylâ ("night," vv. 11, 12)	
yaḥšîk ("is dark," v. 12)	
ḥōšek ("darkness," vv. 11, 12)	*ḥōšek* ("darkness," v. 21)
ḥăšêkâ ("darkness," v. 12)	*'ōpel* ("darkness," v. 22)
	ṣalmāwet (vv. 21, 22)
	("deep darkness")
(*šĕ'ôl* ["Sheol"], v. 8)	*'ereṣ ḥōšek* (v. 21)
	("land of darkness")
	'ereṣ 'êpātâ (v. 22)
	("land of gloom")
	lō' sĕdārîm (v. 22)
	("without order")

LIGHT

'ôr ("light," v. 11)	*tōpa'* ("shines," v. 22)
'ôrâ ("light," v. 12)	
yā'îr ("is bright," v. 12)	
yôm ("day," v. 12 [v. 16])	

With one notable exception, the language of perception is more varied in Job's discourse than in the psalmist's. This is particularly evident in Job's detailed description of darkness. Whereas the psalmist predominantly employs the root *ḥšk* in both nominal and verbal forms, Job heaps five distinct terms to limn the darkness and chaos of the underworld.

While the psalmist celebrates the fact that God penetrates the darkness, apprehending it as light (Ps. 139:12), whether in the womb or in Sheol, Job yearns for the darkness that is devoid of God's presence (Job 10:19-22). Job concludes with a paradox that literally reads "[the land of gloom] shines *(yp')* like darkness" (v. 22), an ironic twist of Psalm 139:12b. It is no accident, then, that Job avoids all reference to light, for his deliverance lies in the darkness of the underworld where God has no business being. The psalmist, by contrast, rejoices over God's omnipresence, even in the confinement of Sheol (Ps. 139:8b). For Job, since the womb has forsaken him (Job 10:18), Sheol is the one domain that can offer respite from his misery (cf. 3:13-19).

Related to these contrasting images are the expressions for divine and human perception. The psalmist holds in awe the fact that though the fiber of his being was woven in secret, he was not hidden from God (Ps. 139:15-16). God's perception is by nature approbatory (cf. Gen. 1:4, 10, 12, 18, 25, 31; Hab. 1:13). Job, by contrast, accuses God of shortsightedness (Job 10:4), which leads to arbitrary and, thus, false moral judgments. Like the friends who cannot see beyond Job's suffering to discern his integrity, God, so Job reasons, suffers from a tunnel vision that precludes apprehension of Job's undeserved misery (v. 18). God has willfully put on blinders, thereby concealing Job's integrity from all, including God's self (vv. 12-13)! God has buried Job's integrity deep in God's heart of darkness. Job has, in effect, turned the psalmist's "genesis of secrecy" from a reason for praise and self-wonder into an accusation of character assassination. Only Job can look upon the self (v. 15b) and thus fully comprehend his condition and its scandalous theological implications. While Job knows himself better than God knows him, the psalmist praises God for knowing him better than he knows himself (Ps. 139:1-5). Like the intimate bond established in the act of creation, knowledgeable perception is fundamental to both the psalmist's praise-filled appeal and Job's bitter complaint.

Language of the Self

The sage and the psalmist are farthest apart in their use of self-referential language. Derived from the wondrous nature of divine activity, the psalmist's self-image is squarely rooted in his self-wonder (Ps. 139:14). At the other extreme is the self-abasement that so dominates Job's discourse (Job

10:1, 2, 8, 15, 20). With unabashed confidence the psalmist enjoins God to probe and test his integrity, to find any hurtful (or idolatrous) way that would mar his character (Ps. 139:23-24). In stark contrast, Job begins with a statement that undercuts the self-referential confidence that pervades the psalmist's rhetoric: "I loathe my life" (*nāqĕṭâ napšî bĕḥayyāy*, Job 10:1). Job rejects what the psalmist rapturously affirms, namely, his identity before God and humanity. Whereas the psalmist gratefully acknowledges the protection afforded him, Job laments his beleaguered condition. Where the psalmist discerns the aesthetic intricacy of his physical being, knit and woven by God, Job finds only frayed threads. All creative care to which Job can lay claim in his inception is now lost. The basis of Job's self-loathing lies in an irreparable rupture in his life, a life that began in the same way as the psalmist's, but with a decidedly different outcome. Job was born into disgrace and self-hatred. Yet the language of loathing finds a suggestive correlation in the psalm: as the self-confident petitioner is filled with indignation against God's enemies, his accusers (Ps. 139:21), Job's indignation is turned wholly inward before God the Accuser (cf. Job 7:16; 9:21).

IV. The Covenantal Bond of Creation

Both Job and the psalmist share a common storehouse of related terms that find their greatest concentration in the language of conception or personal genesis. And thus it is entirely possible — though difficult to prove conclusively — that the Joban poet was intimately familiar with Psalm 139 and, similar to his use of Psalm 8:5-6 in Job 7:17-18, constructed a "parody" of it. The intent, however, behind this essay is not so much to demonstrate linear dependence of one text upon the other as to highlight how the psalmist and the sage utilized common language and concepts to achieve their respective rhetorical aims. Employing the language of personal creation, both are intent on demonstrating their integrity.

For both supplicants, creation in the womb constitutes an act of divine commitment, indeed a pledge, to justify and safeguard the moral constitution of an individual throughout life. It is an act that adumbrates vindication when one's integrity is attacked. Vindicated righteousness is the consummation of the individual's creation. Both the sage and the psalmist associate the intricate beauty of their physical constitution, crafted by God, with the inviolability of their moral constitution. From the perspective of both authors, the womb is the home of God's creation and sustenance. It is here that physical nature and moral nurture coalesce. The womb is a refuge, impregnable from both physical and moral harm. That is why the psalmist remains in this haven, as it were, confident in his appeal to God; no mention is made of his birth, for even in darkness there is the light of God's enlivening beneficence (Ps. 139:11-12). Conversely, Job rails against God for having delivered him *from* the womb and, in turn, for rejecting him (Job 10:18). Severed from the womb to suffer the bellicose aspersions of his peers, Job finds God willfully concealing his integrity from public reach. All Job can hope to do is jolt God's memory (v. 9) and thereby compel God to act with judicious authority to sustain him in his eleventh hour as God had created him in the womb.

Perhaps the primary difference between Job and the psalmist is one of temporal perspective. Whereas the psalmist's discourse seems to be suspended at the moment *prior to* rendered judgment, Job's discourse targets God at the moment in which judgment seems *already* rendered, hence Job's strident disputation and the psalmist's hope-filled praise. In both, however, reference to personal genesis is presented as sufficient evidence of moral integrity. Neither offers here a litany of righteous deeds submitted as proof of integrity.[36] Moreover, the sage and the psalmist find in their creation a pledge that ensures them of resting secure within the protective sphere of righteousness. Personal creation entails a binding obligation of sustained moral leading on the part of the sovereign creator.[37] This covenantal ethos, established in the womb, as it were, is reflected in Job's appeal to God's steadfast *ḥesed* or loyalty in 10:12 and in his reference to the court witnesses (*ʿēd*) arrayed against him (v. 17; cf. 16:8). Deploying the language of litigation, Job asks why God contends (*rîb*) against him (10:2). Finding no justification, Job delivers a countersuit, charging God to *remember* a commitment once conceived (vv. 9, 12), and offers, in effect, his own conception as a covenantal sign (cf. Gen. 9:12-17).

For the psalmist, there is (yet) no breach of which to accuse God; no covenant is abrogated. Rather, he confidently proclaims God's knowledge

---

36. Compare Job's final defense in 31:1-40.

37. Moshe Weinfeld identifies the defining characteristic of the so-called covenant of grant in ancient Near Eastern and biblical sources as the self-obligation of the sovereign to provide for the recipient, as in the figures of Noah, Abraham, Phineas, and David ("The Covenant of Grant in the Old Testament and in the Ancient Near East," *JAOS* 90 [1970]: 184-203).

of him, not unlike the way David extols Yahweh's personal knowledge of him as God's faithful servant (2 Sam. 7:20). Moreover, the characterization of God's incomparability found in certain covenantal contexts (e.g., Deut. 4:32-40; 2 Sam. 7:22-24; Ps. 89:5-8) resonates also with the psalmist's appeal (Ps. 139:6, 13-18). Indeed, the *Leitmotif* of God's preserving hand, a palpable symbol of commitment, is found in another covenantal context, Psalm 89:13, 21. In both Job and Psalm 139, conception is not only a granting of life but a granting of commitment, of "life *and* loyalty" (Job 10:12). Is it any wonder, then, that the psalm is attributed to David, the beneficiary of God's covenantal grant?

Also shared by the royal covenant of grant and by Job's and the psalmist's appeal is a familial ethos. In biblical and extrabiblical sources, the recipient of divine protection is frequently cast as begotten by God.[38] Although Job and the psalmist do not employ such terms as "son" and "father," they both vigorously affirm that their conception was divinely wrought (cf. Ps. 2:7; 110:3[39]). The public proclamation of "adoption"[40] is replaced with the personal language of conception and gestation, effectively democratizing any royal particularity that may lie behind the authors' covenantal expectations of God. Both Job and the psalmist presume that their personal creation reflects an unconditional commitment on the part of God to preserve and uphold them.

On what basis can such a presumption be valid except on the assumption that God's personal creation of the individual is the mark of a divine pledge of sustenance and protection? Personal creation is the divine charter of life and loyalty by which God becomes bound to a particular life, ensuring that the individual flourishes within the protective sphere of righteousness. Job's caustic language reflects a perceived abrogation of that charter,[41] one that breaches the protective womb and mars his moral integrity. Whether for weal or for woe, both Job and the psalmist regard *creatio corporis* as the sign and seal of God's unconditional pledge of support. It is God's covenantal grant *in utero*.

---

38. See 2 Sam. 7:14; Ps. 2:7-8; 89:26-27. For a discussion of extra-biblical parallels, see Weinfeld, "The Covenant of Grant," pp. 189-94.

39. Corrected by the Old Greek: "Like dew I have begotten you." See William P. Brown, "A Royal Performance: Critical Notes on Psalm 110:3aγ-b," *JBL* 117 (1998): 93-96.

40. I use the term reservedly. See J. J. M. Roberts, "Whose Child Is This? Reflections on the Speaking Voice in Isaiah 9:5," *HTR* 90 (1997): 115-29.

41. Compare Job 10:2, 12 with Ps. 89:38-51 for a similar use of *ḥesed*.

"Earth Has No Sorrow That Earth Cannot Heal":[1] Job 38–41

Karen Pidcock-Lester

"The universe is wider than our views of it."

HENRY DAVID THOREAU

As I walked into the community board meeting, my eyes fell upon William, whom I had not seen since the week before Christmas when his seventeen-year-old son was killed in a bizarre private plane accident. I went up to him, extended my hand to shake his, and remarked gently, "William, I haven't seen you in several months, not since Michael's death. How are you?"

"You don't want me to answer that," he replied. William's eyes, normally fringed with trademark smile lines etched by fifty years of cheerful living, now had a hard, crazed look in them; and his voice, which had always brought a lilt to board discussions, now had an edge of bitterness in it. Those eyes darted about the room as he made a few scattered comments about his wife and daughter, who "weren't doing well at all." Then he turned his eyes directly upon me, and with an accusing intensity that bore into my soul, he said: "You know, we had the kids in all kinds of activities, 4-H clubs, Meals on Wheels. We took them to church all the time; they were in youth group and everything that came along. We did it by the book

1. John Muir, *John Muir in His Own Words,* ed. Peter Browning (Lafayette, CA: Great West Books, 1988), p. 24.

125

— by MORE than the book! We were doing it right. And then this happened." And, after a pause, William got to the heart of the matter: "It makes no sense. No sense at all."

It does not make sense, this suffering of good people. It makes no sense at all. It makes no more sense for William Bartlett to suffer the death of his radiant son Michael than for God's servant Job to suffer the loss of his children, his wealth, and his health. And, much as I would like to give the man an explanation he can live with, it is no more possible for me to make sense of things than it is for Job's friends. They, too, can give no adequate explanation for their friend's anguish, though it is not for lack of trying. For thirty-seven chapters they try to make sense of Job's suffering: they subscribe to the worldview that suffering is direct punishment for sins; they urge Job to examine himself to discover his transgressions; and they instruct him to repent so that his suffering will end.

But Job will have none of this. He knows that he has done nothing to deserve the horrors that have befallen him. "I am blameless" (9:21). "Show me what I have done!" he demands. "If my ground has any complaints about me, tell me!" (31:38). There are no scales of justice that can balance any wrong Job has done with the suffering he now endures. His lot simply does not make sense, and the question will not go away: "Why do the innocent suffer so?"

It is a raw question. It is a question hurled against the skies by people who have come to "loathe their life" (10:1), whose nights are "full of tossing until dawn," whose lives stretch before them as "months of emptiness" (7:3-4). It is the question cried out by those whose understanding of the world has been shattered by a suffering they cannot comprehend, and they want to contend with the Almighty — "Oh, that I knew where I might find him, that I might come even to his dwelling! I would lay my case before him, and fill my mouth with arguments" (23:3-4). "Why?" It is the cry of those who stand shaking their fist at the sky overhead, while the foundations of life quake underneath.

And all too often, God seems deaf to the cry. God "hides his face" (34:29). All too often, God is silent.

But in chapters 38–41, God breaks the silence. Out of the whirlwind, God responds to Job, and to William, and to the countless sons of Adam and daughters of Eve who shake their fists at the heavens, demanding a response.

God responds. First of all, that is no mean thing. God does not have to respond, but God does. God comes to Job, as God came to Noah and Abraham, heroic figures who enjoyed God's respect.[2] And when God comes, God does not condemn Job for his questions. Neither does God deny Job's innocence. God "takes his plight so seriously" that God "manifests himself to Job personally and instructs him at length."[3] God does not try to convince Job that his sin balances his suffering. God understands the existential question that plagues the human soul, and God responds.

It is not with an explanation that God responds. For the time being, the suffering of innocent people remains inexplicable. However, while God does not give Job an explanation that satisfies the searching mind, he does give a response that brings a measure of healing to the raging soul. After God's response Job no longer raises his fist toward heaven in righteous anger; after God's response Job casts his eyes upon the ground and utters statements of submission and trust. Job's world is not the same as it had been before the tragedies, and Job's view of it must be rearranged. But in God's response, the man whose foundations had been shaking finds solid ground upon which to stand and an assurance in which he can rest.

What is it that transforms rage to trust? Where does God point Job to find quiet for his suffering soul? God points to the creation. Chapters 38–41 comprise one great, long outpouring from the mouth of God extending for 127 verses, one glorious hymn of creation blending "multiple genres — a theophany, a hymn of praise, legal dispute and interrogation, myths of divine battle between primordial monsters."[4] In this ending to the book of Job, it is as though God has listened long enough. God has heard Job's friends peddle their neat, tidy views of the world and their self-assured opinions about the way God works. God has heard Job's accusations, and now God has something to say.

And when God does, Job may almost wish God were still silent. Once unleashed, God "relentlessly pursues Job as an eagle pursues a trembling mouse. God thunders at the shrinking man."[5] Like a parent whose child accuses him of "never giving me anything," God's nerve has been hit. God makes a list of all that he has done: "Where were you when I laid the foun-

2. Norman C. Habel, *The Book of Job* (Philadelphia: Westminster, 1985), p. 527.

3. Sibley Towner, *How God Deals With Evil* (Philadelphia: Westminster, 1976), p. 113.

4. John E. Hartley, *The Book of Job* (Grand Rapids: Eerdmans, 1988), p. 488.

5. Richard E. Singer, *Job's Encounter* (New York: Bookman Associates, 1963), p. 89.

dation of the earth? . . . On what were its bases sunk, or who laid its corner-stone? . . . Or who shut in the sea with doors when it burst out from the womb? . . . Have you commanded the morning since your days began and caused the dawn to know its place? . . . Have you entered into the springs of the sea? . . . Have you entered the storehouses of the snow? . . . Can you send forth lightnings? . . . Do you know when the mountain goats give birth?" Have you . . . can you . . . do you?

In typical ancient Near Eastern fashion,[6] the writer of Job compiles a list of all that is under God's charge: earth and sea, dawn and deeps, light and darkness, the heavens, the stars and clouds and water, animals, and heavenly beings and monsters. The list keeps washing over Job in relentless waves of passion, and when God pauses to take a breath, when God breaks the rhythm of the barrage with a demand for a reply — "Anyone who argues with God must respond" (40:2), that is, "What do you have to say for yourself, Job?" — Job can hardly get a word out before the poetic interrogation takes off again: "Gird up your loins like a man; I will question you. . . . Have you an arm like God, and can you thunder with a voice like his?" At the opening of chapter 40, it is as though God is saying, "I am not finished with you yet! There's more."

The effect of God's outpouring in chapters 38–41 is to yank Job's focus away from himself and his plight. God's response turns Job's vision toward the vastness of the universe, where Pleiades and Orion spin in their courses and ordinances beyond our knowing rule the heavens, where planets are born and die every minute and where galaxies, which harbor 100 billion suns, emerge and disappear. God's outpouring yanks Job's perspective out of his meager human days and years and places it within the span of time, which began when the foundations of the earth were laid and the morning stars sang together, and when the only ones to sing for joy were the heavenly beings because no one else had as yet been created. I am reminded of Stephen Hawking's claim that if all of history since the dawn of creation were recorded so that it would fill a stack of papers standing shoulder-high, then human history would be a single sheet of paper.[7] "Where were you when I determined the measurements of the earth and laid its cornerstone and caused the dawn to know its place?" It is as though

---

6. Gerhard von Rad, cited in Hartley, *The Book of Job*, p. 88.

7. Cited by Ken Groff at a retreat with First Presbyterian Church, Pottstown, PA, January 1988.

God is saying, "Who do you think you are, Job? You are not the center of the universe."

God is.

And what's more, the God who is at the center is not cold or distant, not deaf or even silent. The God who is at the center of the universe is in love with the world. Every bit of it.

This God watches over the world and takes care of it. This God knows when the mountain goats give birth and counts the number of months until the deer crouch alone in the woods to calve (39:1-3). This God tells the eagle where to nest and commands the hawk to spread its wings toward the south (39:26-30). This God "tilts the waterskins of the heavens and numbers the clouds." This God cuts a channel for rain "to bring rain on land even where no one is" (38:25-27). Though we humans think the world was made especially for us, that "is a presumption not supported by all the facts. . . ."[8] This God at the center of the universe wants to satisfy and provide for every creature and crevice of creation, even the waste and desolate places (38:25-27), even the ravens and their young, even the lion and animals we humans do not like (38:39-41). This God delights in creation, plays with it (41:5), chuckles at it (39:13-18), marvels at it, and sleeps with it (39:9). This God rules over its forces, good and evil, and though this God does not eliminate chaos, God keeps chaos under control (40:15–41:34).

When God responds to Job's angry question, God points to the creation to impress upon Job that he is only a minute part of a complex universe that is "wider than our views of it." As Norman Habel has noted,

> [P]aradox and incongruity are integral to the design of the world. . . . The baby eagle survives because another young creature dies. God does not eliminate the forces of chaos, the role of Death, or the presence of the wicked. They operate within the eternal constraints of his design. . . . In his design there is a measure of the comic with the controlled, the bizarre with the beautiful, the serendipitous with the serious. . . . Job's complaint that the innocent suffer unjustly is never refuted. It stands side by side with the answers of YHWH as part of the paradox of that design.[9]

8. Muir, *John Muir in His Own Words*, p. 4.
9. Habel, *The Book of Job*, pp. 534-37.

In this complex creation, there is no simple explanation for why young men die in the twinkling of an eye, or why good people lose everything while the wicked prosper. These are questions Job will have to live with. But at the same time, chapters 38–41 reveal a God who is in charge of the world and loves the world. These are truths Job can live with.

God's response takes the wind out of Job's sails. Job is struck dumb. Job admits, "I have uttered what I did not understand, things too wonderful for me which I did not know" (42:3). After all, when one has encountered the awesome majesty of the Ruler of the universe, there is little left to say. God is God, and we are not.

But as Job's speech evaporates, so does his anger. In humility, Job musters some reply: "I know that you can do all things, and that no purpose of yours can be thwarted. . . . I despise myself, and repent in dust and ashes" (42:2, 6). Where before there had been rage and defiance, there are now trust and submission. After his encounter with the God of the universe, Job is put in his place.

And it is a goodly place. It is a place in which Job knows his life is upheld, cared for, loved, watched over, and controlled by the God who sets the flicker of each firefly and the flight pattern of each bird, who choreographs the dance of the bee and the migration of the monarch, who spreads the branches of sequoias through the waste of the winter wren, who chisels canyons out of rock with tools of water and wind, who numbers the hairs on our heads and notices when a sparrow falls.

Creation offers no explanation for our suffering, but it does offer a balm for our woe. When trials assail us and our suffering is inexplicable, God points to creation to remind us of the One at the center of all things who holds life and the universe together, and loves it. For when we cling to the One who creates, then we know what John Muir once knew: "the pure rest, the healing power of Nature."[10]

God's response to our cries does not always come to us as loudly as it did to Job. In a quiet way, God pointed the gaze of another suffering servant toward creation and gave her a balm for her wounded soul. Nien Chang was imprisoned in China during the Cultural Revolution because of her refusal to bow to a lesser god, Mao Zedong. At a time when the foundations of her world were shaking and she was tortured despite her

---

10. Muir, *John Muir in His Own Words*, p. 34.

innocence, Chang remembers a quiet encounter with creation, which helped her find her place in the hands of the God who creates. She writes:

> One day, in the early afternoon . . . a small spider crawled into view, climbing up one of the rust-eroded bars. The little creature was no bigger than a good-sized pea. . . . I watched it crawl slowly but steadily to the top of the iron bar. . . . When it reached the top, suddenly it swung out and descended on a thin silken thread spun from one end of its body. With a leap and swing, it secured the end of the thread to another bar. The spider then crawled back along the silken thread to where it had started and swung out in another direction on a similar thread. . . . It seemed to know exactly what to do and where to take the next thread. There was no hesitation, no mistake, and no haste. It knew its job and was carrying it out with confidence. When the frame was made, the spider proceeded to weave a web that was intricately beautiful and absolutely perfect, with all the strands of thread evenly spaced. When the web was completed, the spider went to its center and settled there.
>
> I had just watched an architectural feat by an extremely skilled artist, and my mind was full of questions. Who had taught the spider how to make a web? Could it really have acquired the skill through evolution? . . . Did it act simply by instinct, or had it somehow learned to store the knowledge of web making? . . . I knew I had just witnessed something that was extraordinarily beautiful and uplifting. . . . I thanked [God] for what I had just seen. A miracle of life had been shown me. It helped me see that God was in control. Mao Zedong and his Revolutionaries seemed much less menacing. I felt a renewal of hope and confidence.[11]

In the midst of our suffering, God points us toward creation, so that we will remember this: though the ways of this God are often inexplicable, inscrutable, and confounding, they are not malicious, capricious, or cruel. God is not arbitrary, but ordered. God is not deaf, or silent, or cold, or absent, but God hears, and answers. God loves and comes. This One who comes to Job comes at last to all people in Jesus Christ. And in Christ, one day all shall see fully the awesome power and the infinite love of the God who creates, and all shall be made well.

Until that time, I wait with my friend William. I will look for a gentle way to share with him these words of the poet Wendell Berry:

---

11. Nien Chang, *Life and Death in Shanghai* (New York: Grove, 1986), pp. 142-43.

When despair for the world grows in me
and I awake in the night at the least sound
in fear of what my life and my children's lives may be,
I go and lie down where the wood drake
rests in his beauty on the water and the great heron feeds.
I come into the peace of wild things . . .
I come into the presence of still water.
And I feel above me the day-blind stars
waiting with their light. For a time
I rest in the grace of the world, and am free.[12]

And perhaps one evening William and I will make our way to the top of a hill, or the edge of a canyon, or a dune by the sea, and we will lie on our backs under the canopy of the One who creates, who creates life, even out of death. And lying there, we will remind one another of what we may have forgotten:

His eye is on the sparrow
and I know He watches me.

12. Wendell Berry, "The Peace of Wild Things," in *The Collected Poems of Wendell Berry, 1957-1982* (San Francisco: North Point, 1984), p. 69.

PROPHETS

Stars, Sprouts, and Streams:
The Creative Redeemer of Second Isaiah

Thomas W. Mann

Is it nothing to you, all you who pass by?
Look and see if there is any sorrow like my sorrow,
which was brought upon me,
which the Lord inflicted on the day of his fierce anger.
For these things I weep;
my eyes flow with tears.
For a comforter is far from me,
one to revive my courage;
my children are desolate,
for the enemy has prevailed.

(LAMENTATIONS 1:12, 16, NRSV)

These words of a personified Jerusalem reflect on the profound despair that overwhelmed the people of Israel with the destruction of the city by the Babylonians in 586 B.C.E. The defeat of Judah's forces and the exile of its prominent citizens and royalty who were spared execution seemed to spell the end of Israel as a national and political entity. Likewise, the burning of the temple suggested either the defeat of Yahweh or Yahweh's abandonment of Israel, both options being part of a common ancient Near Eastern theology. Israelite prophecy, both before and after the fact, chose the latter, claiming that Yahweh had *sent* the Babylonians against them as punishment for their corporate sin.

135

Despite the official theology of divine abandonment, however, the temptation to assume a theology of divine defeat would have been enormous. The exiles were exposed to the elaborate processions of the Babylonian deities (i.e., their statues) through the streets of that magnificent city (parodied in 46:1-7).[1] The Babylonians proclaimed their god, Marduk, to be the creator of the universe and the agent of their political triumphs. At their new year festival they faced the statue of Marduk and recited their epic myth, *Enuma Elish,* which concludes with Marduk ruling supreme from his temple in Babylon. The Israelites were captives in a city of great political power and daunting religious traditions. No wonder their sense of identity was reduced to that of a "worm" (41:14; cf. Job 25:6; Ps. 22:6).

How do you convince people who think of themselves as worms that they are, instead, still the beloved people of God? How do you encourage people who see themselves under a divine curse to believe that they are the recipients of a renewed divine blessing? In the language originating in contemporary African-American culture, how do you persuade people who think of themselves as "nobodies" that they are "somebodies"?

In answering these questions, Second Isaiah (hereafter, SI) refers to a variety of traditions from Israel's past — the Noachic covenant, Yahweh's promise to the ancestors (Abraham and Sarah), and the everlasting covenant with David — although only in brief allusions (Noah, 54:9; Abraham, 41:8; 51:2; David, 55:3). In contrast, the figure of Zion/Jerusalem plays a major role in the collection, beginning with 40:9 and especially after 44:28.[2] In addition, SI invokes Israel's God as "the creator of the ends of the earth" and as "the creator of Israel" (40:28; 43:15). In fact, SI is likely among the first (if not the first) of all biblical writings to use the verb *bārā'* to speak of God as creator.[3] This prophet of the exile also refers frequently to God as the redeemer of Israel, evoking the story of the exodus from

---

1. All textual references are to Isaiah unless otherwise specified.

2. Although the figure of Zion derives from traditions associated with David, the dynastic covenant nowhere appears. In 55:3 the Davidic covenant is offered to the entire people, and when Second Isaiah uses the term "messiah," it is for the pagan ruler Cyrus (45:1)!

3. Elsewhere, the word is used by P and in other literary settings that appear to reflect the exilic setting (e.g., Deut. 4:32). However, in his study of the hymns in Amos, Hans Walter Wolff suggests that *bārā'* "belongs to preexilic, Canaanite cultic language," and could easily reflect a correspondingly early polemic (*Amos the Prophet* [Philadelphia: Fortress Press, 1973], pp. 216, 223). See Carroll Stuhlmueller, *Creative Redemption in Deutero-Isaiah* (Rome: Biblical Institute Press, 1970), p. 209 n. 676.

Egypt, and can use the terms creator and redeemer as virtual synonyms (43:14-15). This paper will discuss the language of creative redemption that is so prominent in the opening chapters of the collection, especially in 40:12-31 and 43:14-21.[4]

I. "The Creator of the Ends of the Earth" (40:12-31)

The opening chapter of SI introduces a number of themes that will dominate the book. In the first lines (vv. 1-2), we hear God speaking to the heavenly council, ordering them to "comfort my people," whose sins are now fully recompensed. The "comforter" who was far from the author of Lamentations is now close at hand. Israel is again called "my people," a phrase that reflects traditions of redemption and covenant (e.g., Exod. 3:7-8; 6:7; 19:5-6). In the next unit (vv. 3-5), the divine order now puts in motion the construction of a "highway" in the wilderness. The highway image serves two functions: it evokes the wilderness traditions of Israel and it implies a critique of the statue processions of the Babylonians (cf. especially 46:1-7). The next section (vv. 6-8) uses images from nature — grass and flowers — to express the transitory condition of humankind, contrasted with the permanence of "the word of God." Later such imagery is used to characterize the impermanence of "princes" and "rulers" (v. 24). Verses 9-11 introduce the figure of Zion, who is summoned as a "herald of good tidings" to the cities of Judah (cf. 49:14), proclaiming the return of God as a mighty victor and yet also as a gentle royal shepherd.

The opening unit (vv. 1-11) is thus composed of a series of proclamations of "good tidings" (v. 9). The rest of the chapter is held together formally by a series of rhetorical questions: "Who has measured the waters?" (v. 12), "To whom then will you liken God?" (v. 18), and "Why do you say, O Jacob?" (v. 27).[5] There is an argument going on here, and we are hearing one side of a dispute. The disagreement has to do with nothing less

---

4. The major study of our topic is that of Carroll Stuhlmueller, *Creative Redemption*.

5. The form and content of the rhetorical questions in vv. 12-14 are most reminiscent of the "whirlwind speech" in the book of Job (chs. 38-41; cf. especially 38:4-7 and Isa. 40:12). Moreover, they both address a complaint (for SI, 40:27). The function in each, however, is quite different. In Job the creation language serves to relativize Job's complaints in the face of God's overwhelming power. In SI the creation language *leads into* the complaint and serves as the warrant for the implicit promise of redemption.

than who is in control of the world. Power is thus the central issue. From the arrangement of the questions and answers and from their content, we can infer the counter claims that prompt them. The arrangement produces a structural pattern of nations/isles (vv. 12-17), princes/rulers (vv. 18, 21-24), the heavenly host (vv. 25-26), and Israel (vv. 27-31). The "principalities and powers," as the apostle Paul would say, compete with Yahweh for the status of universal sovereign. The very substance of the dispute, after all, is the major problem posed by the exile. The power of Babylon and its gods seems to be absolute, and Israel despairs of ever again benefiting from Yahweh's power, even if it exists. The entire unit focuses on Yahweh as "the creator of the ends of the earth" (v. 28) and how Yahweh's identity as cosmic creator affects political powers, divine powers, and Israel (v. 26, see below).

In the next unit,[6] vv. 12 and 15 form a frame around the center (vv. 13-14), followed by a conclusion (v. 17). The frame employs a sweeping panorama of nature: seas, sky, dust of the earth, and mountains/hills. Each image suggests immensity: the enormous expanses of sea and sky, the incalculable volume of the dust of the earth, the soaring height and mass of mountains and hills. Yet Yahweh is incomprehensibly more vast than all of these put together. All of the waters can fit in the palm of Yahweh's hand; the sky is but the distance between Yahweh's thumb and little finger ("span"); all the dust of the earth Yahweh can fit into, say, a pint jar; and, like a vendor, Yahweh can weigh all of the mountains on a scale. The nations are like a drop of water, the isles like dust on a scale (v. 15). The nations are as incomprehensibly insignificant as Yahweh is incomprehensibly vast.

The center of the unit (vv. 13-14) moves, as it were, from brawn to brain. The language of the two verses derives from the wisdom tradition: "counsel" (two times), "knowledge" (three times), "understanding" (two times), and "teach" (two times). Yahweh is not only immeasurably vast but also immeasurably wise. At the heart of the universe is a brilliant and totally self-sufficient intelligence at work, the Spirit of Yahweh.

Compared to the cosmic dimensions of Yahweh's power and wisdom, "the nations are as nothing," indeed, "less than nothing [a negative number!] and emptiness" (v. 17). The rare word "emptiness" *(tôhû)* occurs

---

6. Verse 16 may be an insertion. It shifts from the weighing metaphor of vv. 12 and 15 and introduces an awkward specificity.

eight times in SI, more than in any other book. As in Genesis 1:2, it can refer to the shapelessness of chaos before Yahweh formed the world (*yṣr*, cf. 45:18-19), or the vacuousness of idols (44:9), or of rulers (see below on 40:23). Thus the quasi-philosophical language of the conclusion deepens the significance of the metaphorical language of "drop" and "dust" in 40:15.

Having reduced the nations to a mere speck of dust, the argument now turns explicitly to a rhetorical question about Yahweh's incomparability (v. 18). "To whom then will you liken God?" The corresponding noun "likeness" in the second line apparently prompted an insertion of the polemic against idols.[7] The rest of the unit is very much like the preceding. The words for knowledge and understanding reappear in v. 21. The questions are followed by a hymnic response in vv. 22-23. The exiles should be able to deduce from what they have been told about the founding[8] of the world that the power of God ('El, v. 18) literally dwarfs that of princes and rulers. Again, the metaphors suggest immensity. From God's cosmic perspective, such august figures seem to God the way mere grasshoppers seem to humans. The infinite expanse of the sky is God's tent. The metaphorical argument is again followed by the more abstract language of nothingness and emptiness (v. 23, as v. 17), only to be bolstered by the additional metaphor of vegetation that withers under Yahweh's breath (v. 24, cf. v. 7). The rulers are like grass that has dried up and blown away.

Now virtually the same question that was asked in v. 18 is repeated: "'To whom will you liken me that I should be like him?' says the Holy One." The exiles are invited to become stargazers. "Lift up your eyes on high and see: who created these?" As the next verse suggests, the referent is to the heavenly "host," which includes not only stars but sun and moon. The reference serves two purposes. First, it continues the metaphorical description of Yahweh's immensity from the previous units. For an intima-

---

7. If these lines are original, however, we could delineate a somewhat different structure to the larger unit: AB A′ B′ C — that is, nations (vv. 12-17), gods (idols; vv. 18-20), rulers (vv. 21-24), gods (vv. 25-26), Israel (vv. 27-28).

8. There is slight difference in Hebrew between "founding" and "foundation." The former would refer to creative action, the latter (the received text) to the result of that action. The former then would refer to hearing the story of God's creating the world, the latter, to inferring from the presumed physical structure of the world. The combination of foundation(s) of the earth and spreading out the heavens appears in a comparable setting in 48:13 (cf. 48:13c and 40:24b).

tion of infinity, there are few experiences that can match looking up at a star-filled sky. (Indeed, *our* knowledge of the vastness of the universe with its billions of galaxies should only enhance this experience.)[9] Yet to the Holy One, this celestial host is like a set of tiny toy soldiers. They appear at Yahweh's summons, each one recorded by number and called by name (cf. 45:12; 48:13).

Second, not only are the celestial host part of the natural world, they also had long been seen as divine powers, as well as the subject of astrological speculations — at least, to the Babylonians[10] (and sometimes to heterodox Israelites).[11] Astrology, of course, is based on the presumption that stars exercise some control over events on earth, or at least can reveal the most prudent course for human decisions. But in SI's critique, if stars reveal anything it is again the enormous power of the God of Israel. Furthermore, the claim that Yahweh created the celestial host stands in direct contradiction to the Babylonian *Enuma Elish,* in which it is Marduk who "fixes the astral likenesses," sets up constellations, and makes the moon to shine.[12] Second Isaiah, thus, demythologizes the astral powers by reducing them to a part of the natural world created by the sovereign power of Israel's Holy One.

We pause for a moment to review the effect of the argument in vv. 12-26 on the opening proclamations of vv. 1-11. The latter announce the reconciliation between Israel and Yahweh, the construction of a "processional way" through the wilderness, the reliability of the word of God, and the return of Yahweh to Zion "with might" as Israel's shepherd king. These grandiose proclamations and the very situation of the Exile raise a critical question: *Can* Yahweh deliver on these promises? In vv. 12-26, the grandiosity of the proclamations is warranted by the majesty of "the cre-

9. For an eloquent description of the abiding wondrousness of stars, see David Brendan Hopes, *A Sense of the Morning: Inspiring Reflections on Nature and Discovery* (New York: Simon & Schuster, 1988), pp. 61-70. The opening line of the chapter, "Who first looked up?" resembles SI's invitation: "Lift up your eyes on high." Another sentence — "Out there dwells the Magnificence" (p. 66) — also evokes the same sense of wonder and awe.

10. A. Leo Oppenheim, *Ancient Mesopotamia* (Chicago: University of Chicago Press, 1964), p. 308. In Isa. 14:4b-21, an Assyro-Babylonian ruler is identified with the "fallen" deities "Day Star" and "son of Dawn."

11. 2 Kings 17:16; 21:3; 23:5; Jer. 8:1-2 (including astrology); projected as part of exilic situation in Deut. 4:19; prohibited in Deut. 17:3; cf. Amos 5:26. The doxologies in Amos suggest a resemblance to SI as well (note 5:8-9).

12. *ANET,* pp. 67, 68 n. 94.

ator of the ends of the earth." The cumulative metaphors of immensity produce a sense of awesome power, a power infinitely greater than that of nations, rulers, and even rival deities, the latter being not deities at all but the very products of the Holy One's creativity. The conclusion of SI's argument is stated explicitly and succinctly in the closing line: "because [Yahweh] is great in strength, mighty in power."

Yet SI has not presented his argument in vv. 12-26 as an abstract, independent theology of creation. Rather, the purpose of demonstrating Yahweh's power *as creator* is to legitimate the proclamation that Yahweh "comes with might, and his arm rules for him" and for Zion (v. 10) — that is, that Yahweh is *able* to come as *redeemer*.[13]

The first stage in Israel's redemption is not their release from exile, but their release from the spiritual alienation caused by exile. To use the words of Martin Luther King, Jr., it is "to lift [them] from the dark valley of despair to the bright mountain of hope."[14] This "lifting" is precisely the purpose of the concluding unit in 40:27-31. For the first and only time in SI, we hear the words of Israel quoted directly: "My way is hidden from the Lord, and my right is disregarded by my God" (cf. 49:14). These are the words of lament, the cry of abandonment.[15] The response is a repetition of the question in v. 21: "Have you not known, have you not heard," followed by a hymnic description of Yahweh as "the everlasting God, the creator of the ends of the earth." But here the power of Yahweh as creator is connected existentially to Israel. The powerful creator is one who empowers those who "wait" for him.

The final unit is stitched together with the preceding one by the key word "power" (*kōaḥ*; vv. 26, 29, 31). The awesome power that creates and controls the stars is now given to those who are "faint and powerless." In-

---

13. *Contra* Stuhlmueller, who insists that SI's argument for Yahweh's power to redeem is based on Yahweh's faithfulness in history and not on Yahweh as creator of the world (*Creative Redemption,* pp. 137, 146). He suggests that in the Babylonian setting, any claim that Yahweh was creator "might even have seemed ridiculous" (p. 137). Yet would not a claim to Yahweh's power to act in history also be in question? Clearly SI understands Yahweh as both creator *and* lord of history; here (40:12-31) I see the emphasis on the former (cf. Claus Westermann, *Isaiah 40–66,* OTL [Philadelphia: Westminster, 1969], pp. 56-57, 62). See n. 16.

14. United Church of Christ, *Book of Worship* (New York: Office for Church Life and Leadership, 1986), p. 553.

15. Compare Pss. 13:1; 89:46; 102:2; Job 27:2; 34:5-6 (contrast Isa. 49:4).

deed, the antonyms for power, "faint" and "weary," are skillfully interwoven ("faint" four times) to show that they never apply to Yahweh and they need not apply any more to Israel. Untroubled by mixed metaphors, the author compares the rejuvenated Israel to flying eagles and Olympic runners!

The position of 40:12-31 in the introductory chapter of SI is highly significant. As we have seen, the proclamations in vv. 1-11 announce what God is about to do in history, although these actions are at best implicit. Immediately after vv. 12-31, SI turns to that historical event that will be decisive for the release of the exiles: the approach of Cyrus, the "one from the east" whom Yahweh has "stirred up" (41:2; 44:28; 45:1). Yet the position of vv. 12-31 suggests that whatever actions in history may be attributed to Yahweh, they are grounded in a theology of Yahweh as "creator of the ends of the earth." In this sense, a theology of creation is prior to and foundational for a theology of history.[16] This fundamental importance of God as creator in SI's theology is unprecedented within the prophetic corpus of ancient Israel. Second Isaiah is the first prophet to ask Israel to look at the stars before recovering the story that provides their identity. Or better, it is because the one who created the stars is the subject of their story that they have any future at all.[17]

---

16. As Rolf Knierim suggests, "For the Old Testament, just as for the New Testament, the most universal aspect of Yahweh's dominion is not human history. It is the creation and sustenance of the world . . . because creation does not depend on history or existence, but history and existence depend on and are measured against creation" (*The Task of Old Testament Theology* [Grand Rapids: Eerdmans, 1995], p. 13). Note also p. 164, where he talks about the "collapse" of revelation through Israel's history in the exilic period and the rise of the revelation of God as cosmic creator. Compare Stuhlmueller, who argues that "the idea of creation must be accepted as a secondary motif, thoroughly subservient to that of redemption and quite inexplicable without it" (*Creative Redemption*, pp. vii, 5).

17. Space does not allow us to discuss at length the similarities in the use of creation language elsewhere, especially in the Psalms. In Psalm 8, the vastness of the moon and stars suggests that human beings are too insignificant to merit God's concern (vv. 3-4). Like Isa. 40:12-31, the exilic Psalms 74 and 147 also contain a combination of lament and praise, along with appeals to God's power as creator of the stars or luminaries. Psalm 74 also refers to the cosmogonic battle (cf. 51:9-11). Of course, the Priestly story of creation in Genesis 1 also alludes to the cosmogonic battle and demythologizes the luminaries. Given the likely exilic setting of P, the similarity in function to 40:12-31 is all the more apparent. For a lucid discussion of the theological tension between lament and praise in these texts, see Jon D. Levenson, *Creation and the Persistence of Evil* (San Francisco: Harper & Row, 1988).

II. "Your Redeemer — the Creator of Israel" (43:14-21)

The first text presented Yahweh as creator of the universe in order to demonstrate Yahweh's power to redeem Israel from the historical situation of exile. Our next selection presents Yahweh's *historical* acts of redemption as the inseparable counterpart to Yahweh's continuing *creativity.* The two passages differ in terms of focus and emphasis, but they do not present different, much less distinct, dimensions of divine activity. That is, there is no theology of creation in SI that stands alone, independent of a theology of history. At the same time, there is no theology of history apart from a theology of creation.

The unit 43:14-21 is composed of two passages, each introduced by a messenger formula: vv. 14-15 and 16-21. After the messenger formula, a chiastic structure is discernible in the first section:

divine self-identification	"your redeemer, the Holy One of Israel" (v. 14a)
defeat of Babylon	"Babylon . . . break down" (v. 14b)
divine self-identification	"I am the Lord, your Holy One, the creator of Israel, your king" (v. 15)

The center contains the first explicit reference to Babylon and its imminent collapse. The frame represents perhaps the most graphic example of the way in which SI combines redemption and creation: "Thus says the Lord, your redeemer . . . I am the Lord . . . the creator of Israel." The "creator of the ends of the earth" (41:28) is also the "creator of Israel" and their redeemer. The literary structure demonstrates that the imminent defeat of Babylon is Yahweh's action, one which is at once redemptive and creative.[18]

While divine redemption *(g'l)* is based on a human act and institution (Ruth 4:1-7; Lev. 25:25-28, 47-49), creation is uniquely divine: the word *bārā'* is never used with a human subject. In this sense human beings cannot be "creative." Both words are used proportionately more in SI than in any other book in the Hebrew Bible, especially with Israel as the object. Indeed, the very portrayal of Yahweh as "creator of Israel" is unique to SI (cf. 43:1, 7).

---

18. The use of the word "send" may suggest here what is clear elsewhere, that Yahweh's action will be accomplished through the (unwitting) agency of Cyrus (cf. 45:1-7).

The duality of Yahweh as creator and redeemer for Israel in Babylon now leads into the next section, which is a classic example of SI's "new exodus" theology — or perhaps better "new exodus/wilderness" theology, since SI refers both to ancient Israel's liberation from Egypt and their journey through the wilderness to the promised land. In fact, allusions to exodus (vv. 16-17) and wilderness (vv. 19b-21a) frame the central claim of SI's theology: Yahweh is doing a new thing (v. 18).

After the introductory messenger formula, vv. 16-17 are composed of a series of hymnic allusions to Israel's exodus from Egypt, in particular, to the climactic confrontation with Pharaoh at the sea. In fact, it almost seems as if SI had before him the text of the Song of the Sea in Exodus 15, for there are several expressions in common:

Chariot and horse, army	Isa. 43:17; Exod. 15:1b, 4a
"The people whom" (ʿam-zû)	Isa. 43:21; Exod. 15:13, 16b

Moreover, there is a similarity between the overall movement of our text and the ancient Song (although the third element is not present in this passage):[19]

Defeat of the enemy	Isa. 43:16-17; Exod. 15:1-12
Way in the wilderness	Isa. 43:19b-21a; Exod. 15:13-16
Mountain sanctuary	Isa. 45:28b; Exod. 15:17
Praise	Isa. 43:21b; Exod. 15:18

The fusion of creation and redemption, of course, is not original to SI. As numerous studies have shown, the combination was already present in the ancient Song of the Sea, a text that many scholars date to the beginning of Israel's literature. In that Song, the author alludes to the even more ancient mythic tradition of the cosmogonic battle. In fact, the *Enuma Elish* is the parade example of this mythic tradition. In this epic, Marduk becomes the champion of the gods over against the rebellious challenger, Tiamat. Identified with the sea (or the "deep" [*tĕhôm*]), Tia-

---

19. The scenario that leads from victory in battle to the construction of a temple appears in the Baʿl epic from Ugarit, in *Enuma Elish*, and here in Exod. 15, as well as in the story of David (2 Sam. 2–7; Pss. 78, 132). See Arvid S. Kapelrud, "Temple Building, a Task for Gods and Kings," *Orientalia* 32 (1963): 56-62. Note also that the combination of human ruler, gods, and nations that appears in 40:12-26 also appears in Exod. 15.

mat represents the powers of chaos. Marduk defeats her forces, slaughters Tiamat, and creates the universe out of Tiamat's dismembered body. Then the grateful gods build a temple for Marduk, situated in none other than the historical city of Babylon. Another version of such a battle was prominent in Canaanite mythology, in which Ba'l defeats the powers of chaos personified by Prince Sea/Judge River, and then has a house built for himself (although this version is not cosmogonic). Thus, in the Babylonian version of this cosmogonic epic we already see the combination of creation and redemption (note that the gods praise Marduk for their "deliverance," *Enuma Elish* 6.49). We also see the connection between the mythic time and historical reality.

The Song of the Sea alludes to the cosmogonic battle, yet makes a dramatic transformation. While the imagery of the sea and the deep evokes cosmogony (Exod. 15:5, 8, 10), they are not the enemy; they are Yahweh's weapons. Rather, the enemy is the historical force of Pharaoh, and, of course, it is Israel who is delivered. Instead of cosmogony, the Song more accurately presents ethnogony, the "creation" of Yahweh's people through redemption: "the people whom you redeemed" (v. 13); "the people whom you acquired" (v. 16).[20] In addition to the echoes of the Song of the Sea in 43:15-21, SI explicitly invokes the cosmogonic myth in 51:9-11. The "arm of the Lord" is summoned to repeat the act "of old" when it "cut Rahab in pieces, [and] pierced the dragon" (v. 9). That act is then identified with the exodus deliverance by Yahweh, "who dried up[21] the sea, the waters of the great deep; who made the depths of the sea a way for the redeemed to cross over" (v. 10). And the repetition of the past act is proclaimed now for the imminent future: "so the ransomed of the Lord shall

20. See most recently the commentary of Terrence Fretheim, *Exodus* (Louisville: John Knox, 1991), pp. 166-68 and the literature cited there. The verb *qānâ* in Exod. 15:16 rendered "purchased" in the RSV and "acquired" in the NRSV is translated as "created" by Frank M. Cross (*Canaanite Myth and Hebrew Epic* [Cambridge: Harvard, 1973], p. 130). It appears as "create" in the NRSV translation of Deut. 32:6, parallel to "make" (*'śh*). Although the text refers to God as father, the poem subsequently uses a maternal image to refer to God as giving birth to Israel (v. 18). Second Isaiah also uses the language of "begetting" and giving birth for God's creative action (42:14; 45:10, the latter referring to Cyrus). On this, see Phyllis Trible, *God and the Rhetoric of Sexuality* (Philadelphia: Fortress, 1978), pp. 62-64.

21. Here SI shares the language of Exod. 14:16, 21. Note in v. 21 how the term "divided" may reflect the mythic splitting of the body of Tiamat (or the Ugaritic monster), like the reference to Rahab in 51:9. The image of *drying up* the sea is thus distinctly Israelite (cf. 42:15; 50:2).

return, and come to Zion" (v. 11). Verse 9 alone would seem to refer to creation, v. 10 to redemption; *together* the subject is the creative redemption of Israel, the re-creation of Israel. Moreover, there is again an irony: the mythic story that concluded with the rise of Babylon now tells of the fall of Babylon and the rise of Jerusalem (cf. 44:27).

From a "way in the sea" (v. 16a) the text now turns to "a way in the wilderness" (v. 19b), a metaphor initially announced in 40:3. In Israel's traditions this way led from Egypt *through* the wilderness to their settlement in the promised land. For SI the way through the wilderness is the "highway" (40:3) that leads from Babylon through the desert to Jerusalem. While the wilderness way is the path of the redeemed (cf. 35:9), it is also the place where Yahweh provides Israel's sustenance. Second Isaiah especially evokes ancient traditions of Yahweh's provision of water in the wilderness (explicitly in 48:21; cf. Exod. 15:22-25; 17:1-7; Num. 20:2-13; Deut. 8:15). The desert — a place normally without water — is the place where Yahweh will "give drink to my chosen people" (v. 20). Yet SI goes further with the imagery of water. Yahweh will make "rivers in the desert" (v. 20) and springs of water (35:7). It seems that the "highway" will have frequent "rest stops" with drinking fountains all along the way (49:10)!

In his development of both exodus and wilderness traditions, it is clear that SI's interest is far from antiquarian. In alluding to the ancient exodus, he is proclaiming a new exodus that is even now "in process." The exodus story is not simply a history of what happened long ago and far away. The exodus story is about something that is always happening. Exodus is not "was" but "is."

One of the ways in which SI conveys a sense of presentness to the exodus story is his use of participial verb forms at home in a particular hymnic tradition that praises God's activity in nature.[22] The verbs in v. 16, usually translated "who makes," "who brings out," could also be read as "who is making" or "who is bringing out." Some verb forms express finite actions that happened or will happen once and for all. Others express finite actions whose effect continues. But the participle expresses perennial actions.[23] The prophet knows that God is primarily a participial being, a being of uninterrupted activity — or, as the central verse of our text says, one who is always "doing a new thing." Since the word "do-

---

22. Wolff, *Amos*, p. 217.
23. See Stuhlmueller, *Creative Redemption*, p. 49.

ing" here (*ʿāśâ*) also means "making" and is often used for creation,[24] we can say that Yahweh is a God who is continually creating new possibilities. Creation is not an isolated "event" that happened at the beginning of history; it is more like a process in which God is always engaged.[25] In 40:12-31 the emphasis was on Yahweh as *creator;* here the emphasis is on Yahweh as *creating.*

The whole of SI's message can be summed up in these words: "I am doing a new thing." For the prophet it is absolutely critical that his audience is oriented toward this new thing. To be is to "be toward" what is about to happen.[26] So insistent is the prophet that Israel focus on this new thing that he makes a radical and ironic demand: Israel must forget the past. Having just used language that evokes the exodus of the past (vv. 16-17), and about to use language that evokes the wilderness journey of the past (vv. 19b-21a), the prophet demands that the people "not remember the former things, or consider the things of old" (v. 18). Although in the immediately preceding passage the people's memory of the former things provides the evidence of Yahweh's historical supremacy (vv. 8-13), here they are commanded *not* to remember.

Memory of the past can play two different roles. On the one hand, memory can degenerate into nostalgia. The nostalgic person is one who "lives in the past." Their memories may be very warm and comforting, but they are also a trap. Nostalgia shuts one up in the past so that one can no longer live for the future and see any new possibilities. In such a situation, memory prevents hope and becomes painful instead of healthful. Nostalgia, after all, has the suffix (-algia), which means "pain." On the other hand, memory can also be the basis for hope. Such memory recalls the past, but only as a way of recognizing the future. The former activity of God (i.e., exodus liberation, wilderness sustenance) provides the paradigm for discerning the current activity of God. Thus, without memory hope is impossible, but memory without hope leads to despair.

Coupled with the announcement of Yahweh's "doing a new thing" is

24. Gen. 1:7 and passim; Pss. 95:5; 104:24; 124:8; etc. Note how "maker" is used in parallel with "redeemer" in Isa. 54:5.

25. Indeed, it is possible to identify God with this process. See, for example, Gordon Kaufman, *In Face of Mystery* (Cambridge: Harvard University Press, 1993), p. 322.

26. For this image (taken from Dilthey) see Ray Hart, *Unfinished Man and the Imagination* (New York: Herder & Herder, 1968), pp. 143-44. To use Hart's terms, Israel in exile has "background" but no "foreground."

the verb "spring up" (ṣmḥ). The word can be used for various forms of new growth, but the primary meaning seems to be botanical,[27] translated "sprout." The new thing that Yahweh is doing "sprouts now." In the concluding chapter of SI, the analogy between nature and Yahweh's creative word is clear: "as the rain and snow come down from heaven, and do not return there until they have watered the earth, making it bring forth and sprout, giving seed to the sower and bread to the eater, so shall my word be . . ." (55:10-11). There is a reliability inherent to the process that we call germination. Once water meets seed, the process seems to be automatically effective, producing sprouts. At the same time, there is something unfailingly wondrous about the production of plants from seeds buried in the ground, or for that matter, the reappearance of perennials like the crocus that seemed to be dead (35:1). To SI, the reliability of this natural process points to the reliability of the new thing that Yahweh now proclaims and to its perennial freshness. God is the one who is always at work, "sprouting" new things, no matter how unlikely the situation, no matter how dead the things. Sprouting is a metaphor for divine creativity. If the ordinary process of germination is wondrous, it is all the more so in the desert, where the necessary water is absent. This is the subject of 43:19b-21a.

In the larger unit (vv. 16-21), SI has created a richly complex interweaving of water images from both history and nature. "A way in the sea" and "mighty waters" refer to the new exodus; "quenched" implies water; "rivers in the desert," "water in the wilderness," and "to give drink" allude to the wilderness traditions. As with the exodus imagery, the wilderness imagery refers both to ancient Israel's experience (cf. 48:21) and to the imminent journey of the exiles to their homeland. Yahweh provided water then (Exod. 15:22-25; 17:1-7; Num. 20:2-13) and will do so now, and all the more spectacularly in the form of rivers (cf. 35:6; 43:2; 44:3-4). Indeed, in 41:18-19 there are not only rivers but fountains, pools, and springs of water, so much so that the once barren earth will become like a forest or a garden (cf. 35:1-2 [Carmel means "garden"]). The language of provision in the wilderness incorporates not only the traditions of Yahweh as redeemer but also those of Yahweh as creator (41:20) — "the Holy One of Israel has created it." Similarly, in 44:3-4 the water and streams "poured" on the dry ground stand in parallel to Yahweh's spirit and blessing that is "poured" on Israel, causing

27. Lev. 13:37, hair; 2 Sam. 10:5, beard; Gen. 2:5; 41:6, 23, vegetation.

them to "sprout." Again, in 51:3-4 the wilderness of Zion will become "like Eden, her desert like the garden of the Lord." Related to this creation language are the hyperbolic images by which SI calls upon nature — seas, hills, trees, and so forth — to join in exuberant rejoicing over Israel's redemption (41:10; 44:34; 49:13; 55:12-13).

Finally, the unit of 43:14-21 closes with two purpose clauses: "to give drink to my chosen people, the people whom I formed for myself, so that they might declare my praise." The purpose of Yahweh's continuing creation is to benefit Israel and for Israel to praise Yahweh, as in 40:12-31, where the power of Yahweh the creator was proclaimed on Israel's behalf. Here the work of the creative redeemer is for the sake of the "elect" people. The connection between universal creator and a particular human community is intrinsic in the combination of the two phrases, "creator of the ends of the earth" and "creator of Israel." The claim made here is not without the problems inherent in the notion of being chosen. At times it seems that all nations will be the recipient of God's redemptive activity (49:6; 42:4, 6), yet elsewhere Israel's redemption will be accompanied by the humiliation, if not destruction, of the nations (49:22-26). While we cannot engage the larger issue here, it is clear once again that SI's theology of creative redemption is pastoral and political, the result of the correlation of nature and history. This correlation is vividly apparent when SI names Cyrus, the conqueror of Babylon, Yahweh's messiah or "anointed one" (45:1), and understands his political activity as a manifestation of Yahweh's creative activity (*br'*, 45:7, 8).[28] Indeed, in the immediately preceding verses (44:27-28), SI draws a close correlation between the cosmogonic battle motif, Cyrus as Yahweh's shepherd, and the restoration of the Jerusalem temple. None of this should surprise us, for, as noted above, the political consequences of the association of creation and redemption were already set in the Song of the Sea.

III. Conclusion

Given the attractions of what is now called "creation spirituality," perhaps we would prefer to find in SI a theology of creation unsullied by the messy events of history and the embarrassment of national interests, but we

---

28. Especially if "it" in v. 8 refers back to the entire pericope beginning with v. 1.

would have to look elsewhere for such a theology.[29] If some of us have trouble with the political implications of SI's creation theology, it may suggest the extent to which we are immune from political oppression and thus desensitized to the primary significance for SI's audience. In this case, SI's theology of creative redemption provides another instance in which liberation theologians, for example, could remind us of a fundamental dimension of religious experience, and of the Bible.[30] Yet, if SI were only applicable to people in political exile, many people would not find it spiritually helpful for their own situation. Fortunately, it is of the very nature of Scripture that its significance for us is not limited to literal interpretations or particular historical settings.

The spiritual malaise that SI addresses — failure, alienation, despair, abandonment — is part of the human condition. Exile is existential as well as political. That is why during every Advent we may sing the words "O come, O come Emmanuel, and ransom captive Israel, that mourns in lonely exile here." That is why an old gospel hymn, "The Haven of Rest," begins with these words: "my soul in sad exile was out on life's sea." The creation imagery — stars, streams, and sprouts — of SI can speak to these personal evocations of exile as well as to the political. Images of nature, from the infinite to the infinitesimal, speak to our yearning for redemption.

In one of her books, novelist Madeleine L'Engle traces her relationship with husband Hugh Franklin until his death from cancer. Her description of his grueling battle with this ugly disease produces a harrowing account. In one passage where L'Engle wrestles with questions of theodicy and the presence of God, she writes: "any God worth believing in is the God not only of the immensities of the galaxies I rejoice in at night . . . , but also the God of love who cares about the sufferings of us human beings and is here, with us, for us, in our pain and in our joy."[31] Elsewhere, she tells how as a child she was taken out at night to see the stars, given a glimpse of something "awesome and wonderful" — in a word, "numinous." As a parent she would take her own children to the top of a moun-

---

29. For example, Pss. 8, 104. Others, however, include some reference to Israel's special status, e.g., Ps. 19 (nature, vv. 1-6; Israel's torah, vv. 7-13); Ps. 33:12.

30. See Gustavo Gutierrez, *A Theology of Liberation* (Maryknoll, NY: Orbis, 1973), pp. 153-57.

31. *Two-Part Invention: The Story of a Marriage* (New York: Harper & Row, 1988), p. 123.

tain to look at the stars whenever there were tragedies in their lives. There they would "try to put whatever it was in the context of a universe created by a loving God." "So," she says, "whenever I have attacks of faithlessness, which I think we all get, if I can go see stars, that will almost always bring me back."[32] This combination of divine immensity and caring, of power and empowering, is the heart of SI's theology in 40:12-31.

In *The Waste Land,* T. S. Eliot describes that existential place "where the sun beats,/and the dead tree gives no shelter," a place where there "is no water but only rock."[33] It is to such barren, spiritual dryness that SI addresses his imagery of streams in the desert and new things sprouting. Thirst, after all, is a familiar metaphor for spiritual yearning (cf. Pss. 42:2; 63:1; 143:6). "When the poor and needy seek water, and there is none, and their tongue is parched with thirst, I the Lord will answer them" (41:17; cf. 55:1). Similarly, dryness and the resultant failure of things to grow suggest spiritual barrenness. My denomination's *Book of Worship* (United Church of Christ) has this confession of sin: "we confess what seems always with us: . . . things like buds within us that seem never to flower" (p. 533). Few can avoid the aching sterility of the soul reflected by this confession. Consequently, "*all* flesh" can welcome the sprouting created by the Word, as the dry grass welcomes the rain (cf. 55:10-12). Second Isaiah, I think, would like this anonymous saying: "This is the daily miracle, that glancing off each granite face the seed at last finds lodging in the broken place, and from the heart of the cleft sprouts grace, springs green."

32. "Who is God?" in *Questions of Faith,* Video (Nashville: Ecufilm, n.d.). Compare n. 9.

33. Louis Untermeyer, ed., *Modern American Poetry, Modern British Poetry* (New York: Harcourt, Brace & World, 1962), p. 383.

Jeremiah: *Creatio in Extremis*

Walter Brueggemann

The book of Jeremiah offers a clear test case and model for the shift in scholarly paradigms in Old Testament study. In the "history of traditions" perspective dominated by Gerhard von Rad, the tradition of Jeremiah is firmly situated in the exodus and Sinai-covenant traditions of Moses, but with some engagement with the Davidic-messianic traditions as well.[1] This entire phase of scholarship has resulted in a lopsided emphasis upon the traditio-historical background of the book.

We may notice, however, an addendum to von Rad's perspective that has controlled Jeremiah studies. Because of the three-source theory of Bernhard Duhm and Sigmund Mowinckel, the Deuteronomic redaction of the book and the so-called Baruch document left the way open to discerning evidence of sapiential influence in the literature.[2] On the one hand, Moshe Weinfeld has urged a linkage between wisdom and the traditions of Deuteronomy.[3] On the other hand, James Muilenburg has explored the scribal role of Baruch and has linked scribal activity to the more general

---

1. Gerhard von Rad, *Old Testament Theology* (London: Oliver and Boyd, 1965), vol. 2, p. 217 and passim.

2. The three-source theory that has dominated Jeremiah studies is now, of course, open to widespread question. See a summary of that scholarship in Brevard S. Childs, *Introduction to the Old Testament as Scripture* (Minneapolis: Fortress, 1979), pp. 342-45.

3. Moshe Weinfeld, *Deuteronomy and the Deuteronomic School* (Oxford: Clarendon, 1972).

category of wisdom.[4] Thus it is possible to see a development in the Jeremiah traditions toward wisdom influence that in turn suggests an openness to creation. This possibility, however, has been a quite subordinate point in the interpretive models that situated Jeremiah in the Mosaic-covenantal-levitical matrix reflected in the Deuteronomists and voiced in the tradition of Hosea.[5]

I.

The important shift in interpretive models, evidenced by the theme of this volume, permits us to pay much more sustained attention to creation themes in the tradition of Jeremiah.[6] While it is clear that "creation" is an ill-defined rubric and therefore may include many diverse elements, and while there is at the moment a temptation to pan-creationism (like an earlier pan-covenantalism), it is unmistakable that this general perspective on Yahwism pervades the book of Jeremiah, a pervasion mostly denied and kept invisible by the once dominant history-of-traditions perspective.

Leo Perdue has provided a convenient overview of "creation theology in Jeremiah" in terms of (a) creation and history, (b) creation and the destiny of the individual, and (c) wisdom and creation.[7] Of particular interest is his discussion of "the chaos tradition" concerning the divine war-

---

4. James Muilenburg, "Baruch the Scribe," in *Proclamation and the Presence: Old Testament Essays in Honour of Gwynne Henton Davies,* ed. John I. Durham and J. Roy Porter (London: SCM, 1970), pp. 215-38. For a more rigorous historical assessment of the scribes in the world of Jeremiah, see J. Andrew Dearman, "My Servants the Scribes: Composition and Context in Jeremiah 36," *JBL* 109 (1990): 403-21.

5. For the locus of Hosea (and derivatively Jeremiah) in the circles of levitical priests derived from Mosaic traditions and voiced in the Deuteronomists, see Hans Walter Wolff, "Hoseas geistige Heimat," *ThLZ* 81 (1956): 83-94. It is surely more compelling to conclude that Jeremiah was nourished and evoked in these circles than to imagine that the Deuteronomic focus was artificially imposed on the tradition of Jeremiah.

6. The studies in this volume are reflective of a radically shifted paradigm in Old Testament interpretation. See Walter Brueggemann, "The Loss and Recovery of Creation in Old Testament Theology," *ThT* 53 (1996): 177-90, and "A Shifting Paradigm: From 'Mighty Deeds' to 'Horizon,'" in *The Papers of the Henry Luce III Fellows in Theology,* ed. Gary H. Gilbert (Atlanta: Scholars Press, 1996), pp. 7-47.

7. Leo G. Perdue, *The Collapse of History: Reconstructing Old Testament Theology,* OBT (Minneapolis: Fortress, 1994), pp. 141-50.

rior that shows up both in the so-called Scythian Songs and in the Oracles against the Nations.[8] It is telling that this theme, especially in light of the work of Frank Cross, Patrick Miller, and Paul Hanson, can be understood in terms of "creation-chaos," whereas von Rad linked these same texts to holy war, a clear illustration of how particular methodological assumptions mandate and preclude certain readings.[9]

We may list some of the rich variety of creation motifs evident in the Jeremiah traditions, in part informed by Perdue's exposition:

- An emphasis upon *land* can be understood in terms of the Moses-Joshua historical traditions but can also be seen as the space for life willed and maintained by the creator God (2:7; 3:19; 4:3; 33:12; 45:4)[10] and made possible by Yahweh's guarantee of *fertility* (8:13, 20; 22:6; 31:5).
- Fertility in turn is made possible by the assurance of *rain,* a matter of great significance in a marginal, arid climate (2:1-3; 3:2-3; 5:24; 14:4, 22).
- Focus upon land, fertility, and rain, is also confirmed by the utilization of concrete "metaphors of nature," for example, horses and birds (8:6-7), plants and wild animals (1:11; 5:6; 12:9; 24:1), and grain, wine, and oil (31:12). Such imagery saturates the poetry.
- More generally we notice, along with Perdue, linkages to wisdom, that is, regular, orderly patterns of reality (8:7; 15:14; 17:11).
- Perhaps most interesting is the claim of 5:22 that Yahweh's ordering of the sand of the seashore creates a boundary and a limit to chaos, thus providing a safe, viable, fruitful place for human habitation.

8. More generally on the so-called Scythian Songs, see Brevard S. Childs, "The Enemy from the North and the Chaos Tradition," *JBL* 78 (1959): 187-98; on the Oracles against the Nations, see Childs, *Introduction,* pp. 352-53.

9. Frank Moore Cross, "The Divine Warrior," in *Canaanite Myth and Hebrew Epic: Essays in the History of the Religion of Israel* (Cambridge: Harvard University Press, 1973), pp. 91-112; Patrick D. Miller Jr., *The Divine Warrior in Early Israel,* HSM 5 (Cambridge: Harvard University Press, 1973); Paul D. Hanson, *The Dawn of Apocalyptic* (Philadelphia: Fortress, 1975), pp. 123-26, 182-85 and passim; von Rad, *Old Testament Theology,* vol. 2, p. 199.

10. See Walter Brueggemann, "Israel's Sense of Place in Jeremiah," in *Rhetorical Criticism: Essays in Honor of James Muilenburg,* ed. Jared J. Jackson and Martin Kessler (Pittsburgh: Pickwick Press, 1974), pp. 149-65; Peter Diepold, *Israel's Land,* BWANT 15 (Berlin: W. Kohlhammer, 1972).

This listing is only representative. It is sufficient nonetheless to indicate that the tradition of Jeremiah places Yahweh on a wide, panoramic screen, as wide as all creation, and situates Judah in its theo-political crisis amid the guarantees and threats that are as large as all creation. Because it is not possible to explore all such uses, I want to focus only on three cases that I take to be "limit expressions" of the "limit experiences" of Judah living in a creation that is fully dependent upon Yahweh and fully open to Yahweh's singular guarantee of life.[11]

II.

In any consideration of creation themes in Jeremiah, an important reference point is 4:24-29, which is situated in a series of poetic units concerned with foreign invasion.[12] Historically this poetic unit refers to the threat of a foreign invader (apparently Babylon) who will at the behest of Yahweh terminate life in the world and, consequently, life in Jerusalem. Canonically this text and the themes it presents function as *judgment* in a two-stage "final form" text of *judgment and hope*.[13] Special attention may be paid to this text, both because it is an epitome of the ominous quality of life in jeopardy from Yahweh and because of its wondrously symmetrical mode of articulation.[14]

The poem proceeds in four parallel lines, together with a fifth line naming Yahweh as the sole agent of the dismantling of creation, even as Yahweh had been the sole agent of creation. The first four lines are introduced by *rā'îtî*, the report of an observer who anticipates the destruction, accented in each line by *hinneh,* bespeaking the surprise, intensity, and ex-

---

11. The terms "limit expression" and "limit experience" that are crucial to my argument are drawn from Paul Ricoeur, "Biblical Hermeneutics," *Semeia* 4 (1975): 107-45.

12. On this larger unit of poetry, see Childs, *Introduction,* pp. 352-53.

13. See Childs, *Introduction,* pp. 345-54, and more specifically, Ronald E. Clements, "Patterns in the Prophetic Canon," in *Canon and Authority: Essays in Old Testament Religion and Theology,* ed. George W. Coats and Burke O. Long (Philadelphia: Fortress, 1977), pp. 42-55.

14. William Holladay (*Jeremiah,* Hermeneia [Philadelphia: Fortress, 1986-89], vol. 1, p. 163) speaks of "the stark sublimity" of the poem. The use of the term "sublime" recalls the sense of Emmanuel Kant and Rudolf Otto that "the Sublime" is not only awesome in beauty but also profound in its threat. Thus "sublime" is exactly the correct term here.

tremity of the destruction. The lines proceed from the most general (heavens and earth) to the landscape of earth (mountains and hills), to the inhabitants (human and birds), and finally to the specific land of well-being *(karmel)* that Yahweh has guaranteed and that Judah now inhabits. These elements of creation are matched and trumped by the terms of negation, "waste and void" *(tōhû wābōhû)* at the outset, "quaking and moving" as signs of elemental instability, and a double negation, *'ên*.[15] Every line except the first summarizes with "all" — all hills, all birds, all cities — nothing spared, nothing held back, nothing protected, nothing guaranteed.

It is unmistakable that the dismantling described here witnesses in calibrated ways to the creation strategy of Genesis 1. Jeremiah 4:24-26 is a step by step subtraction from the "very good" creation upon which Israel has counted and in which its own life is lived. It is of course sensible to say with Perdue that such rhetoric of "the cataclysmic upheaval of nature is obvious hyperbole."[16] Such a verdict, however, misses the cumulative intent of the rhetoric, which is to imagine and invite the listener of the poem to host a scenario in which nothing reliable or life-sustaining is left. Creation theology here functions to voice a complete, unreserved, elemental negation of all that makes life livable, a negation that could hardly be uttered without such large language. Conversely, the rhetoric makes the theological point that Yahweh is fully capable of termination, and in this circumstance ready to terminate an awesome, sublime articulation of sovereignty. Those addressed are pressed to discern themselves in a moment of radical rejection, more radical and wholesale than any "historical tradition" could possibly voice. This is the most imaginable discontinuity that could be uttered. When the text is seen as a limit articulation designed to lead Judah beyond its conventional imagination, there is nothing hyperbolic about it. This is the real thing for Yahweh the creator, the real thing for creation that has no autonomous existence, and unmistakably the real thing for Judean listeners.

---

15. Childs ("The Enemy from the North") has paid careful attention to the term *rʿš* that occurs in this text and links it to the ancient tradition of chaos.

16. Perdue, *The Collapse of History*, p. 143.

III.

Given this intense portrayal of demolition, we cannot be emotionally or cognitively prepared for the assurance of 31:35-36, 37, which I take to be an antithesis to 4:23-26. These two brief oracles in ch. 31 appeal to the stability and reliability of creation as a ground from which to assert the stability and reliability of Yahweh's promise of durability to "the offspring" of Israel. Whereas 4:23-26 voices Yahweh's destruction of creation, these oracles assure that such demolition is precluded, prohibited, and made impossible in the economy of Yahweh.

This oracle that stands in penultimate position in "the Book of Comfort" (chs. 30–31) makes what may be regarded as the most extreme guarantee of well-being in creation theology. It is viewed by contemporary scholarship as a later part of the "rolling corpus" of the Jeremiah tradition.[17] The oracles may be treated as distinct, isolated units or as confirmation of the promise of new covenant in 31:31-34.

In any case, each oracle, termed by Herbert Huffmon as an "impossible promise," is organized around an "if" of impossibility (in each case an impossibility for creation) and taken as an assurance of the impossibility of the cessation or rejection of "the offspring" of Israel.[18] In the first oracle, the authorization formula (v. 35a) is supported by the doxology (v. 35bc) and reinforced by a reiteration of the divine name (v. 35d). The doxology consists of two participial verbs, the first concerning sun, moon, and stars together with the crucial term "fixed order" (*ḥûqqôt*), the second concerning the sea (see Ps. 146:6). The four elements of creation here mean to comprehend the entire scope of creation. The whole of v. 35 only certifies who it is who speaks, the one with power to resolve to initiate, sustain, and guarantee the created order.

It is this one who speaks the "if . . . then" of v. 36. The "if" that is taken to be "not possible" is the cessation of these "fixed orders" from before the face of Yahweh.[19] On the basis of the fixed order of creation that

17. On that contemporary judgment, see the commentaries of Robert Carroll, William Holladay, and William McKane. In older scholarship, Paul Volz and Wilhelm Rudolf held to the early "authenticity" of the oracles.

18. Herbert B. Huffmon, "The Impossible Word of Assurance: Jer. 31:34-36 (35-37)," paper delivered at the Society of Biblical Literature meeting in New Orleans, 1996.

19. It is perhaps not unimportant that the double use of *pnh* (face) has a counterpart in 4:26 wherein the destruction of creation is "from before Yahweh." That both the destruc-

cannot cease, the "then" is the equally impossible thought that Israel will cease; Israel is grounded in the bottom-line claim concerning the indelible sureness of creation.

The same structure pertains in the oracle of v. 37, presented as it is, sandwiched between two formulas of authorization. Here the impossible "if" is the measuring and exploration of unfathomable creation that is beyond all human measurement. It is the creation impossibility that provides the ground for the "then," the impossibility of the ending of Israel's existence. The power of these assurances, unlike either vv. 31-34 or vv. 38-40, is the wonder of the "natural order," a wonder of regularity and dependability that would seem to be nourished and noticed in something like wisdom teaching.

The juxtaposition of 4:23-26 and 31:35-37 suggests the extreme interpretive possibilities of creation theology hosted within the tradition of Jeremiah. It is likely that 4:23-26 is "authentic" to the prophetic person and is surely "early," concerned with *judgment* upon a recalcitrant community; it is probable that 31:35-37 is a later utterance from a subsequent generation, designed to offer *hope* to an exilic or postexilic community when the very existence of that community is unmistakably in jeopardy.

Thus the two texts reflect chronologically a movement from early to late, together with very different circumstances. Canonically, they move from judgment to assurance. Something like a two-stage understanding of life with Yahweh is surely indicated.[20] If, however, we take a synchronic view of the tradition and see the two accents together in the final form of the text, then an unrelieved "tension between present misery and future property" is evident in the book, as noted by Robert P. Carroll.[21] The juxtaposition of these two "limit expressions" of utter demolition (4:23-26) and total assurance (31:35-37) suggests that neither the demolition nor the as-

---

tion and the assurance are "before Yahweh" points to the Yahwistic, theonomous focus of both realities.

20. On such a "two stage" presentation of Judah's theological reality in the tradition of Isaiah (with special reference to Isa. 8:23b), see Hugh G. M. Williamson, "First and Last in Isaiah," in *Of Prophets' Visions and the Wisdom of Sages: Essays in Honour of R. Norman Whybray on His Seventieth Birthday,* ed. Heather A. McKay and David J. A. Clines, JSOTSup 162 (Sheffield: Sheffield Academic Press, 1993), pp. 95-108. It is likely that such a two-stage presentation became dominant and "canonical" for the prophetic perspective in general.

21. Robert P. Carroll, *Jeremiah: A Commentary,* OTL (Philadelphia: Westminster, 1986), p. 616.

surance is the proper focus of creation theology in the tradition of Jeremiah. Rather both claims are instrumental and point beyond themselves to the one who speaks, Yahweh, the one who presides over creation and over the destiny of Judah. Thus both extremes of expression bear witness to the theological claim that finally Israel must come to terms with Yahweh upon whom its future well-being solely depends. Both the coming destruction and the subsequent assurance are functions of Yahweh's sovereign governance that Israel cannot evade and without which it cannot live.[22]

IV.

In the context of these two most extreme statements, we may now consider one other recurring hymnic assertion of creation theology that will call attention to three texts (10:12; 32:17; 51:15). I take up these three texts because they roughly echo the same cadences of what must have been a more or less stylized doxological assertion. The subject of that stylized assertion is clearly creation in its linkage to the creator, and the matrix of the recurring formulation is clearly sapiential.[23]

Thus if we are to look for the natural habitat of this rhetorical pattern, we will likely find it in wisdom materials that are at the same time instructional and liturgical. It is not our purpose to trace the antecedents of the uses of Jeremiah, except to contend that the doxological articulation is an older formulation situated outside conventional "prophetic" discourse that revolves around speeches of judgment and promise. One such reference point for such antecedent sapiential articulation is in Proverbs 3:19-20:

The Lord by wisdom founded the earth;
by understanding he established the heavens;

---

22. I use the term "subsequent" because it is not possible in the tradition of Jeremiah to deny that there was a rejection in the events of 587; see Walter Brueggemann, "A Shattered Transcendence? Exile and Restoration," in *Biblical Theology: Problems and Perspectives,* ed. Steven J. Kraftchick, et al. (Nashville: Abingdon, 1995), pp. 169-82. The subsequent character of the assurance is more explicit in Isa. 54:9 with its "never again" *('ôd);* see also Gen. 9:11.

23. The intimate connection between creation and wisdom reflection is now commonplace, as in Perdue's discussion (*The Collapse of History*). Reference may also be made to the works of von Rad and Walther Zimmerli.

by his knowledge the deeps broke open,
and the clouds drop down the dew.

This formulation begins with the naming of Yahweh and identifies three agencies whereby Yahweh creates: wisdom, understanding, and knowledge. Beyond the triad of agents, the third portion of the statement (v. 20) departs from the parallelism of the first two lines in two ways. First, the third statement of agency (knowledge) includes two objects in parallel lines (deeps, clouds), so that the match of agent and object in the first two lines (wisdom-earth, understanding-heavens) is violated. Second, the verbs in v. 20 have the created objects as their subjects, and not Yahweh, as in the first two lines. Thus the third element of the unit breaks what seems to be the natural cadence by greater variation.

This small textual unit is regarded by R. Norman Whybray as a part of a second larger expansion in the development of Proverbs 1–9.[24] More importantly, William McKane, along with Whybray, observes that the purpose of the unit is to link wisdom to Yahweh, so that Yahweh is seen to be the agent of the reliable, dazzling order of creation.[25] McKane, moreover, suggests that these verses belong to an editorial piece closely connected to Proverbs 8:22-31. And because Proverbs 8:22-31 figures large in any theological assessment of sapiential tradition, we are able to suggest that Proverbs 3:19-20 articulates a pivotal theological claim.

In Proverbs 8:22-31, wisdom is reckoned to be an intimate of Yahweh in the work of creation. In Proverbs 3:19-20 the same claim is made, except that "wisdom," not yet "personified," is here richly expressed by three agencies, wisdom and the two parallel terms. These two verses, then, make a primal statement about lived reality as creation and provide the base line for thinking theologically and ethically about cosmic and social reality with its orderliness, its uncompromising requirements, and its unfathomable gifts.[26]

24. R. Norman Whybray, *Wisdom in Proverbs*, SBT 45 (Naperville: Alec R. Allenson, 1965), p. 75.
25. William McKane, *Proverbs*, OTL (Philadelphia: Westminster, 1970), pp. 296-97; Whybray, *Wisdom in Proverbs*, pp. 75, 95-104.
26. It is clear that this articulation has close linkages to materials in Second Isaiah. It is not possible, however, to demonstrate the direction of influence.

V.

It is clear that the Jeremiah tradition takes up this doxological, sapiential claim that redefines the world as creation and asserts the connection between Yahweh and the world through the verbs and agents of creation. It is clear that while the Jeremiah tradition recontextualizes such a sapiential formulation, it is no longer intended simply as a doxological base line. Rather, the rhetoric is drawn into the socio-political crisis with which the Jeremiah tradition is preoccupied. The first such use of this doxological formula is found in 10:12:

> It is he who made the earth by his power,
> who established the world by his wisdom,
> and by his understanding stretched out the heavens.

The larger unit of 10:1-16 is peculiar in its context, offering a deeply polemical and doxological contrast between the idols (who are powerless, false, and merit no attention) and Yahweh (who is incomparable, true, living, and powerful). The polemic against idols (cf. Pss. 115, 135; Isa. 44:9-20) is not usual in traditions as early as Jeremiah, and the weight of scholarly opinion has been against the "authenticity" of the passage. Be that as it may, the final assertion of v. 16 draws even the religious polemic into a Jeremianic matrix.[27]

More specifically, vv. 12-15 sharply contrasts Yahweh and the idols. In vv. 12-13, Yahweh is the creator God who works with immense power through all creation. Indeed, the large rhetorical claims here correspond to facets of the Joban speeches of the whirlwind. The counter-assertion of vv. 14-15 is a stark contrast made with an inventory of negatives: stupid, without knowledge, shame, false, no breath, worthless, and delusion. The contrast is detailed, absolute, and sustained.

The precise doxology of v. 12 is more consistent in form than is the sapiential model cited from Proverbs 3:19-20. Our verse in Hebrew lacks the divine name (present in LXX as in Prov. 3:19), but there can be no

---

27. One of the primary grounds for taking 10:1-16 as later is the theme of the treatment of idols. Such a literary judgment based so tightly upon a view of the history of Israelite religion, however, is not necessary. Current interpretation is not inclined to hold literary judgments so closely to historical judgments, if indeed it matters much anyway about what is early and what is late.

doubt who, in context, is asserted as the living, true God. It is this God who acts through three agents: power, wisdom, and discernment. Two of these elements are parallel to those of Proverbs 3:19-20, but here "power" displaces "knowledge" as the third agent. Moreover, this articulation has three verbs, of which Yahweh is the subject — "makes," "establishes," "stretched out" — so that only the middle verb, *kûn,* is parallel to Proverbs 3:19-20. The structure of this verse features three well-delineated parts. The third line, unlike that of Proverbs 3:19-20, stays closely parallel to the first two lines and has only one object, thus yielding a triad of objects — earth, world, heavens — to stay congruent with the three verbs and three agents.

The claim of the whole is that the world, and therefore the world of Israel, and therefore the world of Jeremiah's seventh-century crisis, is completely at the behest of Yahweh, who is the subject of all the verbs. It is indeed the decisive governing capacity of Yahweh that is featured, though in the poem we are given no tilt toward either demolition (as in 4:23-26) or guarantee (as in 31:35-37), for both demolition and guarantee are free choices for the living God.

It is evident that the poem, in its doxology and its polemic, takes a curious turn in v. 16. It is possible to regard this verse as an addendum for the sake of tribal chauvinism. It is also possible, however, to see v. 16 as the climactic point of the entire poem. The specialness of Israel to Yahweh is clear; but the double claim for Jacob — Yahweh as *Jacob's portion,* Israel as *Yahweh's inheritance* — is intertwined with more "creation" claims: "Yahweh of Hosts" has "formed all," thus echoing the great doxological claims linked to Yahweh's power and authority as creator.[28] The claims made for the creator in v. 16 are completely congruent with the doxology of v. 12, thus making Yahweh's attentiveness to Israel not a belated "election" but a factor in the very fabric of creation. Because the verbs of v. 12 are all positive, with no hint of negation or destruction, the purpose is to assure Israel of Yahweh's reliable attentiveness in all of his vitality and power. The poem, of course, is a bid for loyalty to Yahweh and an insistent warning against idols that perish, but the ground for appeal for loyalty to Yahweh is not threat but guarantee. The doxological affirmation of Yahweh as creator is here voiced as the ground for Israel's steadfast reliance upon Yahweh, a ground that is intrinsic to the primal work of the creator.

28. See James L. Crenshaw, *Hymnic Affirmation of Divine Justice,* SBLDS 24 (Missoula: Scholars Press, 1975).

VI.

It is discerned by scholars that 10:12-16 is reiterated in 51:15-19.[29] The entire corpus of the Oracles against the Nations (chs. 46–51) has a problematic linkage to the Jeremiah tradition, particularly chs. 50–51 concerning Babylon. Nonetheless, it is clear that 51:15-19 is a peculiar feature in this extended oracle.[30] The weight of the entire oracle is the devastation of Babylon; the counter theme here is the enduring commitment of Yahweh to Israel in v. 19.

The opening verse (v. 15) reiterates 10:12. Again Yahweh's name is lacking; again three verbs with three agents and three objects are present. Together they constitute the sum of all creation. The larger unit of vv. 15-19 again divides into an affirmation of Yahweh (vv. 15-16), an attack on alternative loyalties (vv. 17-18), and an affirmation of Jacob-Israel as the peculiar object of the creator God (v. 19).

In 51:15-19 the verses of 10:12-16 are set in the oracle against Babylon. The horizon of the oracle is very large, anticipating the demolition of the hegemonic power of the time. At the threshold of the oracle, more reticent than Second Isaiah, is the anticipation of the coming Persians who will do the work of destruction. Thus in the prose of v. 11 it is the coming "Medes"; in vv. 12-14 it is the invading empire that will come with troops; and in vv. 20-23 "you" (unspecified) will fight for Israel. The title "Lord of Hosts," sounded in 51:19 and in 10:16, is also voiced in v. 14.

The unit makes clear that the creator God is larger, stronger, and more determined than even this awesome, brutalizing superpower. The doxological and polemical rhetoric of the oracle must find a way to affirm Yahweh as more absolute than the seemingly absolute superpower, and the only way to do that is to seize upon the creation themes of wisdom that are not tamed by historical references to Yahweh. Of course, vv. 19 and 20 refer to Israel, thus drawing the doxological tradition close to the crisis of exile. All of the powers of the creator are mobilized for the sake of Israel, for Israel before the might of Babylon has no alternative way to the future.

The relationship between the uses of the creation doxology in 10:12-16 and in 51:15-19 is not obvious. In the first usage, the assurance is of-

---

29. See Alice Ogden Bellis, *The Structure and Composition of Jeremiah 50:2–51:58* (Lewiston: Mellan Biblical Press, 1995), pp. 136-39.

30. Bellis regards these verses as a belated intrusion in the text.

fered as a basis for exclusive loyalty to Yahweh against all alternative possibilities, together with a summons. In the second usage, the assurance is offered without any such summons to loyalty, as a ground of hope and a resistance against despair and docile submission to the empire. It is possible and perhaps likely that the doxology of 10:12-16 is simply taken up later and reused by a subsequent poet. Alternatively William McKane, following Bernhard Duhm, suggests that the redactors of 51:15-19 "did not know that it had appeared at chapter 10."[31] The question of the relationship between the two uses is beyond resolution. What is clear is that in making its sweeping Yahwistic claim, the tradition finds a way of pushing behind any historical possibility to the creator, who is the only source of comfort and strength, a source found by these voices to be adequate in more than one crisis.

VII.

A third, truncated use of the same doxological formula is found in 32:17, in the narrative that stands amid the poems of hope in the Book of Comfort (chs. 30–31) and the collection of promises in ch. 33. Chapter 32 is organized around the narrative concerning land entitlement in vv. 1-15 that yields the reiterated summons of v. 25 and the promise of v. 44.[32] Within the specific, anticipated land transaction, the chapter offers a prayer (vv. 16-25) and an oracle (vv. 26-41) that express both the extremity of destruction and the extremity of new possibility. Given both extremities, it is asserted that "Nothing is too hard for you," first as an affirmation (v. 17) and then as a question that implies an affirmation (v. 27). This material thus ponders Yahweh's extreme possibilities in the depths of the exile, including the possibility of Yahweh abandoning his people (a termination of the assurances in 10:12; 51:15) and the possibility of Yahweh regathering his scattered people.[33] This long prose unit is

---

31. William McKane, *A Critical and Exegetical Commentary on Jeremiah II*, ICC (Edinburgh: T&T Clark, 1996), p. 1309.

32. See Walter Brueggemann, "A 'Characteristic' Reflection on What Comes Next (Jer. 32:16-44)," forthcoming from Sheffield Academic Press.

33. On the category of "impossibility," see Walter Brueggemann, "'Impossibility' and Epistemology in the Faith Tradition of Abraham and Sarah (Gen. 18:1-15)," in *The Psalms and the Life of Faith*, ed. Patrick D. Miller Jr. (Minneapolis: Fortress, 1995), pp. 167-68.

indeed a limit expression required to voice the limit experience of Israel in the sixth century.

I suggest that 32:17 is a pivot point in this meditation upon Yahweh's extremities: "Ah Lord God! It is you who made the heavens and the earth by your great power and by your outstretched arm! Nothing is too hard for you." This verse is uttered at the beginning of Jeremiah's prayer, which voices a recital of Israel's past with Yahweh (vv. 18-23a), a speech of judgment (vv. 23b-24), and a reiteration of Yahweh's promise (v. 25). The function of the opening doxology appears to be a motivation, linked to the promise of v. 25.[34] That is, the concrete historical promise of v. 25 would appear to be impossible, but the creator God is the one who does the impossible. The prayer reaches outside historical possibility to move Yahweh into the larger arena of the possible.

Thus creation itself is a sign and measure of Yahweh's capacity to do beyond what the world thinks is possible. In the doxological formulation, the opening is more focused and more powerful than those already cited in 10:12 and 51:15. Yahweh is addressed with the title *'adonai.* This usage of the doxological formula is cast as a prayer; therefore, direct address is especially appropriate. The address is reinforced by the attention-getter *hinneh.* The substance of what is to be said to Yahweh is introduced by the emphatic pronoun *'attâ* followed by a perfect verb.[35] The doxological affirmation has only one verb and two objects, heaven and earth. Moreover, the agents (great power and outstretched arm) are different from the other uses, except that "power" is also an agent in 51:15.[36] Thus the formulation is quite different, but the structure of the utterance is close enough to be considered in the same thematic field. The point here is not simply an assurance (as in 51:15-19) or an assurance with summons (as in 10:12-16). Because of the form of address, the purpose is to remind Yahweh of his capacity to do something.

34. On motivation, see Patrick D. Miller Jr., *They Cried to the Lord: The Form and Theology of Biblical Prayer* (Minneapolis: Fortress, 1994), pp. 114-26.

35. The lead verb in the other two uses of 10:12 and 51:15 is a participle.

36. It is worth observing that the phrase "outstretched arm" has been characteristically taken as exodus terminology. This is yet another case where the historical paradigm has dictated the terms of interpretation when, under another paradigm, the phrasing may relate to creation. Terence Fretheim ("The Plagues as Ecological Signs of Historical Disaster," *JBL* 110 [1991]: 385-96) has proposed a rereading of the exodus narrative in the categories of creation. Such a rereading would, in a small detail, reassign this phrasing to creation theology.

The motivation of this truncated doxology is reinforced by the second half of the sentence: Yahweh does impossibilities! The impossibility celebrated in this verse is the powerful action of the creation of heaven and earth; the impossibility in which Israel now lives is "these disasters," the end of Jerusalem and the ensuing exile. The impossibility anticipated here is restoration:

> Yet you, O Lord God, have said to me, "Buy the field for money and get witnesses." (32:25a)

> Just as I have brought all this great disaster upon this people, so I will bring upon them all the good fortune that I now promise them. Fields shall be bought in this land . . . (vv. 42-43)

The impossibility for which petition is made flies in the face of the concessive clause ("though") of v. 25b: "though the city has been given into the hand of the Chaldeans." The impossibility and the petition for it constitute a counter-reality, counter to the exile, countered only on the ground of the power of the creator.

The rhetoric that stretches from v. 17 to v. 25 has the force of voicing the hope of rehabilitation in the land as a miracle commensurate with the act of creation. Appeal is made to the one as ground for the other, ground out of which Israel hopes and out of which Yahweh may act.

VIII.

While it is clear that the Jeremiah tradition in many incidental ways (as mentioned above) appeals to creation thought, the most important point is that creation themes are of structural importance to the theological accents of judgment and hope in the final form of the text. Four conclusions may be drawn in that regard.

(1) It is clear that the tradition of Jeremiah is familiar with and knows how to use effectively available themes and images of creation thought. It is now clear in biblical scholarship, as evidenced by this volume, that Old Testament theology through the twentieth century, largely propelled by Gerhard von Rad's determinative essay of 1936, stands in need of a major correction. In the battle of the German Church with National Socialism von Rad had linked creation theology with fertility reli-

gion, as it was manifested in the "Blood and Soil" ideology regnant in Germany. In response to that crucial church crisis, von Rad drew an important theological conclusion about the Old Testament:

> Our main thesis was that in genuinely Yahwistic belief the doctrine of creation never attained to the stature of a relevant, independent doctrine. We found it invariably related, and indeed subordinated, to soteriological considerations . . . because of the exclusive commitment of Israel's faith to historical salvation, the doctrine of creation was never able to attain independent existence in its own right.[37]

In retrospect it is evident that von Rad overstated the distinction between creation and soteriology.[38] And in the United States the same judgment was forcefully made by G. Ernest Wright.[39] That judgment, for several generations, has caused scholars to overlook the appeal to creation in biblical literature.

At the same time, if cautiously construed, von Rad's judgment has merit. It is clear in the texts we have considered that creation is "invariably related" to Israel's place in Yahweh's economy. It is surely true that "the doctrine of creation was never able to attain to independent existence in its own right." It is not clear, however, that such thought is subordinated to soteriology. I should argue rather that it is subordinated to the claim that Yahweh is the governor of all of reality, both what we have come to call history and what we call creation. That is, creation theology is an instance of the theonomous character and quality of all of reality, including the reality of Israel's life.

(2) In the tradition of Jeremiah, there is no doubt that the core themes are demolition and rehabilitation. Creation themes in Jeremiah, I suggest, are designed to affirm that the experience and reality of demoli-

---

37. Gerhard von Rad, "The Theological Problem of the Old Testament Doctrine of Creation," in Gerhard von Rad, *The Problem of the Hexateuch and Other Essays* (New York: McGraw-Hill, 1966), p. 142.

38. It is clear than von Rad took his cue from the categories of Karl Barth. For a polemical review of Barth's categories, see James Barr, *Biblical Faith and Natural Theology: The Gifford Lectures for 1991* (Oxford: Clarendon, 1993). Of particular interest is Barr's assertion, "Thus the understanding of pro-Nazi theology as basically a kind of natural theology was probably a vast misdiagnosis" (pp. 112-13).

39. G. Ernest Wright, *The Old Testament Against Its Environment*, SBT 2 (London: SCM, 1950), and *God Who Acts: Biblical Theology as Recital*, SBT 8 (London: SCM, 1952).

tion, while serious, is *only penultimate*. Similarly, the prospect of return and restoration is also real and serious, but *also penultimate*. Undermining the ultimacy of both demolition and rehabilitation is the more extreme claim of Yahweh the creator, who can do the impossible by dismantling creation (and Israel's life) and who can do the equally impossible act of revamping creation (and Israel's life). All of life is referred to the creator God, who is not restrained or restricted by any "given" of either creation or history. Thus the doxologies we have cited counter the absolute autonomy of Israel, the absolute despair of Israel, and the absolute hegemony of Babylon. Nothing is absolute, except the "Thou" who occupies the transformative verbs of power.

(3) It is important that the theological claim not be separated from the rhetorical act. The doxologies may be about creator and creation, but they are said, sung, and spoken acts. The deabsolutizing of the penultimate realities of demolition and rehabilitation takes place through an extreme statement of wonder. The rhetoric may strike us as so familiar and conventional that we do not notice. In fact, the claims are extreme. In 4:23-26, it is extreme to say "behold" four times to dismantling. In 31:35-37, it is extreme to speak an "if-then" assurance that rates the durability of Israel with the durability of creation. It is extreme when the claim for Yahweh subverts the alternative of idols (10:1-16), when the claim of Yahweh overrides the landless present tense of the exiles (32:17), and when the claim of Yahweh trumps the hegemony of Babylon (51:15-19). It is an extremity of rhetoric in which the tradition asserts what the world cannot reasonably entertain.

The rhetoric must be so extreme, however, because the tradition offers *speech* that matches *experience*. The extremity of expression is required in order to make available the extremity of experience, which in Judah is the loss of a safe world and the prospect of a new world.[40] With this rheto-

---

40. It may be possible to suggest an analogue between the losses of sixth-century Judah and contemporary losses in the immense suffering of Auschwitz, Hiroshima, and Vietnam, to name only the most prominent examples. Robert Jay Lifton has identified "psychic numbing," that is, to cease to notice or to care, as a strategic response to evil that threatens to overwhelm. He suggests that such "psychic numbing" produces a "symbol gap," wherein there are no adequate symbols to mediate the experience. Such a situation of deficiency of speech and expression requires fresh utterances to break the numbing. *Mutatis mutandis,* I suggest that the limit expressions of the Jeremiah tradition are addressed to the limit experiences of Judah that perhaps produced such numbing.

ric it is possible to make available the loss and the future prospect. Such expression makes the density of the experience inescapable. The enduring effect of such rhetoric is to press the listening community to face its own lived life, to ensure Yahweh as the pivotal player in that lived life, and to certify to coming generations that lived reality presided over by Yahweh is a reliable lens through which to engage other crises that have the same world-ending and world-making scope. Indeed, it is the richness of the limit expression that causes this Jeremiah tradition to be canonically perceived as revelatory.

(4) It is important to recognize the odd, subversive world given in this extreme rhetoric. It is unmistakable that Yahweh the creator is the subject of every verb. Heaven and earth, like Israel, are always on the receiving end of that activity, always the object acted upon. The most extreme form of rhetoric is that of creation, in which all imaginable reality is object. It does not surprise us, in this context, that Judah and Jerusalem are objects in the same way.

Such a view of reality contends against the conventional Enlightenment notion of autonomy that perhaps echoes the ancient anti-Yahweh claims. In a splendid articulation of the grammar of Enlightenment, Nelida Pinon urges:

> You must know who is the object and who is the subject of a sentence in order to know if you are the object or subject of history. If you can't control a sentence, you don't know how to put yourself into history, to trace your own origin in the country, to vocalize, to use voice.[41]

One can hear here echoes of Karl Marx's urging that human persons must become subject of their own history!

I happen to agree with that human mandate. However, the covenantal traditions of Judaism and Christianity, voiced in the magisterial I-Thou of Martin Buber and more recently in the "religion of the face" in Emmanuel Levinas, insist that below that emancipated autonomy there is an inescapable Holy Other.[42] The creation theology of Jeremiah attends to

41. Quoted in David E. Purpel, *The Moral & Spiritual Crisis in Education: A Curriculum for Justice & Compassion in Education*, Critical Studies in Education Series (New York: Bergin & Garvey, 1989), p. xiii.

42. Martin Buber, *I and Thou* (New York: Charles Scribner's Sons, 1937); Emmanuel Levinas, *Totality and Infinity: An Essay on Exteriority* (Pittsburgh: Duquesne University Press, 1969).

the Holy Other, who ends every dysfunctional effort at autonomy, only to authorize again an emancipated, rehabilitated history, which gives great play to the voiced subject beloved by the inscrutable Thou. It is a reality Israel mostly refuses, learning again and again that this reality is the only source of comfort and hope, a reality in which the creator offers the only possibility for creation.[43]

43. I am glad to join in a salute to Sib Towner, long-time friend and colleague. Sib's way in our common scholarship is deeply marked by gentleness, caring, and humaneness, a model for us in an enterprise inevitably permeated with tension and dispute.

The Rivers of Paradise:
Ezekiel 47:1-12 and Genesis 2:10-14

Steven Tuell

In the vision described in Ezekiel 47:1-12, the prophet sees a wondrous stream emerge from the temple and flow out through the eastern gates of the temple courts. The stream courses through all the land, deepening and broadening as it flows until it becomes a mighty river. This awesome flood of water transforms the Dead Sea into a freshwater lake teeming with fish, even while brackish marshes are miraculously preserved as a source of salt. Along the river's banks sprout trees that bear fruit continually and whose leaves can be used for healing.

Students of Scripture have long understood the river of Ezekiel's vision, with its life-giving waters and miraculous trees, to be related to the river of Paradise, which watered the garden of Eden (Gen. 2:8-14).[1] Of

---

1. For the association of Ezek. 47:1-12 with Gen. 2:10-14, see Rudolph Smend, *Der Prophet Ezechiel*, KEH (Leipzig: S. Hirzel, 1880), p. 387; Johannes Herrmann, *Ezechiel übersetz und erklärt*, KAT 11 (Leipzig: A. Deichert, 1924), p. 295; Georg Fohrer and Kurt Galling, *Ezechiel*, HAT 13 (Tübingen: J. C. B. Mohr, 1955), p. 245; Herbert G. May, "Ezekiel," *Interpreter's Bible*, ed. George Buttrick (Nashville: Abingdon, 1956), vol. 6, p. 326; John W. Wevers, *Ezekiel*, NCBC (Greenwood, SC: Attic, 1969), p. 229; Walther Eichrodt, *Ezekiel*, trans. Cosslett Quin, OTL (Philadelphia: Westminster, 1970), pp. 583-84; Jon D. Levenson, *Theology of the Program of Restoration of Ezekiel 40–48*, HSM 10 (Missoula: Scholars Press, 1976), p. 27; Walther Zimmerli, *Ezekiel*, trans. James E. Martin, Hermeneia (Philadelphia: Fortress, 1983), vol. 2, p. 510; Katheryn Pfisterer Darr, "The Wall Around Paradise: Ezekielian Ideas about the Future," *VT* 37 (1987): 276-77; Ronald Hals, *Ezekiel*, FOTL 19

course, this need not mean that Ezekiel and Genesis have any explicit, deliberate connection. Both texts could allude, independently, to the image of the river flowing from Zion, as conveyed in the Judean royal theology (Ps. 46:5 [46:4]; Zech. 13:1; 14:8; Joel 3:18 [4:18]).[2] Note, however, the use of *nepeš ḥayyâ* ("living creature") in Ezekiel 47:9, an expression found in the primordial stories of creation (Gen. 1:20, 21, 24, 30 [P]; 2:7, 19 [J]) and the flood (Gen. 9:10, 12, 15, 16), and of the term *šrṣ* ("swarm"), which likewise appears in the Priestly creation and flood accounts.[3] These explicit terminological connections strongly suggest that more is at work in the association of Ezekiel 47 and Genesis 2 than simply allusions to a common stock of images. Ezekiel, it seems, deliberately evokes not merely Zion imagery in general, but *Eden* imagery in particular.

Further support for this connection comes from Revelation 22:1-5, which artfully unites Ezekiel's vision and the Genesis account. In Revelation 22:2, the trees of Ezekiel's vision, growing along either bank of the river, become the (singular) tree of life, which in Genesis 2:9 grows in the midst of the garden.[4] Although this image is literally nonsensical (how can

---

(Grand Rapids: Eerdmans, 1989), p. 339; Joseph Blenkinsopp, *Ezekiel*, IntBC (Louisville: John Knox, 1990), p. 231; Leslie Allen, *Ezekiel 20–48*, WBC 24 (Dallas: Word, 1990), p. 280; and Wolfgang Zwickel, "Die Tempelquelle Ezechiel 47: Eine traditionsgeschichtliche Untersuchung," *EvT* 55 (1995): 140-54.

2. So Gustav Hölscher, *Hezekiel: der Dichter und das Buch*, BZAW 39 (Giessen: Töpelmann, 1924); George A. Cooke, *Ezekiel*, ICC (Edinburgh: T. and T. Clark, 1936), p. 517; and Richard J. Clifford, *The Cosmic Mountain in Canaan and the Old Testament* (Cambridge, MA: Harvard University Press, 1972), pp. 102-3, 160.

3. Apart from the texts noted above, *nepeš (ha)ḥayyâ* appears only in Lev. 11:10 and 46, with reference to priestly dietary laws. Note that *nepeš ḥayyâ*, without the article, appears only in the creation and flood accounts and in Ezek. 47:9. Similarly, apart from the Priestly stories of creation (Gen. 1:20, 21) and the flood (Gen. 7:21; 8:17; 9:7), the term *šrṣ* as noun or verb is found in Exod. 1:7 as a description of the Israelites "swarming" over the land of Egypt (cf. Gen. 9:7; Exod. 8:3 [MT 7:28]; Ps. 105:30), and in the kosher laws of Leviticus (5:2; 11:10, 20-23, 29-31, 41-44, 46; 22:5) and Deuteronomy (14:19). The term appears in conjunction with *nepeš ḥayyâ* only in Gen. 1:20 and Ezek. 47:9 (in Gen. 1:21 and Lev. 11:10, 46, *šrṣ* appears in conjunction with *nepeš haḥayyâ*).

4. The singular is used in the NRSV and is presupposed by M. Eugene Boring (*Revelation*, IntBC [Louisville: John Knox, 1989], p. 221). Note that J. Massyngberde Ford translates "on either side of the river, there was a tree of life," resolving the problem by imagining one tree on each side of the river (*Revelation*, AB 38 [Garden City, NY: Doubleday, 1975], p. 332). The proposal that the singular here is generic and collective, referring to a particular type of tree (so for instance Martin Rist, "Revelation," in *Interpreter's Bible* [Nashville:

one tree grow on both sides of the river?), it reveals that John understood Ezekiel's vision with explicit reference to Genesis 2. Indeed, he has harmonized the two passages.

Such odd harmonization of texts is not unique to Revelation. Michael Fishbane identifies a similar compositional technique at work in the Chronicler's text regarding the preparation of the Passover. Confronted with conflicting authoritative traditions in Exodus 12:9 (which directs that the Passover must not be boiled in water but rather roasted in fire) and Deuteronomy 16:7 (which directs that the Passover is to be boiled), the Chronicler describes the Passover of Josiah thusly: "Then they boiled the Passover in fire" (2 Chron. 35:13)! The Chronicler insists that this self-contradictory act was performed in order to fulfill the requirements of the law "as it was written in the book of Moses" (35:12). As Fishbane observes, "Evidently the Chronicler knew two distinct sets of ritual norms, and, regarding both as authoritative traditions, preserved them by an artificial, exegetical harmonization."[5] Similarly, with his tree of life growing on both sides of the river, John has produced a harmonization of Ezekiel 47 and Genesis 2 that, while literally nonsensical, is religiously meaningful. In John's view, the river flowing from Ezekiel's temple and the river flowing out of Eden are one and the same, suggesting that, in the first century at any rate, Genesis 2 and Ezekiel 47 were read together.

Walther Zimmerli argues that the connection between Ezekiel 47 and Genesis 2 is a late, secondary feature of Ezekiel's vision. Indeed, he proposes that the prophet's originally succinct description of the river (Ezek. 47:1-8) was expanded by a series of four separate additions: v. 9, an elaboration on the life-giving quality of the river in "the language of P"; v. 10, which elaborates on the boon the waters will provide for fishermen; v. 11, an even later supplement, which declares that the marshes, with their

---

Abingdon, 1957], vol. 12, p. 542; Mathias Rissi, *The Future of the World: An Exegetical Study of Revelation 19:11–22:15*, SBT, Second Series 23 [Naperville, IL: Allenson, 1972], p. 80 and n. 248; and Bruce Metzger, *Breaking the Code: Understanding the Book of Revelation* [Nashville: Abingdon, 1993], p. 102 n. 2), might at first seem apt, given the collective usage of the Hebrew *ʿēṣ* in Ezek. 47:7 and 12. However, the same formulation found in Rev. 22:2, *xulon zōēs*, appears in the LXX of Gen. 2:9, where it clearly refers to a single tree of life that grows in the center of the garden. Note, too, that in *1 Enoch* 24:4–25:5, only one tree of life is in view in the world to come.

5. Michael Fishbane, *Biblical Interpretation in Ancient Israel* (Oxford: Clarendon, 1985), p. 134.

life-preserving salt, will not be lost; and v. 12b, which gives the purposes of the fruit (for food) and the leaves (for healing) of the trees that thrive alongside the waters.[6]

The laconic phrasing of the earlier temple description (Ezek. 40–42) would at first seem to support Zimmerli's analysis.[7] There, very little descriptive detail is given at all, and the prose is stark. However, as will be argued below, the supposed addenda in Ezekiel 47:9-12 are not mere descriptive details. Ezekiel 47:1-12 as a unit is an expression of an image found elsewhere in the ancient Near East: the river as the symbol of the life-giving presence of the god in the temple. However, Ezekiel's use of terminology from the creation narratives, his rejection of the term "Zion,"[8] and his disassociation of the mountain and its temple from the royal palace, indeed from *Jerusalem,* all indicate that something more than appeal to the standard temple imagery is at work. Arguably, here as elsewhere in his prophecy, Ezekiel is cutting the imagery associated with Zion free from its historical and political referent in favor of the mythic image of Zion as Eden, the home of God.[9]

---

6. Zimmerli, *Ezekiel,* vol. 2, pp. 513-14. Zimmerli's analysis is assumed by Zwickel ("Tempelquelle," pp. 142-43); note, however, that Zwickel understands the redacted form of Ezekiel's vision to be the source of Gen. 2:10-14 ("Tempelquelle," pp. 145-46). Wevers also regards Ezek. 47:9 as an accretion (*Ezekiel,* p. 230).

7. Compare the discussion in Steven Tuell, *The Law of the Temple in Ezekiel 40–48,* HSM 49 (Atlanta: Scholars Press, 1992), pp. 26-31, 49.

8. As well as the related divine title, *Yhwh ṣĕba'ôt.* See Tryggve N. D. Mettinger, *The Dethronement of Sabaoth: Studies in the Shem and Kabod Theologies,* trans. Frederick H. Cryer, ConBOT 18 (Lund: C. W. K. Gleerup, 1982), especially pp. 11, 109-13.

9. Note that this article deals with the function of Ezek. 47:1-12 in its original context, as a part of Ezekiel's original vision report. That vision, as I have elsewhere argued, is to be found in 40:1–43:7a (with minor insertions at 40:5 and 42:13-14); 44:1-2; 47:1-12; and 48:30-35 (Tuell, *Law,* p. 75). Clearly, in its final form, Ezek. 40–48 is very much concerned with political and cultic realities, specifically those of the Judean Restoration in the reign of Darius I (Tuell, *Law,* p. 14). The original vision, however, dealt with the promise of the divine presence with the exiles, in fulfillment of YHWH's promise in 11:14-16 (Steven Tuell, "Ezekiel 40-42 as Verbal Icon," *CBQ* 58 [1997]: 649-64 and "The Temple Vision of Ezekiel 40-48: A Program For Restoration?" *Proceedings of the Eastern Great Lakes Biblical Society* 2 [1982]: 96-103).

I. Eden as Zion

This proposal, of course, presumes that Eden was believed to be located on Zion. This identification is made explicitly in Ezekiel 28:13-14[10] and is at least implied in the Paradise imagery of Isaiah 11:6-9 and 65:17-25 (cf. Gen. 1:29-30). The association of Eden and Zion is presumed in *1 Enoch* 25:3-5. There, the visionary sees the tree of life planted on a beautiful mountain situated among six other beautiful mountains in the northeast. The angelic interpreter Michael tells him, "This tall mountain which you saw whose summit resembles the throne of God is (indeed) his throne, on which the Holy and Great Lord of Glory, the Eternal King, will sit when he descends to visit the earth with goodness."[11] Although (as in Ezekiel) the name is not used, Zion is clearly the referent; hence, in this second- or third-century B.C.E. apocalypse, Eden and Zion seem to be identified.

However, in *Jubilees* 8:19, Eden and Zion, although closely associated with one another, remain distinct:

> And [Noah] knew that Eden was the holy of holies and the dwelling of the LORD. And Mount Sinai (was) in the midst of the desert and Mount Zion (was) in the midst of the navel of the earth. The three of these were created as holy places, facing each other.[12]

The concept of Zion as "the navel of the earth" also may point toward a connection with Eden. The myth of the center or "navel" of the earth as the source of life and meaning for all creation has been identified by Mircea Eliade as a common theme in the history of religions, particularly in the ancient Near East.[13] Jon D. Levenson identifies several references in rabbinic literature to

10. Although, of course, the term "Zion" is not used. Clifford regards this identification as a peculiarity unique to Ezekiel (*Cosmic Mountain*, p. 103).

11. E. Isaac, trans., in *The Old Testament Pseudepigrapha*, ed. James H. Charlesworth (Garden City, NY: Doubleday, 1983), vol. 2, p. 28.

12. "Jubilees," trans. O. S. Wintermute, in *The Old Testament Pseudepigrapha*, ed. James H. Charlesworth (Garden City, NY: Doubleday, 1983), vol. 2, p. 73.

13. Mircea Eliade, *The Myth of the Eternal Return, or Cosmos and History*, trans. Willard Trask (Princeton: Princeton University Press, 1974), pp. 12-17. For example, the temple area in Nippur was called *Dur-an-ki*, "the bond of heaven and earth." Clifford (*Cosmic Mountain*, pp. 14-15) observes that it marks the spot where Enlil cut the navel string binding heaven and earth.

Zion as the navel of the world.[14] Midrash *Haššēm Běhokmâ Yāsad 'Āreṣ* speaks of the Lord creating the world from the navel outward, just as an embryo grows. Another midrash, *Tanhumâ: Kĕdōšîm* 10, cites Ezekiel 38:12 to demonstrate that Israel is the center of the world, just as the navel is the center of a human being.[15] Little wonder, then, that according to Rabbi Eliezar the Great, creation began with Zion (*b. Yoma* 54b).

The Rivers of Eden

In short, it is clear that Zion and Eden came to be associated as early as the sixth century B.C.E. However, do we have any evidence that Genesis 2 also imagines this association? Perhaps the notion of Eden as a source of rivers provides such an indication. In addition to Ezekiel 47:1-12, several biblical texts identify Zion as a source of rivers. In Psalm 46:5 (46:4), the psalmist affirms, "There is a river whose streams make glad the city of God, the holy habitation of the Most High" (see also Zech. 13:1 and Joel 3:18 [4:18]). The image of the mountain of God as a source of waters likely derives from the Canaanite 'El's dwelling: "at the source of twin rivers, by the pools of the double-deep."[16] This idea of double streams flowing from the mountain

---

14. Jon D. Levenson, *Sinai and Zion: An Entry Into the Jewish Bible* (San Francisco: Harper & Row, 1985), pp. 117-18.

15. Ezek. 38:12, where the people of Israel are said to dwell "at the center of the earth," is one of two places where *ṭabbûr* appears in the Hebrew Bible; the other is Judg. 9:37, where the NRSV reads a place name (Tabbur-erez). Both times, the term appears in construct with *'ereṣ*. The LXX *omphalon tēs gēs* and the Vulgate *umbilici terrae* for *ṭabbûr hā'āreṣ* in Ezek. 38:12 suggest the likelihood that *ṭabbûr* means, literally, "navel." The postbiblical use of *ṭabbûr* for navel is well attested (see the discussion of the rabbinic literature, above). The earliest such use would appear to be *Jub.* 8:19, also cited above, which places Zion at "the navel of the earth." Given the probable parallel to Ezek. 5:5, where the Lord says that Jerusalem is set "in the center *(bĕtôk)* of the nations," Ezek. 38:12 should be understood to refer to the navel of the earth as well. This reading is also to be preferred in Judg. 9:37 (*contra* Clifford, *Cosmic Mountain*, p. 135), where the Vulgate has *umbilico terrae* and the LXX reads *omphalon tēs gēs*. Abimelech is coming against Shechem from Mt. Gerizim, which is roughly in the center of the land. Indeed, Gerizim comes to represent for the Samaritans what Zion represents for the Jews: the mountain at the center of the earth and the one place where God's temple can be set (cf. John 4:20). Eliade (*Myth*, p. 13) records a tradition from Peter Comestor, who says that at the Fountain of Jacob near Gerizim the sun casts no shadow at the summer solstice — meaning that this spot is the *umbilicum terrae*.

16. *CTA* 4.4.21-22.

lies in the background of Zechariah 14:8: "On that day living waters shall flow out from Jerusalem, half of them to the eastern sea and half of them to the western sea; it shall continue in summer as in winter." Eden is also the source of rivers. The river that flows out of Eden divides into four branches — the Pishon, the Gihon, the Tigris, and the Euphrates (Gen. 2:10-14). The identification and location of the Tigris and Euphrates are, of course, obvious, prompting many to look to Mesopotamia for the location of Eden.[17] The Gihon and the Pishon have prompted far more controversy.

Gihon. The association of the Gihon with Cush (Gen. 2:13) suggests that the Gihon is the Nile.[18] Perhaps the earliest evidence for this proposal is the Septuagint text of Jeremiah 2:18, which reads *Gēōn* for the Hebrew *šiḥôr* (Nile).[19] Similarly, in the *Genesis Apocryphon* from Qumran, Abraham tells of a journey along the frontier of the land that God had promised him, beginning from the Gihon River (apparently identified with the Nile).[20] However, Sirach 24:23-27 argues against this identification. In this text, the rivers of Eden are joined to the Jordan and the Nile as images of wisdom's abundance pouring forth from torah.[21] The additional mention

17. So Clifford, who urges that Eden and Zion must be viewed separately: Zion relating to Canaanite myth, and Eden to Mesopotamian (*Cosmic Mountain*, pp. 101-3). Ephraim A. Speiser (*Genesis*, AB1 [Garden City, NY: Doubleday, 1979], p. 16) connects the name Eden with the Akkadian *edinu* and Sumerian *eden*, meaning "plain steppe"; however, see nn. 33 and 38 for a more probable Aramaic etymology. The location of Eden "in the east" in Gen. 2:8 has usually prompted the identification of Eden with an imagined site in Mesopotamia. However, the verse does not require this interpretation.

18. So Brevard Childs, "Eden, Garden of," in *The Interpreter's Dictionary of the Bible*, ed. George A. Buttrick (Nashville: Abingdon, 1962), vol. 2, p. 23. Denis Baly ("Gihon," in *Harper's Bible Dictionary*, ed. Paul Achtemeier [San Francisco: Harper and Row, 1985], p. 347) observes that, although Gihon was once commonly identified as the Nile, "it almost certainly indicates a now unidentifiable irrigation channel in southern Iraq, 'Cush' being the land of the Kassites." Note, however, that Baly's only evidence for this assertion would appear to be the association of the Gihon with the Tigris and Euphrates: an association that, as we shall see, seems to owe more to mythology than to geography.

19. For the use of *šiḥôr* meaning "Nile," see also Josh. 13:3; Isa. 23:3; 1 Chron. 13:5.

20. *Genesis Apocryphon* 21:15-20, in Joseph A. Fitzmeyer, *The Genesis Apocryphon of Qumran Cave 1: A Commentary*, Biblica et Orientalia 18 (Rome: Pontifical Biblical Institute, 1966), pp. 60-61. On the Gihon as the Nile, see also Josephus, *Ant.* 1.1, 3.

21. Of course, the torah connection could suggest an association with Sinai rather than Zion. However, Sirach elsewhere establishes a firm link between divine wisdom and Zion (Sir. 24:8-11).

of the Nile and the Jordan shows that neither of these was identified with the rivers of Eden by Sirach.[22]

Another possibility is that the Gihon of Genesis 2:13 is the spring of the same name in the Kidron Valley (1 Kings 1:33; 2 Chron. 32:30; 33:14), which served as the primary water source for Jerusalem.[23] In keeping with the identification of Zion as a source of waters, it could be argued that Gihon here provides a clear link between Zion and Eden. Three major objections can be raised against this idea: the spring of Gihon is not a river, it does not flow around Cush, and it does not actually flow from Zion! Yet in Isaiah 8:5-8 the waters of Shiloah, fed by the Gihon spring, are used as a symbolic representation of God's assurance, contrasted with the flood waters of the Euphrates, representing the might of Assyria.[24] We thus have clear precedent for the waters of the Gihon being used in comparison to the Euphrates, and with reference to the presence and blessing of God. For Isaiah, it appears, the Gihon-fed stream was the "river whose streams make glad the city of God" (Ps. 46:5 [46:4]).[25] Although the spring was outside the city, it was regarded as part of the Zion complex, and indeed, following the completion of Hezekiah's tunnel, its waters were collected within the fortified area of the city. The geographical impossibility of the Gihon watering Cush should not concern us overmuch. After all, even if we propose that the Gihon is the Nile, that does not remove the difficulty of the Tigris and Euphrates somehow emerging from the same source as that African river! Genesis

22. *Contra* Fitzmeyer (*Genesis Apocryphon*, p. 135) and W. H. Gispen ("Genesis 2:10-14," in *Studia biblica et semitica T. C. Vriezen dedicata*, ed. Willem C. van Unnik and A. S. van der Woude [Wageningen: H. Veenman en Zonen, 1966], p. 120), who evidently understand Gihon in parallel with the Nile in Sir. 24:27. Note, however, that this is not an instance of parallelism. Sir. 24:23-25 begins with the Pishon and concludes with the Gihon, with the Tigris, Euphrates, Jordan, and Nile sandwiched in between. If we understand Sir. 24:27 to identify the Gihon with the Nile, we must also conclude that the Pishon is identified with the Tigris in 24:25 and the Jordan with the Euphrates in 24:26!

23. For more on the water system of ancient Jerusalem, cf. Avraham Negev, ed., *The Archaeological Encyclopedia of the Holy Land* (Nashville: Thomas Nelson, 1986), pp. 199-200; John Rogerson and Philip R. Davies, "Was the Siloam Tunnel Built by Hezekiah?" *BA* 59 (1996): 138; and the response to Rogerson and Davies by Ronald Hendel in *BA* 59 (1996): 233, which rejects their late dating of the Siloam Inscription and supports the accepted seventh-century date for the tunnel.

24. An association also made by Zwickel, "Tempelquelle," p. 147.

25. So also Zimmerli, *Ezekiel*, vol. 2, pp. 510-11.

2, like Ezekiel 47, belongs to the realm of the supramundane. The point made in Genesis 2, as in Ezekiel 47 and other related texts, is that the divine presence is the source of life for all the world.

Pishon. The Pishon is mentioned in the Hebrew Bible only in Genesis 2:11. This river, we are told, "is the one that flows around the whole land of Havilah, where there is gold; and the gold of that land is good; bdellium and onyx stone are there" (Gen. 2:11-12). These clues should suffice to identify the Pishon for us; however, the task proves far harder than it appears. Apart from Genesis 2:11, Havilah is mentioned six times in the Hebrew Bible. First, in Genesis 10:7 Havilah is said to be a descendant of Cush the son of Ham, brother to Egypt (see also 1 Chron. 1:9). The association with Egypt is also found in Genesis 25:18, where Havilah is the place opposite Egypt in the direction of Assyria where Ishmael's descendants settled. In 1 Samuel 15:7 the same location ("Havilah as far as Shur") is described as the territory of the Amalekites east of Egypt, where Saul was victorious. In Genesis 10:29, however, Havilah is the descendant of Joktan (so also 1 Chron. 1:17), among the inhabitants of the "hill country of the east," from Mesha toward Sephar. Neither location points us clearly toward any river.[26] Once again, given the connections with Egypt, the Nile is a possibility,[27] although Sirach evidently considered neither the Pishon nor the Gihon to be the Nile.

If the Gihon of Genesis 2:13 is the Gihon spring, then the Pishon as well may be identified with a spring near Zion. Nehemiah 2:13 mentions a Dragon's Spring, located between the Valley Gate and the Dung Gate, which would place this site to the west of Zion, as Gihon was located to its east.[28] This connection may, in fact, be strengthened by the etymology of the names Pishon and Gihon. Although these terms are usually associated with *pwš* ("leap") and *gyḥ* ("break forth"),[29] David Neiman has proposed that Gihon may rather derive from *gāḥôn*, meaning the belly of a snake

---

26. Note that Targum Jonathan has "Hindiqe" (that is, India) for Havilah, so that the Pishon becomes the Ganges! This interpretation was also adopted by Josephus, *Ant.* 1.1, 3.

27. So Zwickel, "Tempelquelle," p. 145. Note that both Rashi and the Ramban identified the Pishon as the Nile (cf. Yehuda T. Radday, "The Four Rivers of Paradise," *Hebrew Studies* 23 [1982]: 26).

28. It is intriguing to note that in the Herodian period an aqueduct-fed reservoir called the Serpent Pool was situated to the west of Jerusalem. An association with Nehemiah's Dragon Spring seems plausible.

29. W. H. Gispen, "Genesis 2:10-14," pp. 117, 119.

(Gen. 3:14; Lev. 11:42), while Pishon may be cognate to *peten* ("serpent"; Isa. 11:8; Ps. 91:13; Job 20:16) and Ugaritic *btn*[30] — certainly an appropriate designation for Nehemiah's "Dragon's Spring."

The location of two springs identified with serpents on or near Zion would be in keeping with the mythic imagery of the mountain as the place of combat between the creator and the dragon of chaos. In the *Enuma Elish*, a mountain is raised on the head of the slain Tiamat, with the Tigris and Euphrates flowing from her two eyes.[31] Similarly, the home of 'El was located "at the source of the *twin* rivers, by the pools of the *double*-deep," and Zechariah 14:8 describes two streams flowing out of Zion, to the east and to the west. The Pishon and the Gihon could be the streams flowing east and west from Zion, as the Tigris and Euphrates flow north to south.

Of course, the Tigris and Euphrates do not originate on the earthly Zion, but attempts to locate Eden in Mesopotamia or even Africa[32] mistake the symbolic, mythological geography of Genesis 2 for actual geography. It is clear that in Ezekiel's vision terrestrial geography features only superficially: Zion has become a very high mountain with a fabulous temple at its summit, and Jerusalem has been transported some distance away. We could also compare Psalm 48:3, which identifies Zion with Zaphon to the north, and *1 Enoch,* where Zion is nestled among six other very high mountains and shifted to the northeast. It is quite probable that, in Genesis 2 as well, the rivers do not correspond to their terrestrial courses. That the great rivers of Assyria and Babylon flow from Zion makes no sense geographically. However, it makes abundant sense theologically. As creator of the whole earth, YHWH is God of all creation. YHWH's mountain is the source of life and fertility in all the world, not just in Israel.

30. David Neiman, "Gihon and Pishon: Mythological Antecedents of the Two Enigmatic Rivers of Eden," in *Proceedings of the Sixth World Congress of Jewish Studies,* ed. Avigdor Shinan (Jerusalem: Jerusalem Academic Press, 1977), p. 326. Note, however, that Neiman identifies the Pishon as the sea surrounding the Arabian peninsula, while Gihon he believes represents "the circumfluent Ocean Stream which most ancient geographers considered to be the rim of the disc of earth" (pp. 325-26).

31. Tablet 5.55 (*ANET,* p. 501). This idea may also be reflected in Ezek. 47:9, where the MT has the dual form *naḥălayim,* hence "two rivers."

32. So David Tuesday Adamo, "Ancient Africa and Genesis 2:10-14," *JRT* 49 (1992): 37. However, the approach of Yehuda T. Radday, who refers to the "atopism" of Gen. 2 ("Four Rivers," p. 31), is extreme. While the texts frustrate any attempt to locate Eden in terms of terrestrial geography, they do nonetheless point to a place, namely Zion, the home of God and source of life and fertility.

II. The River and Its Abundance as a Symbol of Divine Presence

In Ezekiel 47:1-12, the blessings associated with the divine presence are not limited to fertility: more is involved than fruit trees and fresh water. Material blessings are also represented by an abundant supply of leaves for medicine, of fish for fishermen, and of life-giving salt. This same idea is found in Genesis 2:10-14, where gold and precious stones, as representations of material abundance, appear in conjunction with the agricultural abundance the river naturally represents. As the biblical and extra-biblical parallels for the language in Genesis 2 and Ezekiel 47 demonstrate, such a connection is in keeping with the language of divine presence in the ancient world.

Biblical Depictions of Divine Presence

Eden is, of course, a place of great fecundity, a rich garden in which every kind of fruit tree grows (Gen. 2:9). Indeed, Alan R. Millard and Pierre Bordreuil propose that the name derives from an Aramaic term meaning "fertility."[33] Eden is also, however, associated with wealth. Its rivers flow through a land of wealth (Gen. 2:11-12), and Eden itself is associated with wealth in Ezekiel 28:13-14:

> You were in Eden, the garden of God;
>> every precious stone was your covering,
> carnelian, chrysolite, and moonstone,
>> beryl, onyx, and jasper,
> sapphire, turquoise, and emerald;
>> and worked in gold were your settings
>> and your engravings.
> On the day that you were created
>> they were prepared.

---

33. Alan R. Millard and Pierre Bordreuil, "A Statue from Syria with Assyrian and Aramaic Inscriptions," *BA* 45 (1982): 140. The Aramaic *'dn* appears in lines 4-5 of the Tell Fekhariyeh inscription: *m'dn mt kln,* translated "he who makes all lands luxuriant" by Stephen Kaufman ("Reflections on the Assyrian-Aramaic Bilingual From Tell Fakhariyeh," *Maarav* 3/2 [1982]: 169) and "who enriches all lands" by Millard and Bordreuil ("Statue," p. 137).

With an anointed cherub as guardian I placed you;
    you were on the holy mountain of God;
    you walked among the stones of fire.

The association of the divine blessing with the temple (Ezek. 47:1-12) and with "the holy mountain of God" (Ezek. 28:13-14) prompts comparison with other biblical texts involving YHWH's sanctuary. The description of the tabernacle in Exodus 25–27 and that of Solomon's temple in 1 Kings 6–7 both emphasize precious materials.[34] Note, too, that Haggai 1:2-11 links material prosperity to the divine presence, enshrined and celebrated in the right temple with the right cult.

Ancient Near Eastern Depictions of Divine Presence[35]

Extrabiblical sources likewise equate the presence of the god in the temple both with fertility and with material prosperity. Parallels with the Gudea Cylinders are particularly interesting. Cylinder B, 14.19-24 describes the preparation of a royal bedchamber in the temple for the god and his consort. That accomplished, the material benefits that the temple will bring to the land are recorded:

The marshes stocked
    with marsh carp and giant carp,
Their inspector of fisheries,
    the one stocking (them with) fish, guiding them;
With the grain laden
    for (transport on) the great waters,
With the storage piles and heaps
    of Lagash piled up,
With the river filled with flowing waters,
    the sheepfolds built,
The lambs placed with good ewes,
    the ram released unto its good ewes,
With the calves placed with good cows,

---

34. On the association between temple building and creation, see Jon D. Levenson, "Temple and World," *JR* 64 (1984): 287-88.

35. Compare also the discussion on this point in Tuell, *Law*, pp. 68-71.

and the bull bellowing loudly among them,
With the oxen properly in their yokes,
    and their oxdriver standing by their side,
With the asses saddled with their packsaddles,
    and their drivers who feed them following after them,
With huge copper ingots
    strapped on the jackasses,
With the huge millhouse supported. . . .[36]

Sure enough, once mother Baba and lord Ningirsu had made themselves at home in the bedroom, the jars and goblets of the temple became "(like) the Tigris and Euphrates rivers continually carrying abundance."[37] Although the sexual imagery of the Gudea Cylinders is absent from the biblical texts cited above, the connection made between the presence of the god in the temple and an abundant supply of pure water gives support to the original linkage of the river and the divine presence in our texts as well. Moreover, the explicit mention of fish and of other material blessings brought by the temple to the city and its people provides precedent for the use of these motifs in Ezekiel's vision report.

Fertility in nature and material prosperity are also linked to temple building in Ugaritic mythology. When 'El decrees that a house be built for Ba'l (*CTA* 4.5.68-73), Lady 'Atirat jubilantly responds:

wn'ap . 'dn . mṭrh   Now, indeed, his rainy season[38]

---

36. Cylinder B, 14.25–15.15; Thorkild Jacobsen, *The Harps That Once . . . : Sumerian Poetry in Translation* (New Haven and London: Yale University Press, 1987), p. 438. Compare also George A. Barton, *The Royal Inscriptions of Sumer and Akkad* (New Haven: Yale University Press, 1929), pp. 249-51.

37. Cylinder B, 17.10-11; Jacobsen, *Harps*, p. 440. Compare Barton, *Royal Inscriptions*, pp. 251-53.

38. Frank M. Cross (private communication) suggests interpreting '*dn* here and in the following line as referring to "fertility and the giving of fertility," based on this use of Aramaic '*dn* in the Tell Fekhariyeh inscription (cf. n. 32, above). On the basis of this usage, Cross translates *CTA* 4.5.68-69:

> Now, behold, let Ba'l make fertile with his rains,
> Let him make luxuriant with flowage and torrents.

This rendering, however, depends on reading *ṭrt* instead of *ṭkt* (see following note). If *ṭkt* is indeed the reading, it is best to consider '*dn* as cognate to Aramaic '*iddān*, Arabic '*adān*, and Akkadian *adānu*, and translate as "time" or "season."

bʿl . yʿdn . ʿdn . ṯkt . bglṯ	Baʿl will appoint; the season of ships[39] upon the waves.[40]
w⟨y⟩tn . qlh . bʿrpt	Now he will give his voice in the clouds;
šrh . l'arṣ . brqm	He will loose lightnings upon the earth.
bt . ʾarzm . ykllnh	The house of cedar, he may build it;
hm . bt . lbnt . yʿmsnh	Even the house of brick, he may raise it![41]

39. André Caquot, Maurice Sznycer, and Andrée Herdner (*Textes Ougaritiques, Mythes et Légendes: Introduction, Traduction, Commentaire* [Paris: Cerf, 1974], vol. 1, p. 207) propose reading *ṯrt* here, explained by the Arabic *ṯarra* ("to make water spout"), and translate "the time of gushing floods." Given the close similarity of the cuneiform signs *r* and *k*, this rendering is possible. However, I propose that this reading is prompted as much by translation difficulties as by morphological concerns. With Joseph Aisleitner (*Wörterbuch der ugaritischen Sprache* [Berlin: Akademie-Verlag, 1963], p. 334), Cyrus H. Gordon (*Ugaritic Textbook*, AnOr 38 [Rome: Pontifical Biblical Institute, 1965], p. 502), Manfried Dietrich and Oswald Loretz ("Zur ugaritischen Lexikographie I," *Bibliotheca Orientalis* 23 [1966]: 129), and Edward Lipinski ("Epiphanie de Baal-Haddu RS 24.245," *UF* 3 [1971]: 86), among others, I read *ṯkt* here, which must be understood as an ancient word of indeterminate origin meaning "ship" (note the Egyptian *ṯkti* and the Phoenician city of Shigata). When the context is properly understood, this yields a perfectly natural reading, as the next note reveals.

40. *Glṯ* may be cognate to the enigmatic Hebrew *gālaš*, used twice in the Song of Sol. (4:1; 6:5). In each instance, *gālaš* is used in a simile comparing a woman's hair to the movement of a flock of goats. In the Song, the apparent meaning is "wave." A flock of sheep or goats, observed from a distance as they move down a hillside, appear to flow in a wavelike motion; hence, the point of the obscure simile in the Song would be that the woman's hair is wavy. The reading "wave" for the Ugaritic *glṯ* is further supported by *PRU* 5.1.5, where *glṯ* parallels *thmt* ("the watery abyss"). In light of this parallel, Dietrich and Loretz ("Lexikographie I," p. 129) also propose the translation "The time of the ship on the waves", while Lipinski ("Epiphanie," p. 86) renders the phrase "The time when the ships are caught in the storm." Another, more puzzling use of *glṯ* comes from *KTU* 1.101.7 in a hymn to Baʿl: *rišh bglṯ bšm[m]* ("his head in/ with *glṯ* in the heavens"). The proposed translation in *Ugaritica* 5 (ed. Charles Virolleaud, Mission de Ras Shamra 16 [Paris: Imprimerie Nationale, 1968], p. 558), "his head is in motion in the heavens," seems strange. Given the parallel with Song of Sol. 4:1; 6:5, which describes the beloved's hair, a more likely translation may be "his hair in waves in the heavens." For a complete discussion of the terms *glṯ* and *gālaš*, see Steven Tuell, "A Riddle Resolved by an Enigma: Ugaritic *glṯ* and Hebrew *gālaš*," *JBL* 112 (1993): 99-121.

41. Instead of "build" and "raise," Harold L. Ginsberg reads "destroy" and "remove" (*ANET*, p. 133). Ugaritic *ykllnh* is from *kll* or *kly*, which, like Hebrew *klh*, means "finish, complete" in both the positive and the negative sense. Similarly, *yʿmsnh*, from *ʿms* (cf. He-

The temple of Baʻl at Ugarit was a blessing to merchant as well as farmer, bringing material as well as natural abundance.[42]

Like temple building in the biblical texts, the building of the temples at Lagash and Ugarit called for precious woods, stones, and metals. This is shown both in the list of materials in Gudea Cylinder A[43] and in *CTA* 4.5.74-81, 91-97 (98-102):

lyrgm . lʾaliyn . bʻl	Let it be told to Victorious Baʻl:
ṣḥ . ḥrn . bbht!k	"Summon a caravan[44] into your house,
ʿdbt . bqrb . hklk	Furnishings[45] into the midst
	of your palace.

---

brew *ʿms*), means literally "load up," for which both positive and negative readings are possible. Ginsberg chose to see these texts as descriptive of the destructive power of Baʻl's lightning. However, in their context, they are more likely to refer to the building of Baʻl's temple. Hence, the positive rendering is to be preferred.

42. The thirteen stone anchors left as votive offerings at Baʻl's temple in Ugarit confirm the connection between Baʻl and merchant fleets (cf. Honor Frost, "The Stone-Anchors of Ugarit," in *Ugaritica* 6, ed. Claude F. A. Schaeffer, Mission de Ras Shamra 17 [Paris: Mission Archéologique de Ras Shamra, 1969], pp. 235, 242). Note that four more anchors were incorporated into the actual structure of the temple, with one anchor serving as a cornerstone. The association of Baʻl with merchant fleets is further supported by this ritual curse from a treaty between Esarhaddon and Baal, king of Tyre (ca. 677 B.C.E.): "May Baal-sameme, Baal-malage, and Baal-saphon raise an evil wind against your ships, to undo their moorings, tear out their mooring pole, may a strong wave sink them in the sea, a violent tide [. . .] against you" (*ANET*, p. 534).

43. Gudea Cylinder A, especially 15.1–17.1. Jacobsen, *Harps*, pp. 406-8; Barton, *Royal Inscriptions*, pp. 219-21.

44. Reading the Ugaritic *ḥrn* as a cognate of the Akkadian *ḥarrānu*, "caravan," with Caquot, Sznycer, and Herdner (*Textes Ougaritiques*, p. 208). Aisleitner's proposal *Erdarbeiter* (digger, laborer), from the Akkadian *ḥēru* (dig) and *ḥurru* (hole) and the Hebrew *ḥôr* (hollow), is strained (*Wörterbuch*, p. 116); Ginsberg's reading (*ANET*, p. 133), "Summon *weeds* into thy house," is incomprehensible.

45. Again, following Caquot, Sznycer, and Herdner (*Textes Ougaritiques* p. 208), who render *ʿdbt* as "fournniture," relating the term to Hebrew *ʿizbônîm* ("wares," found only in Ezek. 27:12, 14, 16, 19, 22, 27, 33, and only in the plural, as a description of imported manufactured goods) and to Akkadian *ʿuzubbu* ("payment"). Aisleitner reads "builders," in parallel with his rendering of *ḥrn* in the previous line and in comparison with the Old South Arabic *ʿdb*, "to make" (*Die mythologischen und kultischen Texte aus Ras Schamra*, Bibliotheca Orientalis Hungarica 8 [Budapest: Akadémiai Kiadó, 1959], p. 42). The reading followed here provides a better fit phonetically and better sense contextually, and is bolstered by the citations in Ezek. 27.

tblk . ǵrm . mid . ksp	The mountains will provide you with much silver,
gb'm . mḥmd . ḥrṣ	The hills with the finest gold;
yblk . 'udr . 'ilqṣm	Camels[46] will bring you precious stones.[47]
wbn . bht . ksp . wḥrṣ	Now, build a house of silver and gold,
bht . thrm . 'iqnim	A house of pure lapis lazuli."

In the temple texts from Lagash and Ugarit then, as in Ezekiel 47 and Genesis 2, the presence of the god brings blessings of both fertility and material prosperity. There is no more need to view these elements as secondary in Ezekiel 47 than there is in Genesis 2. In both texts, material blessing and fertility belong to the river image as signs of divine presence.

III. The Significance of Edenic Imagery in Ezekiel 47:1-12

The use of the river image, which elsewhere in the ancient world was linked closely to temples, is not surprising in Ezekiel 47:1-12. However, in Ezekiel's vision the traditional imagery is substantially modified, if not subverted. True, the river flows from the temple on a very high mountain, doubtless Mount Zion. However, here as elsewhere in Ezekiel, the mountain is not *called* Zion; indeed, it is deliberately disassociated from the city of Jerusalem.[48] Further, as Walther Zimmerli in particular has observed,

46. Reading Ugaritic *'udr*, with Aisleitner (*Wörterbuch*, p. 9), as "camel," in comparison with Akkadian *'udru*. Gordon (*Ugaritic Textbook*, p. 353), inferring only from context, reads "quarry," while Ginsberg (*ANET*, p. 133) and Godfrey R. Driver (*Canaanite Myths and Legends*, OTS 3 [Edinburgh: T. and T. Clark, 1956], p. 97), influenced by Hebrew *'dr* ("be great, noble") understand this as the object of the verb in construct with the following *'ilqṣm* and read, respectively, "god's glory aplenty" and "noblest of gems." No such contortions are necessary: this is a perfectly natural parallel to the mention of the caravan in l. 75.

47. No cognate evidence is available for the enigmatic *'ilqṣm*. With the majority of scholars, I have understood it as a reference to some sort of precious stone, paralleling the later mention of lapis lazuli.

48. Note that in Ezekiel's vision the city, described in Ezek. 48:30-35, is not located on the mountain, and the temple is not located within the city. Zimmerli (*Ezekiel*, vol. 2, p. 547) observes that the "last sentence of the book of Ezekiel shows how the old tradition of the city of God has forcibly obtained justice for itself against the priestly reform project, which, through the separation of city and temple, has robbed the city of much of its dignity." He

the temple of Ezekiel's vision has been purged of all royal references.[49] This is particularly intriguing in light of Ezekiel's general avoidance of the term *melek*.[50] Finally, it is surely significant that Ezekiel, a Zadokite priest, should make explicit reference to the priesthood only twice prior to ch. 40 (7:26 and 22:26; elsewhere, the term *kōhēn* is found only in the superscription [1:3]), and that *both* of these references should come in a context of judgment. Ezekiel, it seems, reacted against the institutions and ideology of the Jerusalemite temple even more forcefully than has often been recognized.[51] Perhaps it is in this way that we can understand the explicit use of Edenic imagery in Ezekiel 47.

---

therefore classes Ezek. 48:30-35 with the similar exaltations of the city in Deutero- or even Trito-Isaiah (vol. 2, p. 545). Cooke (*Ezekiel*, p. 536), Wevers (*Ezekiel*, p. 233), Eichrodt (*Ezekiel*, p. 593), Hartmut Gese, *Der Verfassungsentwurf des Ezechiel (Kap. 40–48) traditionsgeschichtlichen untersucht*, BHT 25 (Tübingen: J. C. B. Mohr, 1957), p. 107, and Hals (*Ezekiel*, p. 347) similarly attribute these verses to another, later, hand. May, however ("Ezekiel," p. 337), defends the text as the work of the same redactor as Ezek. 48:1-29, explaining the differences in the tribal listing by suggesting that Joseph has been used to designate both Ephraim and Manasseh, making room for Levi in the naming of the twelve gates. Similarly Fohrer and Galling (*Ezechiel*, p. 262), while denying the Ezekielian authorship of the text, do not propose an additional redactional layer here. On the basis of the parallel between the city (*'îr*) in 48:30-35 and the "construction like a city" *(kĕmibnēh-'îr)* in 40:1-4, I have proposed that 48:30-35 was a part of the prophet's original vision (Tuell, *Law*, pp. 73-74). Only by explicitly describing the city as distinct from the mountain could Ezekiel adequately express his point, namely, that the true dwelling of God has been cut loose from its associations with Jerusalem.

49. Zimmerli, *Ezekiel*, vol. 2, p. 418. Compare also Hals, *Ezekiel*, pp. 306-7.

50. Ezekiel's term of choice for Israel's kings is *nāśî'*. In Ezekiel 1–39 the term *melek* is only used for a past or present monarch when he is listed together with other court officials, making the use of *nāśî'* confusing or impossible (as is the case in both 7:27 and 17:12). Otherwise, *melek* occurs only in the editorial superscription (1:2), with reference to the future Davidic messiah (37:22, 24), and in the redactional expansion of Ezekiel's temple vision (43:7b-9). For a discussion of both terms in Ezekiel, see Tuell, *Law*, pp. 39-41, 105-20.

51. This evidence has led Iain Duguid (*Ezekiel and the Leaders of Israel*, VTSup 56 [Leiden: Brill, 1994]) to quite a different conclusion. Duguid argues that the king and priest, who receive comparatively little criticism in the body of the book, are rewarded with significant roles in the utopian program presented in chs. 40–48. However, the paucity of references to priesthood in Ezek. 1–39 more likely represents a negative attitude on Ezekiel's part than a positive one, particularly since the two attested references are both condemnatory. Similarly, the *nĕśî'îm* are repeatedly charged with injustice and covenant violation in chs. 1–33. That Ezekiel considered them less reprehensible than other leadership groups, as Duguid claims, seems unlikely (cf. my review of Duguid's volume in *JBL* 115 [1995]: 127-28).

Of course, neither temple nor city is found in the primordial earth of Genesis 2; here, the river originates in the garden of Eden before dividing into four branches (Gen. 2:10). However, both in Genesis 2 and in Ezekiel 47 (as the John of Revelation realized), the river's source makes the same point. In Ezekiel 43:7a, YHWH affirms, "Human, here is my throne and my footstool, where I will dwell among the Israelites forever." In Ezekiel's vision the temple itself, indeed the entire mountaintop where the temple is (Ezek. 43:12), takes the place of the lost ark as YHWH's throne and footstool, the place of God's presence. In Genesis as well, the river originates in a place of divine presence: Eden, the garden personally planted by YHWH (Gen. 2:8), where YHWH is accustomed to walk in the cool of the evening (Gen. 3:8).[52]

For Ezekiel, the earthly Zion had ceased to be a place of divine presence. This is apparent from the opening chapters of the book, where Ezekiel encounters the *kābôd* in Babylon, by the river Chebar — far from the Jerusalem temple. Any doubt about the disassociation between the divine presence and the earthly Jerusalem is removed by the vision of the abominations in Ezekiel 8–11, where the *kābôd* departs from the temple, and from Jerusalem itself. However, the true home of God is not affected by the dire consequences of Jerusalem's sin. The heavenly Zion, which Ezekiel visits in his final vision (Ezek. 40–48), still serves as the reliable source for life and meaning.[53] Moreover, as Ezekiel's visionary experience itself confirms, that divine presence is accessible to human beings — even to exiles, cut off from intermediation by cult or king.

---

52. Compare *Jub.* 8:19 (cited above) and 2 Esd. 3:6: "And you led him into the garden that your right hand had planted before the earth appeared." Zimmerli (*Ezekiel,* vol. 2, p. 510) observes, "But paradise, as is shown by many features in Genesis 2f, is the dwelling place of God." Compare also Clifford, *Cosmic Mountain,* p. 159.

53. Darr insists that the paradisial conditions described in Ezek. 47:1-12 are for the land of Israel alone: "We should not, for example, simply reconcile the differences between the description in Gen. ii 10-14 of a river in Eden which eventually divides to water all four regions of the earth, and Ezekiel's description of a sacred stream which flows only toward the east. . . . [W]e cannot avoid hearing the silence concerning any paradisial transformation of land lying beyond the perimeters of Israel's territory" ("Wall," pp. 277-78). However, if this text is a symbolic vision of life brought by the divine presence, rather than a literal vision of a transformed future, this objection fades. As Darr rightly observes, the nations are not in view in Ezek. 47:1-12. This, however, is not because they are polemically excluded, but rather because they are not addressed. The significance of an apolitical, atemporal, "Edenized" Zion lies in the hope that it gives to Ezekiel's audience, the community of the exiles.

As the connections between Ezekiel 47:1-12 and Genesis 2:10-14 reveal, Ezekiel understood the symbol of Zion in a new way. Cut free from explicit reference to the temporal, political realities of kingship, priesthood, and the earthly temple, the temple-mountain and river of Ezekiel's last great vision stand as timeless symbols of divine presence.[54] For Ezekiel, the earthly Zion, with its city and temple, was a bitter disappointment. It was the mythic, heavenly reality — Zion as YHWH's home and, specifically, Zion as Eden — that proved a more worthy ground for hope.

54. Compare Tuell, "Ezekiel 40–42," pp. 657-64. So also Levenson (*Theology of the Program*, p. 33), who writes: "The garden of Eden is an ideal of pre-political existence, and the redemption which ends in the Garden of Eden is deliverance from the tensions of political life."

Creation and New Creation: The Role of Creation Imagery in the Book of Daniel

Robert R. Wilson

In 1983 W. Sibley Towner called the attention of the scholarly world to one of the more curious chapters in the interpretive history of the book of Daniel.[1] To illustrate the difficulties encountered by communities of faith when they attempt to understand and appropriate Israel's eschatological beliefs, Towner focused on the way in which Daniel 7 was understood by antimonarchists in mid-seventeenth-century England. He was well aware that most contemporary critical scholars would judge interpretations from this period to be misguided, if not pernicious, and would not take them seriously. Indeed critical readers of Daniel 7 would be likely to reject most of the premodern interpretations that have been advanced in an effort to explicate this literarily complex chapter.[2] However, at the same time, Towner rightly recognized that modern scholarly understandings of Daniel are not necessarily more useful than earlier readings if the interest of the interpreter is in finding theological meaning in apocalyptic literature. In order

1. W. Sibley Towner, "Were the English Puritans 'the Saints of the Most High'?" *Int* 37 (1983): 46-63.

2. For a survey of the interpretation of Daniel 7, see Klaus Koch, *Das Buch Daniel* (Darmstadt: Wissenschaftliche Buchgesellschaft, 1980), pp. 113-14, 182-213; Arthur J. Ferch, *The Son of Man in Daniel 7* (Berrien Springs, MI: Andrews University, 1983), pp. 4-35; and, more generally, John J. Collins, *Daniel*, Hermeneia (Minneapolis: Fortress, 1993), pp. 72-123.

to see why this is so, it will be helpful to review the basic outline of Daniel 7 and to summarize the standard scholarly approach to it.

Daniel 7 as a whole is cast in the form of a dream report and is full of obscure symbolism. Daniel first tells his readers that in his night vision he saw the four winds of heaven churning up the great sea, from which emerged four beasts. The first of them was like a lion but had the wings of an eagle. The second was like a bear with a voracious appetite, while the third resembled a leopard with four wings and four heads. The fourth beast was so terrifying that it apparently had no analogues in the natural world, and the seer does not even attempt a comprehensive description, but simply notes its strength, its iron teeth, and its ten horns. As Daniel watched, three of the horns were pulled up and replaced by a little horn, having eyes and a mouth speaking arrogantly (7:1-8).

Most modern scholars believe that creation language reinforced by mythological allusions to various ancient Near Eastern cosmogonies lies behind this initial portion of the vision. The churning "great sea" recalls the windswept, chaotic deep of Genesis 1:1-5, which has its Mesopotamian counterpart in the goddess Tiamat, the deified ocean of the Babylonian creation myth *Enuma Elish*. In this myth Tiamat threatens to destroy the young gods, who are disturbing her rest, but she is finally subdued by the warrior god Marduk. Tablets discovered in the Syrian city of Ugarit show that in the second millennium B.C.E. a similar story was told about the sea god Yam, who fought with but was defeated by the storm god Ba'l, who was able to provide the earth with fertility through the life-giving fresh water of the rain. The various animals of Daniel 7 are most often compared with the threatening serpentine monsters created by Tiamat and ultimately slain by the god Marduk in the Mesopotamian myth, although the Ugaritic texts also know of dragonlike monsters, and other sources for the imagery are sometimes suggested.[3] Beyond these specific parallels, the association of the sea with the threat of chaos, with destruction, and with monsters of various types is a common motif throughout the ancient Near East, and traces of it are preserved in the Old Testament outside of Genesis 1 (e.g., Isa. 27:1; 30:7; 51:9-11; Ezek. 29:3-7; Pss. 74:13; 87:4; Job 7:12; 26:12-13).[4]

---

3. For a citation of the relevant extrabiblical texts and a discussion of the possible ancient Near Eastern sources for the imagery in Dan. 7:1-8, see Collins, *Daniel*, pp. 280-94; and Koch, *Daniel*, pp. 113-15.

4. For a discussion of the various mythological motifs associated with the sea in the

Daniel's vision continues with a court scene, in which "an Ancient One" (NRSV), presumably God, is enthroned, and a judgment takes place. As part of the proceedings, the fourth beast is put to death and burned, while the power of the remaining beasts is taken away (7:9-12). Following the destruction of the beast, Daniel saw a figure "like a human being" coming with the clouds and being presented to the Ancient One. With the presentation the figure is given royal power over all of the nations and is granted an eternal kingship (7:13-14). As is typically the case in these visions, Daniel does not understand what he sees and asks one of the visionary bystanders for an interpretation. The interpreter explains that the beasts are four kings, but that the "holy ones of the Most High" will ultimately receive an eternal kingdom (7:15-18). To this rudimentary interpretation is then added a more elaborate one in which the beasts are seen as four kingdoms, with the horns representing individual kings. However, in this interpretation, too, the "people of the holy ones of the Most High" eventually receive an eternal kingdom after being oppressed by the eleventh king, who will change seasons and the law (7:19-28).[5]

The connection that Daniel 7 makes between creation and kingship or enthronement is also to be found in many of the ancient Near Eastern creation myths. In *Enuma Elish*, for example, Marduk's defeat of the forces of chaos represented by Tiamat and her attendants leads directly to the foundation of Marduk's temple in Babylon and to the god's enthronement and the proclamation of his royal names. A similar pattern is probably represented in the Ugaritic texts, although there is some scholarly debate about the proper sequence of the relevant tablets. It is likely, however, that Ba'l's defeat of Yam leads Ba'l's supporters to demand that a "house" or temple be built for him so that he can be properly enthroned. The head of the pantheon, 'El, eventually agrees to this proposition, and a miraculous

---

ancient Near East, see Otto Kaiser, *Die mythische Bedeutung des Meeres in Ägypten, Ugarit und Israel* (Berlin: de Gruyter, 1959); John Day, *God's Conflict with the Dragon and the Sea* (Cambridge: Cambridge University Press, 1985); and Carola Kloos, *Yhwh's Combat with the Sea* (Amsterdam: G. A. van Oorschot, 1986).

5. The identification of the beasts as kings in Dan. 7:17 and as kingdoms in 7:23 may indicate two successive stages in the interpretation, although some Latin and Greek texts of Daniel also refer to kingdoms in v. 17. The Aramaic text, being the more difficult reading, is probably original, although a scribal error in the Aramaic cannot be ruled out. See the discussion of Collins (*Daniel*, pp. 311-12).

house is duly constructed. With his installation in the temple, Ba'l is able to provide the rains that the land requires.

In addition to this common ancient Near Eastern connection between creation and kingship, an increasing number of scholars find in 7:9-14 more specific allusions to Ugaritic cosmogonic texts. Although such scholars admit that the phrase "one like a human being" (7:13) is probably taken from the similar reference in Ezekiel 1:26, they also note that Ezekiel uses these words to refer to God rather than to a human. Following this clue, they then suggest that the picture of one who comes with the clouds is derived from a Canaanite background and describes the interactions between the god Ba'l and the god 'El, the head of the pantheon in the Ugaritic mythological texts. Like the Ancient One in Daniel 7, 'El is portrayed at Ugarit as an old man who is nominally the ruler of the gods but who in fact is in the process of losing his power and authority to a relative newcomer, the god Ba'l. In these texts the young storm god is often given the title "the cloud rider," so, the argument runs, the one who comes with the clouds in 7:13 is most appropriately identified with Ba'l. The scene pictured in Daniel's vision, then, is the formal transfer of power from 'El, the titular head of the pantheon, to Ba'l, the actual ruler of gods and humans.[6]

Beyond the mythological background represented in Daniel 7, most modern scholars agree that the chapter was originally shaped in response to the persecutions of Antiochus IV Epiphanes, who desecrated the Jerusalem temple in 167 B.C.E. and triggered the Maccabean revolt. The first three beasts represent the Babylonian, Median, and Persian empires, while the terrible fourth beast represents the empire of Alexander the Great. The horns are the Seleucid kings who ruled after Alexander's death, with Antiochus IV being the arrogant little horn.

Modern critical readings of Daniel 7, then, recognize the mythological background of the chapter and often explicitly or implicitly regard it as non-Israelite. At the same time, scholars consider the "real meaning" of the chapter to lie in specific events within the Maccabean period.

Against this sort of understanding, the type of interpretation described by Towner stands out in sharp relief. Rather than give Daniel 7 a

---

6. This interpretation has been argued in great detail by John A. Emerton ("The Origin of the Son of Man Imagery," *JTS* n.s. 9 [1958]: 225-42). See also the supporting arguments of Day (*God's Conflict*, pp. 157-67) and the discussion of Collins (*Daniel*, pp. 286-94, 304-10).

mythological reading or one that locates meaning in a particular set of ancient historical circumstances, most interpreters before the modern period treated the chapter as if it were prophecy rather than some sort of coded historiography. The task of the interpreter was not thought to be the discovery of the events that gave rise to the creation of the text, but, on the contrary, the interpreter was expected to clarify the present or future events to which the text referred. However, interpreting the text in this way may carry with it other dangers, including the risk of using the text to justify problematic political or social circumstances. To illustrate this problem, Towner describes in some detail an interpretation of Daniel 7 published in 1654 by the English Puritan divine William Aspinwall.[7] The expansive title of the work provides a good outline of Aspinwall's basic argument: "An Explication and Application of the Seventh Chapter of Daniel: with a Correction of the Translation. Wherein is briefly shewed the State and Downfall of the four Monarchies; but more largely of the *Roman Monarchy,* and the Ten Horns or Kingdoms; and in Particular, the Beheading of *Charles Stuart,* who is proved to be the Little Horn by many Characters, that cannot be applied to any before or after him. . . ." Following many interpreters before him, Aspinwall takes the four beasts of Daniel's vision to be the kingdoms of Babylon, Persia, Alexander, and Rome, the last of which his readers would probably have understood both as a reference to the Roman empire and as a reference to the Roman Church. The three horns that are pulled up by the roots represent to Aspinwall England, Scotland, and Wales, whose "roots" — religion, liberties, and civil rights — have been destroyed by the little horn, the English king Charles I. The prophesied judgment on the little horn has, according to Aspinwall, already been accomplished through the king's execution at the hands of the Puritan Parliament in 1649. All that remains to be fulfilled is the establishment of the eternal kingdom of the Saints of the Most High, who are, of course, to be identified with the Puritans of Aspinwall's own party.

Towner's example demonstrates graphically the difficulties involved in seeing in Daniel prophecies of future events. In retrospect, the interpretation of Aspinwall was not only wrong but had the capacity for justifying civil disorder and supporting a particular religious and political party. In short, no matter what its history, this approach to the text can be danger-

---

7. The following account of Aspinwall's work is taken from Towner, "English Puritans," pp. 47-63.

ous, even though it is not easy to identify what is wrong with the approach from the standpoint of interpretive theory. However, Towner correctly perceives that the standard scholarly approach to the passage runs the risk of locating meaning in past events or of leading the interpreter into other-worldly realms that seem to have little to do with the everyday lives of the people who view the text as Scripture.

Since Towner's sensitive discussion of the issues involved in the interpretation of apocalyptic literature, the interpretive polarities to which he pointed have, if anything, become more marked. On the one side, people wishing to read Daniel as prophecy have become even more active, and the approach of the millennium has generated even more attempts to see current events as those foretold by the biblical seer.[8] Furthermore, it is becoming increasingly clear that the tendency to reinterpret prophetic and visionary texts is one that has been going on since antiquity, even within the Bible itself. Recent work on Isaiah, for example, suggests that in this particular prophetic tradition Isaiah's early oracles, which had already been fulfilled, were reinterpreted several times, and these reinterpretations have left their imprint within the present text of the book. Lying behind this process seems to be the belief that divine predictions have an almost limitless reservoir of meaning and are not exhausted by being fulfilled in a particular historical event. Such a belief may drive both interpretation and literary development in other prophetic books as well, and writers of the Bible's apocalyptic visions may have held similar views about their literature.

A case in point may be Daniel 9, where Jeremiah's prophecy of a seventy-year exile, a prophecy that was more or less correct, is reinterpreted to refer to a later time. The original prophecy was not wrong or unfulfilled; rather it was thought to be capable of supplying additional meaning for a later community.[9] Phenomena such as these within the biblical text make it more difficult for the modern reader to reject out of hand the sorts of interpretations provided by Aspinwall and much of the precritical interpre-

---

8. For examples of the way in which biblical prophecies are being interpreted in contemporary communities, see Paul Boyer, *When Time Shall Be No More: Prophecy Belief in Modern American Culture* (Cambridge, MA: Harvard University Press, 1992).

9. For a discussion of multiple fulfillment in biblical prophetic and apocalyptic texts, see John Barton, *Oracles of God* (New York: Oxford University Press, 1986), pp. 192-210; and Robert R. Wilson, "The Prophetic Books," in *The Cambridge Companion to Biblical Interpretation*, ed. John Barton (Cambridge: Cambridge University Press, 1998), pp. 213-17.

tive tradition. The impulse toward reinterpretation seems to be deeply embedded in both Jewish and Christian tradition, and this impulse must be respected, even if the details of particular reinterpretations cannot be accepted.

On the other side, in recent years scholarly treatments of apocalyptic religion and of Daniel in particular seem to have become even more otherworldly and thus more inaccessible to the modern reader than was the case when Towner wrote his article. One of the factors lying behind this trend is the view that apocalyptic eschatology, which is the subject of much of the Bible's apocalyptic literature, is by its very nature unconcerned with everyday life and the events of history. Scholars who pursue this line of argument believe that while the biblical prophets translated their revelations into historical terms that could be of immediate use to their communities, the apocalyptic visionaries abandoned this task and instead spoke of a world beyond space and time. Characteristic of this turn away from history is the reappearance of mythological language in the Bible's apocalyptic literature. This language, some of which comes from non-Israelite sources and some of which is transmitted but often suppressed within the biblical tradition itself, is sometimes thought to be a departure from Israel's earlier, historically based religion.[10]

Coupled with and perhaps encouraged by this understanding of apocalyptic eschatology, there has recently been a greater tendency to see nonhuman actors in Daniel 7. Clearly the Ancient One of the vision is a reference to God, but the "one like a human being" has often been identified as a human ruler (or a collective representation of Israel), and the "holy ones" have often been interpreted as faithful Israelites. Throughout the history of interpretation scholars have from time to time offered other suggestions and seen in the chapter references to Jesus or to angels, but this was not the predominant interpretation. This state of affairs began to change with an influential article by Martin Noth, who identified the "holy ones" as divine beings and argued that Daniel 7 described the advent of a heavenly kingdom. No human beings were present in the chapter at all.[11] In recent literature on Daniel 7, this interpretation has been accepted by a

---

10. The most detailed presentation of this position is Paul D. Hanson, *The Dawn of Apocalyptic* (Philadelphia: Fortress, 1975).

11. Martin Noth, "The Holy Ones of the Most High," in his *The Laws in the Pentateuch and Other Studies* (Philadelphia: Fortress, 1967 [German original 1955]), pp. 215-28.

number of scholars and has been popularized by the influential commentary of John Collins.[12]

Thus recent developments in scholarship have not helped to solve the interpretive problems that Towner analyzed, and in some ways they have made the situation more complex. On the one hand, attempts to read apocalyptic literature as prophecy referring to the present make the literature relevant to contemporary communities, even though this approach can carry with it the sorts of pitfalls that Towner noted. On the other hand, scholarly approaches to such literature increasingly portray it as otherworldly and therefore not useful to contemporary communities.

The complex issues that Towner has raised cannot be resolved easily, but some progress toward a resolution might be achieved if the use of mythological language in apocalyptic literature were understood more fully. Such language is often thought to be imported from foreign sources and to have no natural place in Israel's theological discourse, but the latter judgment in particular is somewhat wide of the mark. In fact, mythological language is particularly useful in apocalyptic literature and can play important theological roles in that context. To understand more fully why this is so, it will be useful to examine briefly the nature of apocalyptic communities and the literature that they produce.[13]

Apocalyptic groups are often thought to be made up of marginalized individuals who feel that they have been deprived of something that they might reasonably expect to possess. They may lack political power or social standing, or they may be without the basic necessities of life, such as food, clothing, housing, or useful work. This sort of deprivation is most obvious when group members are in the presence of others who are not marginalized; they are most likely to recognize their peripheral status when they see themselves in relation to other people or groups. Relative comparisons of this sort are most likely to occur in times of rapid social change or when different cultures are suddenly brought into proximity with each other.

However, recent research into apocalyptic groups has shown that this understanding of their nature does not explain all of the examples.

---

12. Collins, *Daniel*, pp. 304-18.

13. The following discussion of the characteristics of apocalyptic groups is based on my article, "From Prophecy to Apocalyptic: Reflections on the Shape of Israelite Religion," *Semeia* 21 (1981): 84-87, where relevant anthropological studies are cited.

Some apocalyptic communities seem to be composed of people who are not on the fringes of society but at its center, people whose position, wealth, or power would seem to make them unlikely candidates for membership in such communities.[14] This fact suggests a somewhat broader explanation of the forces that encourage apocalyptic group membership. Rather than speaking simply of "relative deprivation," it might be more accurate to suggest that group members experience an incongruence between the world as their society has taught them to perceive it and the actual world as they experience it. In these terms situations of rapid social change, cultural conflict, or reversal of personal fortune present challenges to the worldview of the people who experience them. The incongruence must then be resolved in some way, and all successful apocalyptic groups provide some means of achieving such a resolution.[15]

Typically the resolution of the group's experience of incongruence is to be found in a program that the group advances either in written or in oral form. The program articulates clearly the group's analysis of the incongruence that it feels and then points the way to some sort of resolution. Such programs are usually both prospective and retrospective. The primary interest of the group is clearly in the future, when the world it experiences will again be brought into conformity with "the world as it should be," a process that will come about through either natural or supernatural means. At the same time, however, the program looks to the past for the picture of the world as it was before contemporary experience challenged it. In this sense the resolution of the incongruity can be spoken of as a return to the past and as a restoration of the traditional worldview. The group in fact may not accurately remember the past, and the traditional worldview may be shaped more by the present than by historically accurate memory, but the program will still be described as a restoration and as an affirmation of what has always been.

In addition to providing a map for resolving the group's experience of incongruence, successful apocalyptic plans also have a practical dimension. They not only outline what will eventually happen to the group, but

14. For a critique of the use of "relative deprivation theory" to account for the formation of apocalyptic communities, see Stephen L. Cook, *Prophecy and Apocalypticism* (Minneapolis: Fortress, 1995), pp. 1-84.

15. An analysis along these lines is suggested by Jonathan Z. Smith in "A Pearl of Great Price and a Cargo of Yams: A Study in Situational Incongruity," in his *Imagining Religion: From Babylon to Jonestown* (Chicago: University of Chicago Press, 1982), pp. 90-101.

they also provide guidelines for group behavior during the time that elapses between the present and the predicted end. In some cases members are informed of specific steps that they are to take in order to help bring about the resolution of the incongruence, while in other cases they are taught what they are to do while waiting for a supernatural intervention that will achieve the resolution.

Given the nature and functions of apocalyptic programs, it comes as no surprise that they often contain a great deal of mythological language and imagery. Myth is itself a notoriously complex phenomenon, which has defied simple definition and triggered numerous debates within the field of Old Testament studies.[16] For our purposes it is not necessary to suggest a comprehensive definition, but it will be sufficient to note that myth is more than a story about the gods, an account of origins, a picture of the supernatural world, or the antithesis of history, although it may be all of those things. Rather it is language that a culture uses to express what it considers the totality of reality to be, whether that reality is natural or supernatural, visible or invisible, perceptible or imperceptible. Because it expresses what the world really is, myth often takes the form of a creation story, an account of how everything came to be what it is and should be, even though the culture's current experience of the world may not match what it believes the world actually is. In the context of apocalyptic literature, myth often affirms the true nature of reality and provides the baseline to which the now incongruent world of contemporary experience will ultimately return.

Against this general background on the nature of apocalyptic programs and the mythological language that they often employ, we are in a position to appreciate more fully the importance of the mythological creation imagery incorporated in Daniel 7. Although this imagery has often been noted, its function within the chapter has not been fully explored. Even though some of the imagery may be borrowed from Mesopotamian, Canaanite, or Persian sources, as scholars have long suggested, it is fair to assume that its presence in Daniel represents a deliberate choice by the author and that the creation references are intended to present an account of what the author thought reality to be. To explore this idea more fully, it

16. For a survey of these debates, see John W. Rogerson, *Myth in Old Testament Interpretation* (Berlin: de Gruyter, 1974). Note especially his list of the various dimensions and functions of myth on pp. 174-78.

will be useful to set Daniel 7 against the background of the biblical creation story that it most explicitly evokes, the Priestly Writer's account in Genesis 1. Because of the late date of Daniel, it is safe to conclude that the author of Daniel 7 would have known the Priestly account, and it is probably also safe to assume that it was understood as a fundamental statement of reality, although not necessarily the only such statement known to the author.

As scholars have long recognized, Genesis 1 is fundamentally an account of the process of imposing divine order on the originally chaotic components of the cosmos. This concept of order seems to have been a fundamental component of the Priestly view of reality and is in marked contrast to the more experimental and haphazard process described by the Yahwist in Genesis 2–4. Genesis 1 opens with a description of the watery chaos with which creation began. While the language of the account evokes the Mesopotamian goddess Tiamat, the deified sea mentioned in *Enuma Elish,* scholars have often noted that in the biblical account the primordial sea is not personified, even though it may retain the evil connotations that it had throughout the ancient Semitic world.

The first creative act is also the first act of ordering: God creates light and then separates light from darkness, thus drawing a boundary between the two and making possible the marking of time through the alternation of night and day (Gen. 1:3-5). Time was particularly important to the writer because it permitted the numbering of days and thus the regulation of the cultic calendar, symbolized in this account by the creation of the sabbath on the seventh day (Gen. 2:1-3). Liturgical time was thus part of the creation itself and was built into the structure of the world as it was intended to be.

The process of ordering continues in Genesis 1:9, when the primordial waters are set within boundaries and separated from the dry land. This description contrasts with the Mesopotamian parallel, where Tiamat is actually killed and then divided. In the Priestly account, the sea is contained, but its potential for evil is not destroyed. This notion that the chaotic forces of the cosmos can be restrained but never eliminated appears elsewhere in biblical thought and seems to imply that creation in some sense is a continuous or cyclical process. The world is always threatened by chaos, but God's power holds it in check. When chaos does break out, God can again restrain it and re-create the world, bringing it back to the orderly form in which it was meant to be. This re-creation of the world is brought about in the human sphere in the cult and in the regular observance of the sabbath, symbolizing the completion of creation.[17]

In Genesis 1:11 plants are created, and they too are carefully regulated. Each type reproduces after its own kind, so, at least in the view of the Priestly Writer, there is no possibility of creating new species through mutation. The same pattern is followed in the creation of animals in 1:20-25. Each reproduces after its own kind, and apparently even the great sea monsters are subject to the divinely imposed order. It has become clear by this point in the account that this ordering of creation is intended to be hierarchical. It moves from the inanimate world to the world of living things, and within the latter, creation moves from water creatures to birds, to wild animals and insects, and then to domestic animals. At the apex of the hierarchy are human beings, who are given dominion over all of the created order. They are described as being made in the image of God and thus are to serve as God's representatives on earth and its surrogate rulers (1:26-28). Elsewhere in the ancient Near East, this same sort of language is applied to kings, and the idea of kingship may also lie in the background of the Priestly account, although no explicit reference to a king is made. Rather, in this original world people as a whole are given royal authority.[18]

Against the background of the Priestly creation account in Genesis 1, the function of the creation language in Daniel 7 can be understood more clearly. While the churning waters of Daniel 7:2 are clearly reflexes of those in Genesis 1, the great sea in Daniel's vision is no longer within its boundaries. It has returned once more to its chaotic state, as it was capable of doing from time to time according to the Priestly worldview. This sense of chaos is reinforced by the description of the beasts that Daniel sees. Although the inspiration for these creatures may lie in Mesopotamian or Persian iconography, their most important characteristic has not been sufficiently appreciated. They are without parallel in the natural order as it is described in Genesis 1. These are composite animals, mutants rather than the products of normal animals each reproducing after its own kind. In

17. For a discussion of the continual threat of chaos within the created order and the role of the cult in ordering that chaos, see Jon D. Levenson, *Creation and the Persistence of Evil* (San Francisco: Harper & Row, 1988), pp. 14-127.

18. For a discussion of the kingship motif in Genesis 1 and its possible Persian background, see Udo Rüterswörden, *Dominum Terrae. Studien zur Genese einer alttestamentlichen Vorstellung* (Berlin: de Gruyter, 1993), pp. 81-130.

short, they are violations of the natural order that God set up in creation, and by implication the kings and kingdoms that they represent are also violations of the order. The world has reverted to its pre-creation state and is clearly in need of re-creation.

That process begins in the next portion of the vision. God in the form of the Ancient One appears, and it is clear from the visionary's description that God is in fact able to reestablish control over the world, imposing on it again the order from which it has departed. The aberrant beasts are destroyed and their power taken away. Then, just as in Genesis 1, God appoints a surrogate to rule the world. The reference in Daniel seems to be to a genuine royal figure, although in 7:18, 27 dominion is apparently shared with the holy ones. The scholarly debate about these figures cannot be resolved on the basis of a comparison with Genesis 1, although the parallels do suggest that the writer in Daniel is talking about a new earthly creation in which the original created order is restored; he is not portraying a strictly heavenly kingdom of some sort. This interpretation would also fit well with apocalyptic programs in general, which usually map out the process of restoring the world to the way it should be, the way in which it was created in the beginning. To be sure, this act of re-creating the world may require direct divine intervention, as it does in Genesis 1, but in the end the new creation is the reimposition of order in this world and not the creation of a heavenly realm. This interpretation of Daniel 7 is reinforced elsewhere in Daniel, particularly in chs. 8 and 9, where the reestablishment of the cult is described. As is also the case in Genesis 1, the cult is an integral part of the created order and is itself a symbolic barrier against chaos.

The creation imagery in Daniel 7 thus seems to have a dual function. On the one hand, by evoking Genesis 1 it restates in clear terms the writer's view of the way reality is supposed to be, even though the writer's experience of the present world does not match that view. On the other hand, by repeating in the vision the sequence of events that took place during the original creation, the writer reminds the readers that just as chaos can return to the world, so also can God restore order and bring the world back to the way it was in the beginning. However, in Daniel 7 a new element is added to the account of Genesis 1. While the Priestly Writer implies that both creation and return to chaos can be repeated throughout human history, the visionary of Daniel 7 speaks of an eternal kingdom (7:14, 27). If this language is not simply hyperbole, the writer may be suggesting that with the predicted new creation the cycle of reversion to chaos and re-creation will finally end. The cosmic order will permanently remain in the form that God intended, and the earth and the faithful of Israel will finally enjoy the divine rest that marks the end of the creative process.

The World of Creation
in the Book of the Twelve

David L. Petersen

Reflection on the nature of the created order looms as an increasingly important arena of religious and theological discourse in the late twentieth century. Ecological concerns among others help to explain the prominence of this topic. Moreover, biblical scholars have realized that the literature with which they have been entrusted can have an important role to play in this discussion.[1]

However, to talk about the world of creation is no easy matter. What texts or topics is one to assess? Richard Clifford and John Collins propose to investigate cosmogonies as the primary resource, a ploy similar to Bernhard Anderson's focus on creation accounts.[2] Others have elected a

---

1. See e.g., Bernhard W. Anderson, "Creation and Ecology," in *Creation in the Old Testament*, ed. Bernhard W. Anderson, IRT 6 (Philadelphia: Fortress, 1984), pp. 152-71; Theodore Hiebert, *The Yahwist's Landscape: Nature and Religion in Early Israel* (New York: Oxford University Press, 1996); James Limburg, "Down-to-Earth Theology: Psalm 104 and the Environment," *Currents in Theology and Mission* 21 (1994): 340-46; Ronald Simkins, *Creator & Creation: Nature in the Worldview of Ancient Israel* (Peabody, MA: Hendrickson, 1994); Gene M. Tucker, "Rain on a Land Where No One Lives: The Hebrew Bible on the Environment," *JBL* 116 (1997): 3-17. Robert Murray has pursued comparable issues in *The Cosmic Covenant: Biblical Themes of Justice, Peace, and the Integrity of Creation* (London: Sheed and Ward, 1992).

2. Richard J. Clifford and John J. Collins, *Creation in the Biblical Tradition*, CBQMS 24 (Washington, D.C.: Catholic Biblical Association, 1992).

style of literature (e.g., Dennis McCarthy on early poetry).[3] Still others have focused on a literature that has been reconstructed by scholars (e.g., Theodore Hiebert on the Yahwist). Equally challenging is the question about what methods or perspectives one should bring to bear on the question. What method or angle of vision will be appropriate to the task? Biblical scholars are most familiar with the methods of their guild. And yet study of the created order challenges the interpreter to offer broader angles of vision, for example, the "model" approach of Ronald Simkins or the reconstructive proposal of Robert Murray.

In this paper, my methodological approach will be modest. I intend to offer a traditio-historical analysis, since this perspective has proven so fruitful for understanding various features of prophetic literature. E. Rohland's formative monograph, which decisively influenced Gerhard von Rad's *Old Testament Theology,* provides a classic exemplar.[4] Attention to the Zion traditions in Isaiah, Priestly traditions in Ezekiel, or lament traditions in Jeremiah has been useful both in determining what influenced a particular prophet and also in assessing how a particular prophet may have revised a normative tradition, for example, the variation wrought by Amos on the day of Yahweh tradition. In this paper, I will examine creation and other traditions that involve the created order (day of Yahweh/theophany).

This paper looks at a distinctive corpus, namely, the minor prophets. Scholars of various methodological persuasions have recently begun to appreciate the ways in which this literature may function together.[5] As a result, a new body of scholarly literature devoted to The Book of the Twelve (hereafter designated the XII) is now emerging. Although the extent to which the minor prophets may be read as "a book" is the subject of consid-

3. Dennis J. McCarthy, "'Creation' Motifs in Ancient Hebrew Poetry," in *Creation in the Old Testament,* ed. Bernhard W. Anderson, IRT 6 (Philadelphia: Fortress, 1984), pp. 74-89.

4. E. Rohland, *Die Bedeutung der Erwählungstraditionen Israels für die Eschatologie der alttestamentlichen Propheten* (Theol. Diss., Heidelberg, 1956, Fotodruck).

5. For example, Paul R. House, *The Unity of the Twelve,* JSOTSup 97/BLS 27 (Sheffield: Almond, 1990); B. Jones, *The Formation of the Book of the Twelve: A Study in Text and Canon,* SBLDS 149 (Atlanta: Scholars Press, 1995); James Nogalski, *Literary Precursors to the Book of the Twelve,* BZAW 217 (Berlin: de Gruyter, 1993); idem, *Redactional Processes in the Book of the Twelve,* BZAW 218 (Berlin: de Gruyter, 1993); Odil H. Steck, *Der Abschluss der Prophetie im Alten Testament: Ein Versuch zur Frage der Vorgeschichte des Kanons,* BTS 17 (Neukirchen-Vluyn: Neukirchener, 1991).

erable debate, attention to these books as a literary entity that would have been written on one scroll offers new and interesting opportunities of interpretation.

The world of creation in the XII is a complicated one. Most of these twelve prophetic books refer at one point or another to elements in the created order — the heavens, the earth, celestial luminaries, mountains, water, animals, and human life. Such references, however, occur in diverse kinds of literature — for example, lawsuits, hymns, and judgment oracles. Instead of focusing on literary type, it seems wiser to attempt to review references to the created order according to the theological traditions they reflect.

Prophetic books appear to draw on (or perhaps contribute to) some of the classic creation texts in the Hebrew Bible (Gen. 1–2; Job 9; Ps. 104). The primary emphasis here is on God's creative activity. In addition, the minor prophets allude to the created order but without explicit reference to the activity of creation. We will examine these texts and attempt to determine their traditional character, since they seem to lie outside the ambit of creation traditions as such.[6]

I. Creation Traditions

When viewing the minor prophets as a Book of the Twelve, the reader encounters a literature that encompasses considerably more history than the so-called major prophets. The XII covers Amos, in the mid-eighth century, and texts like Zechariah 9–14, in the fifth century B.C.E. As a result, one cannot expect much homogeneity of thought or perspective.

I have argued elsewhere that one particular tradition appears with striking prominence throughout the XII, namely, the day of Yahweh traditions.[7] However, other significant traditions are also present. In this portion of the study, I will argue that creation traditions inform the XII.

This claim should be viewed as unusual. There has been something of a consensus that creation traditions were only important fairly late in

---

6. Compare Simkins (*Creator & Creation*, pp. 207-51), who subsumes prophetic literature on the created order under the category of eschatological myth.

7. David L. Petersen, "The Book of the Twelve," in *The Hebrew Bible Today*, ed. Steven L. McKenzie and M. Patrick Graham (Louisville: Westminster/John Knox, 1998), pp. 95-126.

Israelite religion and literature. Though this consensus is breaking up, it remains the case that the most powerful exemplar of creation language in prophetic literature occurs in what has hitherto been known as Deutero- or Second Isaiah, prophetic poetry dating to the mid-sixth century B.C.E. Gerhard von Rad wrote, "Very surprisingly, however, there is still another tradition in Deutero-Isaiah, one upon which no previous prophet had called. It deals with the creation of the world by Yahweh."[8] However, creation traditions and theological perspectives were alive and well before the exilic period, and not just in the minor prophets.

What, then, is the evidence for creation traditions in the XII? We must rely primarily on diction, that is, Hebrew verbs typically used when Israelite writers refer to the generative activities of the deity. So it becomes appropriate to search the XII for that vocabulary associated with creation of the cosmos and all that is within it. One may also look for those instances in which the negation of creation is played out.

Hosea 8:14 presents the first exemplar: "Israel has forgotten his Maker." The language of creation is, at the outset, applied not to the mountains or the clouds, which otherwise appear so prominently in this prophetic book. Instead, Israel is the object of creative activity. Moreover, the prophet uses language of formation to indict Israel. The notion of creation leads toward indictment and sentence, not toward praise, as it does in so many psalms. Hosea serves as an ominous harbinger for the rest of the XII.

Not all books include allusions to creation traditions, and so we must move on to Amos to find the next exemplars. On three different occasions, the book of Amos presents what appear to be fragments of a hymn (4:13; 5:8-9; 9:5-6).[9] Each fragment contains language specific to creation traditions:

> For lo, the one who forms the mountains, creates the wind,
> > reveals his thoughts to mortals,
> makes the morning darkness,
> > and treads on the heights of the earth —
> the Lord, the God of Hosts, is his name! (4:13, NRSV)

---

8. Gerhard von Rad, *Old Testament Theology* (New York: Harper & Row, 1962-65), vol. 2, p. 240.

9. For a recent assessment of this material, see Jörg Jeremias, "Exkurs: Die Doxologien im Amosbuch," in his *Der Prophet Amos*, ATD 24/2 (Göttingen: Vandenhoeck & Ruprecht, 1995), pp. 56-58.

The one who made the Pleiades and Orion,
  and turns deep darkness into the morning,
  and darkens the day into night,
who calls for the waters of the sea,
  and pours them out on the surface of the earth,
The Lord is his name,
  who makes destruction flash out against the strong
  so that destruction comes upon the fortress. (5:8-9, NRSV)

The Lord, God of hosts,
  he who touches the earth and it melts,
  and all who live in it mourn,
and all of it rises like the Nile,
  and sinks again like the Nile of Egypt;
who builds his upper chambers in the heavens
  and founds his vault upon the earth;
who calls for the waters of the sea,
  and pours them out upon the surface of the earth —
the Lord is his name. (9:5-6, NRSV)

These poetic lines present a number of challenges to the interpreter. We can, however, focus on one basic question: What is the role of creation language in this material?[10] In each fragment, such language is juxtaposed with activity that affects humans. According to 4:13, God's very intentions are revealed. Within a prophetic book like Amos, such a statement may well allude to the way in which the deity communicates to humans through the prophet. In 5:8-9, the deity's destruction of the strong involves the decimation of humans. And in 9:5-6, humans will mourn at the suffering they will endure after God "touches the earth." With each hymnic piece, the prophet affirms that God creates as well as destroys.

Yet there are limits to that destruction. In Amos, the picture of destruction is held in check by that which the Lord is described as having created. One senses that the mountains, the wind, the structures of the heavens, the stars, the flow of time, and the flow of water will all perdure. The

---

10. Compare S. Gillingham ("'Der die Morgenröte Finsternis macht' Gott und Schöpfung in Amosbuch," *EvT* 53 [1993]: 109-23), who studies the natural order in Amos and discovers that God's relation to the world is complex, even paradoxical, involving creative, sustaining, and destructive elements. Natural catastrophes play a remarkably prominent role in Amos.

threat envisioned by this poet does not involve the destruction of the cosmos. The situation is, therefore, quite different from the deluge picture in Genesis, according to which the entire cosmos — that which had been created — is washed back to its preformed state. The destruction is itself part of the created order, not a threat to it. In sum, creation traditions in the book of Amos both warrant God to act as destroyer and place limits upon the extent of the destruction that might ensue.

After Amos, there is a major hiatus in the XII. That gap stops at the book of Zephaniah. The use of creation language here is markedly different from that in Amos. The first major oracle in Zephaniah employs creation language, as attested in Genesis 1.

> I will utterly sweep away everything
> > from the face of the earth, says the Lord.
> I will sweep away humans and animals;
> I will sweep away the birds of the air
> > and the fish of the sea.
> I will make the wicked stumble.
> I will cut off humanity from the face of the earth,
> > says the Lord. (Zeph. 1:2-3, NRSV)

To read these lines is to encounter the thought world of the primeval history. As with Amos, the cosmic structure, even "the face of the earth," will remain. However, all life — fish, birds, animals, and humans — will disappear. Commentators have noted that the phrase "from the face of the earth" creates a literary envelope around these verses, a frame for this scene of annihilation. Moreover, this same phrase occurs in the primeval history's deluge scene (Gen. 6:7; 7:4; 8:8). The author of the poetry in Zephaniah may be alluding to the scene of destruction in that primeval age in order to argue that something of comparable scale will happen again. Yet the prophet does not refer to the destruction of either earth or heaven; "the face of the earth" remains.

The book of Zechariah presents the next literary context in which creation traditions appear. In Zechariah 10:1, a Persian-period poet wrote:

> Ask rain from the Lord
> > in the season of the spring rain,
> from the Lord who makes the storm clouds,
> > who gives showers of rain to you,
> > the vegetation in the field to everyone. (NRSV)

Such a command (plural) presupposes a God who not only created the natural order in the past but continues to work in the natural order in the present, that is, by making "storm clouds." Moreover, such activity in the present enables the material of primordial creation to remain intact. For example, the "vegetation in the field" (*'ēśeb baśśādeh*), which benefits from the showers, derives from the primal vegetation (*'ēśeb haśśādeh*, Gen. 2:5). The making of storm clouds now sustains God's original work of creation.

Zechariah 12:1, which introduces the second *massā'* (chs. 12–14), also attests creation language: "The word of the Lord concerning Israel: Thus says the Lord, who stretches out the heavens and founds the earth and forms the human spirit within." The hymnic participial constructions prominent in the Amos doxologies reappear here, though their presence is not evident in the typical English translations. This elegant and compact formulation seems to reflect key aspects of both the Priestly and Yahwistic creation accounts. It refers to the cosmic structure of the heavens and the earth, as in the Priestly creation account. Moreover, it alludes to a spirit that vivifies humanity, as in the Yahwistic creation account.

In neither case, however, does there appear to be a direct allusion to either creation account in Genesis. The imagery of stretching out the heavens, though absent from Genesis 1, appears in Psalm 104:2; Job 9:8; and Isaiah 44:24; 51:13. Zechariah 12:1 is the only biblical text in which this imagery of stretching out the heavens ("like a tent," Ps. 104:2) includes reference to the creation of humanity. Elsewhere, the image is bound uniformly to poems that focus exclusively on the creation of the cosmos. Moreover, the reference in Zechariah 12:1 to humanity appears to be a variant of the tradition attested in Genesis 2. Whereas in Genesis 2:7 God "formed" (*yṣr*) the earth creature . . . and breathed into his nostrils the breath of life (*nišmat ḥayyîm*), according to Zechariah 12:1 God "formed" the human spirit (*rûah 'ādām*) inside him. The object of the verb is different in the two cases. In Genesis, God forms the creature; in Zechariah, God forms the spirit. One has the sense that there is a traditional set of creation vocabulary, but that it could be arranged in various acceptable patterns. Heavens, earth, humanity, and spirit provide the crucial building blocks. Zechariah 12:1 combines them in an innovative and adroit manner.

The final text in the XII that uses creation language is Malachi 2:10. It is embedded in some questions that are being posed to the people.

> Have we not all one father?
> Has not one God created us?
> Why then are we faithless to one another,
>> profaning the covenant of our ancestors? (Mal. 2:10, NRSV)

The image of parent is linked in parallel poetic lines to that of creator. Cosmogony has been replaced by a concern for the origins of the community, the same issue prominent in the first text we examined, Hosea 8:14.

In summary, creation in the XII is something that has occurred in the past. Moreover, it is a kind of activity that includes more than the creation that is described in Genesis 1–2. The *inclusio* created by Hosea 8:14 and Malachi 2:10 highlights the creation of God's people, of community rather than of the cosmos. Moreover, in the other texts, various prophets attest that, despite the evil machinations of humanity and the devastating judgment that will ensue, the created order itself will remain intact.[11] Various life forms may be annihilated, but the structures of God's world will endure.

II. The Created Order

The above survey of those texts that betray explicit linguistic connections with creation language elsewhere in the Hebrew Bible makes it appear as if the cosmos is a stable and reliable entity. Though God may destroy peoples and kingdoms, the natural order might seem to be immune from such activity. However, other texts in the XII that describe the created order do not routinely offer such a picture. If one examines those passages that include specific reference to various elements in the natural order (e.g., mountains, hills, earth), quite a different world emerges, one in which that order is liable to destruction. How is such dissonance about the durability of the created order to be understood? An answer to this question will emerge as we review the key theological traditions that are associated with these texts.

Again, we must offer a brief inventory of the salient biblical texts.

---

11. Texts such as Mic. 6:2 seem to reflect such creation traditions. Mountains and the enduring foundations of the earth will be permanently available as judges for God's lawsuit against Israel.

Hosea 4:3 is the first and in some ways most unusual. The prophet describes the earth as shriveling up, since all life is apparently dying.

> Therefore, the land shrivels up,
>   and all who live in it languish;
> together with the wild animals,
> and the birds of the air,
>   even the fish of the sea are perishing.

From a form-critical perspective, this verse functions as the sentence in a judgment oracle. And yet the sentence seems less an overt punishment by the deity and more an automatic response of the created order to the violations of the decalogue-like ethic by those who live in the land (vv. 1-2). What Yahweh will sweep away à la Zephaniah is described by Hosea as dying out.

With Joel, we enter a different set of traditions, not those associated with creation but those involving the day of the Lord and Yahweh's theophany.[12] Joel describes elements in the natural order — the sun and the moon — and the impact of the appearance of the day of the Lord on them.

> The sun shall be turned to darkness,
>   and the moon to blood. (Joel 2:31a [3:4a], NRSV)

> The sun and the moon are darkened,
>   and the stars withdraw their shining. (3:15 [4:15], NRSV)

> The heavens and the earth shake. (3:16 [4:16], NRSV)

Neither the physical nor the temporal order is immune from radical disturbance when the deity appears. Here there is a striking contrast with the prophetic allusion to creation traditions.

The book of Amos continues in this vein. In at least one reference to the day of the Lord, the prophet says:

---

12. For the purposes of this study, I shall suggest that these two traditions be viewed as one integral complex. Theophany involves the manifestation of the deity in the natural order, and the day of the Lord presumes the presence of the deity, often in a military manner. As a result, there is significant overlap. On theophany, see the classic study of Jörg Jeremias, *Theophanie: Die Geschichte einer alttestamentliche Gattung*, WMANT 10 (Neukirchen-Vluyn: Neukirchener, 1965).

I will make the sun go down at noon,
    and darken the earth in broad daylight. (8:9; cf. 5:18-20, NRSV)

This dangerous day will involve a cessation of the natural orders of time and light.

Micah, Nahum, and Habakkuk offer comparable vignettes of the impact of God's theophany upon the earth:

The mountain will melt under him
    and the valleys will burst open. (Mic. 1:4, NRSV)

The mountains will quake before him,
    and the hills melt,
the earth heaves before him,
the world and all who live in it. (Nah. 1:5, NRSV)

He stopped and shook the earth . . .
    The eternal hills were shattered . . .
    the everlasting hills sank low. (Hab. 3:6, NRSV)

Clearly, these prophets share an expectation that, when God "treads upon the high places of the earth," the created order — as symbolized by the mountains, hills, and valleys — will suffer radically disruptive reorganization.

Haggai moves in a different direction. When describing the way in which Yahweh will endow the new temple, Haggai offers the following divine speech:

I will shake the heavens and the earth,
    the sea and the dry land;
and I will shake all the nations. . . . (2:6b-7a, NRSV)

And then, when offering encouragement to Zerubbabel, the Davidic heir, God repeats,

I am about to shake the heavens and the earth
    and to overthrow the throne of kingdoms. . . . (2:21b-22a, NRSV)

Here one is not in the world of theophany but instead in the world of prophetic woe and weal — woe to the nations, weal to Israel. The heavens and

213

the earth work as a merism to describe the created order, which will be shaken like a box.

With Zechariah we return explicitly to the day of the Lord traditions, the leitmotif for Zechariah. Here, as with Nahum, Habakkuk, and Zephaniah, we hear about mountains being re-formed (Zech. 14:4-5); and as with Joel 3, we are told about a different kind of light and temporal order (Zech. 14:7). The day of the Lord will spell an end to the created order as humans now know it, which makes Zechariah 14 stand in an ironic relationship with the beginning of that "oracle" (Zech. 12:1) and its focus on the God of creation.

In sum, this second set of references to the created order — those not associated with creation traditions as such — in the XII most often occur linked with theophany or day of the Lord traditions. In that nexus, the created order is hardly permanent; it is subject to radical change. This picture of the orders of creation stands at considerable odds with that of the cosmos when it appears within the context of explicit creation traditions. Reflection about the created order can be subject to other powerful theological motifs as well, such as theophany and the day of the Lord.

III. Conclusions

We have discovered that the XII offers ambiguous testimony about the world in which humans live. Ancient Israelites apparently believed that their universe was one in which the heavens and the earth could shake, the mountains could melt away, and the whole earth could be consumed. Such language was at home in the theophanic day of the Lord traditions. There was, however, a counterpoise, namely, explicit creation traditions that bespoke the conviction of "eternal hills," heavenly vaults, Pleiades and Orion, the cycle of day to night, even the creation of a people, Israel. Though there might be "temporary" interruptions (e.g., a solar eclipse or exile of the people), these patterns of creation perdure. Creation traditions provide a check against the cosmic instability present in day of the Lord traditions. Together, these traditions emphasize the permanence but fragility of the created order. The God who creates can destroy. But at least according to the creation traditions in the XII, that destruction can only occur within certain fixed limits.

The Peaceable Kingdom and a Covenant with the Wild Animals

Gene M. Tucker

The most fundamental and dominant view of the world in the Hebrew Bible is that it is God's good creation. History is the sphere in which God and human beings live out their relationship with one another in ever new, always distinct events. But those events occur in place as well as in time. That place is the earth; all who live in it — plants, animals, and human beings — are creatures of God, who sustains them. Thus the Hebrew Scriptures teach its readers, as it taught ancient Israel, to love life, and that there could be no greater blessing than to live out one's life supported by the bounty of God's gifts, especially those of creation.

In his contribution to the recent *Interpretation* issue on "Theology and Ecology," Sibley Towner addressed what is doubtless one of the most difficult issues confronting the Old Testament's affirmation of the goodness of creation: the prophetic and apocalyptic visions of the transformation of that creation.[1] Towner recognized the problems raised by prophetic visions of the transformation of the relationship between human beings and the rest of God's creatures, particularly animals. Among the texts that he considered were Ezekiel 34:25-27; Hosea 2:18 [2:20]; and Isaiah 11:6-9. Although they have in common a vision of the alteration of the typical relationships between human beings and animals, and sometimes even among animals, there are significant differences. On the surface these texts

---

1. W. Sibley Towner, "The Future of Nature," *Int* 50 (1996): 27-35.

share some perspectives, but their differences are at least as important, particularly when one is concerned with their relationship to the biblical affirmation of the goodness of creation.

I. Isaiah 11:6-9

One of the best known of these texts is Isa. 11:6-9.

> The wolf shall live with the lamb,
>   the leopard shall lie down with the kid,
> the calf and the lion and the fatling together,
>   and a little child shall lead them. . . .
> The nursing child shall play over the hole of the asp,
>   and the weaned child shall put its hand on the adder's den.
> They will not hurt or destroy on all my holy mountain. (NRSV)

This is magnificent poetry, but it is not a poem. Nor is it typical prophetic address, for the usual formulas are missing and there is no direct address to an audience. Nonetheless, a prophetic voice speaks, referring to Yahweh in the third person and describing what the Lord will accomplish in the future. This is a promise, or a proclamation of salvation in two parts, the first concerning the messiah of the future or the ideal king (vv. 1-5), and the second concerning security in the animal world (vv. 6-9).

In the context of the announcement of a new Davidic king (11:1-5), verses 6-7 proclaim a dramatic change in the natural, cosmic sphere. Natural enemies in the animal world will live together in peace, even changing their diets. On the one hand, as so frequently shown in the prophetic literature, the poem stresses the relationship between justice, mercy, peace, and harmony in the natural order.[2] Who does not long for a world without fear and violence? On the other hand, the lines suggest that the world may have been created good, even very good, but not quite good enough. The text presumes a negative evaluation of the world as it is, filled with predators and prey, violence and death. One implication of the passage, to put it bluntly, is that there will be a time when the world will be made safe for domestic animals and children.[3] This is the vision of the peaceable kingdom.

2. Compare also, e.g., Hos. 1:8 and Ezek. 34:25.

3. Gene M. Tucker, "Rain on a Land Where No One Lives: The Hebrew Bible on the Environment," *JBL* 116 (1997): 11-12.

Like virtually all the other prophetic texts concerning the transformation of "natural" relationships in the world, this one is distinctly related to the establishment of justice and righteousness, and therefore of peace in the human realm, by means of a just ruler who is to come. It is not universally accepted that Isaiah 11:6-9 is original in terms of "authorship" or its relationship to the promise of the future messiah in 11:1-5.[4] The vision of the peaceable kingdom appears to have no integral connection with the announcement of the messiah. Only the juxtaposition of the verses indicates that the change in the animal kingdom is the result of the ascendancy of the new king. Ronald E. Clements, who takes the entire unit as later than the eighth century, seems to agree with those who conclude that vv. 6-9 were originally distinct from vv. 1-5. However, v. 9b ties the two parts of the announcement together: "for the earth shall be full of the knowledge of the Lord as the waters cover the sea," with the reference to "the knowledge of the Lord" picking up the expression "spirit of knowledge and the fear of the Lord" from v. 2. There is no good reason to treat 11:6-9 either as late or as separate from 11:1-5.[5] They are two parts of the same proclamation concerning the future reign of peace.

This conclusion is confirmed by consideration of the traditio-historical background of the unit. The vision of the peaceable kingdom in Isaiah is distinctly related to the promise of a Davidic messiah — referred to as a "shoot from the stump of Jesse" (v. 1) — and with that to the celebration of kingship in the Psalms (see especially Ps. 72) and the wider ancient Near Eastern tradition.[6]

In view of the comprehensive statement that closes the unit, it is common to conclude that this vision of the change in nature is cosmic, reaching to all creation. But there are two ways in which the scope of the vision is limited. First, it does not encompass all the animals, but only those of the land (not those of sea and air). And the distinction is between wild and domestic animals, with the concern for human security and peace. It is genuinely a "pastoral" concern for the safety of flocks for the sake of humankind. Second, while the "knowledge of God" will fill the earth (v. 9), it is only on "my holy mountain" that "they will not hurt or

4. Hans Wildberger has a list of those who take it as from Isaiah and those who do not and gives the arguments on both sides, concluding that it is Isaianic (*Isaiah 1–12: A Commentary,* trans. Thomas H. Trapp [Minneapolis: Fortress, 1991], pp. 465-66).

5. Ronald E. Clements, *Isaiah 1–39,* NCBC (Grand Rapids: Eerdmans, 1980), p. 112.

6. Wildberger, *Isaiah 1–12,* p. 469.

destroy" (v. 9). Certainly this mountain is Zion. Even if — as seems likely — the mountain stands for the whole of the land of Israel,[7] the envisioned peaceable kingdom is a particular sacred territory and not the whole earth.

Is the prophecy realistic in the sense that its composer expected it to be fulfilled within imminent history? There has been considerable disagreement on this question with regard to the promise of an ideal king (vv. 1-5). Some commentators have argued that this vision, like the one in 9:1-7, is to be related either to the inauguration of an actual king in the time of Isaiah (such as Hezekiah) or to the time of a future king (such as Josiah).[8] Such readings thus take at least vv. 1-5 as connected to actual expectations for the king, even if they were not realized. Others, such as Hans Wildberger, see the promise as related to the prophet Isaiah's disappointment with Hezekiah and his vision for a king in some unspecified future who would embody the Davidic royal ideal.[9] Those commentators who take it to be exilic or postexilic tend to see the promise as an unrealistic hope for the revival of the Davidic monarchy.

Christopher Seitz talks of this transformation of natural relationships in the animal world as mythological, and he gives a fundamentally allegorical reading: the animals are the military powers warring with one another and the vision is one of international peace.[10] Such a reading is hardly justified, however. Isaiah 1–39 does not exhibit this type of broad allegory. When the prophetic voice speaks "symbolically," it is in terms of specific metaphors, and they are never so enigmatic as to identify particular animals with nations without explanation. Typical of the poetry of Isaiah is the "Song of the Vineyard" (5:1-7), in which the concluding interpretation makes clear that the vineyard, whose owner is Yahweh, is the house of Israel and the people of Judah.

While the first part of the promise (vv. 1-5) draws out the implications of the Davidic tradition, the second part (vv. 6-9) depends upon the Zion tradition. Both are central in the thought of Isaiah of Jerusalem. Verses 6-9 recall the vision of the world peace in Isaiah 2:2-5 and its parallel in Micah 4:1-5. Hans Wildberger concludes that Isaiah 11:6-8 is "a de-

---

7. Clements, *Isaiah 1–39*, p. 124.

8. Marvin A. Sweeney, *Isaiah 1–39, With an Introduction to Prophetic Literature*, FOTL 16 (Grand Rapids: Eerdmans, 1996), pp. 196-217.

9. Wildberger, *Isaiah 1–12*, p. 469.

10. Christopher R. Seitz, *Isaiah 1–39*, IntBC (Louisville: John Knox, 1993), pp. 106-7.

11. Wildberger, *Isaiah 1–12*, p. 483.

piction which uses the vocabulary of the paradise myth to announce the radical conquest of evil and injustice."[11] However, this picture of nonviolence among the animals goes far beyond any paradise as characterized in the creation stories of the Hebrew Scriptures. There is, to be sure, no explicit criticism of the world as it is, but the imagery is employed to characterize peace and security under the ideal ruler. In its context, the envisioned future is within history and falls short of an apocalyptic transformation of the world. However, the prophecy of the peaceable kingdom clearly is an expectation that could not be fulfilled within the framework of creation.

II. Hosea 2:18 [2:20]

Within the context of the renewal of the relationship between Yahweh and Israel, we find in this verse the announcement of an almost unexpected covenant:

> I will make for you [Hebrew "them"][12] a covenant on that day with the wild animals, the birds of the air, and the creeping things of the ground; I will abolish the bow, the sword, and war from the land; and I will make you lie down in safety. (NRSV)

What is this covenant? What does a covenant with the wild animals, the birds, and the creeping things of the ground entail? Some commentators suggest that this is a covenant for the end time and that it entails a radical transformation in what we, in our time, would call natural relationships. Accordingly, the covenant is supposed to establish a new world order for the relationship between dangerous animals and human beings, so that the envisioned future will see an end to violence among all living creatures. Although qualifying the interpretation in some of its details, Hans Walter Wolff suggests that this covenant is virtually a cosmic return to a primeval time:

12. The alternation of the pronouns in this section of Hosea is not unusual and probably reflects the process of compiling originally distinct announcements and promises into their present form. In context there can be little doubt that the prophetic speech has the people of Israel in view, whether in direct address or in the third person.

[I]t involves a mediation of peace between Israel and the estranged animal kingdom (cf. Gen. 3:15). Yahweh proves his covenant loyalty toward Israel by mediating a covenant between opposing forces within creation (cf. Ezek. 34:25-30; Gen. 9:8-17). The three phrases naming the animals recall Gen. 1:30, where they and mankind are placed under the same divine regulation concerning food.[13]

Francis I. Andersen and David Noel Freedman see here an even more dramatic change, calling Hosea 2:18-23 [2:20-25] a "little apocalypse." They say: "The vision of the transformation of nature and achievement of universal harmony is unified by the eschatological frame of reference. . . ."[14] And further, "the cosmic scope of Hos. 2:16-25 is unmistakable; it includes an eschatological vision not unlike that of Isaiah (11:6-9; 35:9)."[15]

But it is by no means self-evident that this is a renewal or restoration of an original paradise or that its scope is cosmic, even if one should conclude that it is eschatological, more apocalyptic than prophetic. It is not even clear that Hosea 2:18 [2:20] suggests there will be no killing of animals in the age of this new covenant. This verse needs to be examined in the broader context, including Hosea 4:11-13, as well as in light of other biblical covenants and, particularly, the understanding of animals in the Hebrew Scriptures.

The announcement of the covenant with the animals is part of the fourth of five units that make up Hosea 1-3. Two narratives (1:2-9 and 3:1-5) concerning Hosea's wife and children frame three prophetic addresses: 1:10–2:1 reverses the symbolic announcement of judgment in the initial narrative; in 2:2-15 [2:4-17] Israel as Yahweh's wife is on trial; and in 2:16-23 [2:20-25] there is the announcement of a new covenant. Throughout these chapters the movement is from sin and accusation, to indictment and judgment, to renewal through purchase and purging, and, finally, to announcement of salvation. It is clear that this sequence articulates the theology of only the final editors of the section. Whether or not Hosea himself saw history unfolding in such an order is uncertain.

13. Hans Walter Wolff, *Hosea: A Commentary on the Book of the Prophet Hosea*, trans. Gary Stansell, Hermeneia (Philadelphia: Fortress, 1974), pp. 50-51.

14. Francis I. Andersen and David Noel Freedman, *Hosea: A New Translation with Introduction and Commentary,* AB 24 (New York: Doubleday, 1980), p. 277.

15. Andersen and Freedman, *Hosea,* p. 281.

The unit in question (2:16-23 [2:18-25]) consists of two parts, marked by the formula "On that day" (vv. 16, 21 [vv. 18, 23]). The section picks up and expands the announcement of salvation that concludes the previous unit, an announcement of a renewed relationship between Yahweh and Israel that entails a productive and supportive environment (2:14-15 [2:16-17]). The central proclamation of 2:16-23 is Yahweh's announcement of the covenantal renewal with Israel, characterized in the preceding units as having been broken. These verses combine the traditional language of the covenant with the distinctive vocabulary of love to characterize the promised relationship between the Lord and Israel. Remarkable human analogies ("My husband") point to the depth and intimacy of the love between God and the people. The new covenant will be so broad as to include all living things, and so deep as to establish righteousness and justice. The Lord will take the initiative, thus enabling the people to "know" him. As in Isaiah 11:1-9, the establishment of justice brings both peace and security, and a new relationship between animals and human beings corresponds to peace among human beings.

But the promise of a covenant with the animals in Hosea is distinctly unrelated to the traditions that are foundational to the thought of Isaiah. In Isaiah, the David and Zion traditions form the basis for the vision of the future. Hosea knows neither of these traditions but lives and breathes the air of the Exodus and the subsequent covenant between Yahweh and Israel.

As Hans Walter Wolff points out, "covenant" is used variously in Hosea.[16] The same expression used in 2:18 [2:20] *(kārat běrît)* refers in 12:1 and 10:4 to the establishment of a treaty between Israel and another nation.[17] In 6:7 Israel is accused of transgressing the covenant with Yahweh. Similarly, according to 8:1, "one like a vulture is over the house of the Lord, because they have broken my covenant, and transgressed my law." To say that "covenant" here means "law" in general would be going too far. The accusation is that Israel has not kept its side of the covenant, not followed certain attendant stipulations. And beyond the explicit use of the word, the covenant tradition is reflected in other ways in Hosea, including the allusion in 4:2 to five out of the ten commandments.

Moreover, the unit (4:1-3) that alludes to these laws has a direct bear-

16. Wolff, *Hosea*, p. 48.

17. James L. Mays, *Hosea: A Commentary,* OTL (Philadelphia: Westminster, 1969), p. 49.

ing on the understanding of the covenant with the animals in Hosea 2:18 [2:20]). In that address, which is an indictment of Israel, the "inhabitants of the land" are accused of disloyalty to the covenant with Yahweh (4:1b): "There is no faithfulness or loyalty, and no knowledge of God in the land." Not only is this the language for the covenant relationship, this same language spells out the characteristics of the future covenant announced in 2:17-18 [2:19-20]. The result of this failure are specific crimes of neighbor against neighbor (4:2), and what follows is the desolation of the land and "all who live in it," including "wild animals," the "birds of the air," and the "fish of the sea." This, too, is a close, albeit inexact, parallel to the creatures with whom a covenant will be established in 2:18 [2:20]. Disruption of the covenant with Yahweh leads to the destruction of all living creatures. Consequently, renewal of the covenant with Yahweh entails the restoration of harmony between human beings and nonhuman life, described in 2:18 [2:20] as a covenant.

Such an understanding of the implications of covenant faithfulness for the relationship with the rest of creation runs deep in Israel's traditions. A close parallel that relates the concern with wild animals to peace as well as covenant and obligations is found in Leviticus 26: Yahweh promises, "And I will grant peace in the land, and you shall lie down, and no one shall make you afraid; I will remove dangerous animals from the land, and no sword shall go through your land" (v. 6). The promise continues, "and I will maintain my covenant with you" (v. 9). The other side of the covenant, the penalties for failure to be faithful, include: "I will let loose wild animals against you, and they shall bereave you of your children and destroy your livestock; they shall make you few in number, and your roads shall be deserted" (v. 22).

The Hebrew Scriptures typically distinguish between domestic and wild animals. The animals that dominate the biblical tradition are domestic, living creatures that are owned by and serve human masters. The wild animals are beyond the fringe of culture, for the most part symbolizing danger and destruction.[18] Thus, in prophetic texts wild animals often are instruments of or involved in divinely instigated punishment. The oracle concerning Babylon in Isaiah 13 is the reverse of the promise in Hosea 2:18 [2:20]. Here judgment is proclaimed over Babylon in terms that approach

18. Tucker, "Rain on a Land Where No One Lives," pp. 10-11. In only two texts, Job 38–39 and Ps. 104, are the wild creatures viewed with unambiguous admiration.

but fall short of a cosmic, apocalyptic judgment.[19] The announced desolation is not the pre-creation chaos but a return to the "chaotic" state of the uncultivated and uncultured land (Isa. 13:20-22):

> It [Babylon] will never be inhabited
> or lived in for all generations;
> Arabs will not pitch their tents there,
> shepherds will not make their flocks lie down there.
> But wild animals will lie down there,
> and its houses will be full of howling creatures;
> there ostriches will live,
> and there goat-demons will dance.
> Hyenas will cry in its towers,
> and jackals in the pleasant palaces;
> its time is close at hand,
> and its days will not be prolonged. (NRSV)

We may now return to the question of the meaning of the covenant with the animals in Hosea 2:18 [2:20]. Seen in its context in Hosea 2, it is clear that this promise does not entail the transformation of the relationships between human beings and wild animals. Rather, 2:18 [2:20] is the antithesis of the announcement of judgment in Hosea 2:10-13 [2:12-15]. In v. 12 [v. 14] wild animals are turned loose on the cultivated vines and fig trees; judgment is the destruction of supportive (agri)culture, the return of the land to the status of a wilderness. As James L. Mays points out, "The covenant reverses the role of the beasts as the instrument of judgment (2:12)."[20] Consequently, the promised transformation in Hosea 2 — and in other texts as well — is not a return to paradise but a return to culture and fruitful nature, to the way humans have come to live in positive relationship with the rest of creation. The covenant with the animals in Hosea 2 is not a part of the Urzeit/Endzeit pattern, with its mythological background; animals do not become something they have not been. In the con-

19. Isaiah 13 is a composition that includes features that are proto-apocalyptic in their expectations as well as more specifically historical-prophetic announcements. Otto Kaiser (*Isaiah 13–39: A Commentary,* trans. Robert A. Wilson, OTL [Philadelphia: Westminster, 1974], pp. 8-9, 21-23) points out that the chapter combines a universal with a particular expectation of judgment. The verses in question (vv. 19-22) specifically concern the historical Babylon.

20. Mays, *Hosea,* p. 49.

text, where just before they had been turned loose to destroy, this is rather a return to the situation before the judgment. As in Leviticus 26:6, it is a blessing of the covenant that the people will live in their land without fear of wild animals. So this covenant does something to the behavior of the animals for the sake of human beings. But nature is not transformed. It had been an instrument of punishment, and now it is a vehicle of salvation. Thus the promise of protection from wild animals is part of that vision of abundance in v. 22 [v. 24]: "the earth shall answer the grain, the wine, and the oil. . . ."

This covenant is quite without parallel elsewhere in the Hebrew Bible. This is not the covenant between Yahweh and Israel, but rather Yahweh establishes or mediates a covenant between two other parties, Israel and the wild animals, the birds of the air, and the creeping things of the ground.[21] The alternative view of Francis I. Andersen and David Noel Freedman — that we have here a covenant between Yahweh and the animals for the benefit of "them" — is difficult to justify.[22] To be sure, Yahweh is, as they argue, asserting divine power over all creation, but as the one who establishes a covenant between Israel and the nondomesticated creatures.

The covenant in Hosea 2 recalls, but does not seem to reflect, Priestly traditions in Genesis. In Hosea the promise concerns wild animals of the land, birds of the air, and "creeping things of the ground." Genesis 1 includes the creatures of the water and those of the land, including the domestic animals (1:24). This suggests the possibility that God's promise in Hosea entails only those creatures that pose a threat. Wild animals and reptiles certainly fit that picture, as do other creeping things, but birds as well can pose a threat to human agriculture. Moreover, birds often are listed among the threats to human life: "And I will appoint over them four kinds of destroyers, says the LORD: the sword to kill, the dogs to drag away, and the birds of the air and the wild animals of the earth to devour and destroy" (Jer. 15:3).[23]

The covenant following the flood (Gen. 9:8-11) concerns the same three parties identified in Hosea: God, animals, and human beings.[24] On

---

21. Wolff, *Hosea*, pp. 280-81.
22. Andersen and Freedman, *Hosea*, p. 281.
23. See also Ezek. 5:17; Deut. 28:26; Isa. 18:6.
24. Compare Andersen and Freedman, *Hosea*, p. 281.

the one hand, it includes the divine promise never again to destroy the world; on the other hand, it allows human beings to kill and eat animals, establishing human dominion over other creatures. Nothing in Hosea 2 explicitly contradicts such an understanding of the relationship between human beings and other living things.

III. Conclusions

Isaiah 11:6-9 and Hosea 2:18 [2:20] articulate distinct visions of the future with regard to the relationship between human beings and animals. That they are different in important respects suggests that similar prophetic announcements, commonly taken to be promises of the transformation of the world, should be reexamined closely. There has been a tendency to read these and similar texts as announcements concerning the end times, but both of them stop short of an apocalyptic transformation that presupposes the possibility of rejection of the world as created. Rather, they look either to the restoration of a prejudgment state of the relationship with creation or to an ideal world ruled by a divinely ordained king. The alternatives are neither a corrupt world nor a promise to a return to a primordial paradise. Rather, they are nature and culture, in which a return to an uncultured state of the world, with unrestrained wild animals and unproductive land, is a curse, and a productive, safe, and secure place for human beings within the world is a blessing. It is important to emphasize that the promise of a peaceful relationship between humanity and other creatures is an extension of the establishment of justice and righteousness among human beings and of a faithful relationship of people to God.

Consequently, Sibley Towner's assessment is on target: "The biblical pictures of nature in the future function as incitements toward a style of ethical living in the present that is holistic, interdependent, non-hierarchical, and one that does not reject flesh and matter as corrupt because God does not reject them."[25]

---

25. Towner, "The Future of Nature," p. 33.

NEW TESTAMENT

"Creation Waits with Eager Longing"

David L. Bartlett

In his careful and helpful study, *How God Deals with Evil*, Sibley Towner points to a tension in Paul's understanding of the created order and its redemption.

> First, *Paul cannot be called a straightforward and consistent universalist in his eschatological expectation. . . .* [H]e considered judgment and the destruction of evil to be a given and essential part of both the present and future activity of God. Second, *the epistles nonetheless contain inescapable evidences that Paul could conceive of the ultimate redemption of the entire universe, and that because of the utterly new situation created by the New Adam.*[1]

I think that Towner is right that the tension in Paul's writing is inescapable, but in this essay I will look at the second pole of the tension — that strain in Paul's writing suggesting that in Jesus Christ God works toward the redemption of the whole cosmos. Paul most consistently addresses this issue through the motif of new creation, and a look at that motif in his writings may help us to understand further the radical implications not only for his

---

1. W. Sibley Towner, *How God Deals with Evil* (Philadelphia: Westminster, 1976), pp. 132-33.

Scripture quotations in this essay are taken from the NRSV, occasionally with slight modifications.

understanding of redemption but also for his understanding of the ethics of the Christian life and of the nature and mission of the church.

I. 2 Corinthians

The appropriate starting point for understanding some of the nuances of Paul's proclamation of the new creation is the familiar passage in 2 Corinthians 5:16-21:

> From now on, therefore, we regard no one from a human point of view; even though we once knew Christ from a human point of view, we know him no longer in that way. So if anyone is in Christ, there is a new creation: everything old has passed away; see, everything has become new! All this is from God who reconciled us to himself through Christ, and has given us the ministry of reconciliation; that is, in Christ God was reconciling the world to himself, not counting their trespasses against them, and entrusting the message of reconciliation to us. So we are ambassadors for Christ, since God is making his appeal through us; we entreat you on behalf of Christ, be reconciled to God. For our sake he made him to be sin who knew no sin, so that in him we might become the righteousness of God.

In 2 Corinthians Paul is defending his ministry against charges that he is not equal to other apostles who have come after him and preached their own version of the gospel to the Corinthian Christians. Apart from what Paul considers a too high view of the "super" apostles, we are not sure about the content of this competing gospel. But the content of Paul's gospel is clear enough: God in Christ reconciles the world to his own self. Right ministers are those who pronounce that word, as ambassadors declare the message of the monarch who commissions them.

One way to talk about the content of this message, with which Paul and other true apostles are entrusted, is to say that it is the message of new creation. The "old" RSV and the NRSV translate 2 Corinthians 5:17 rather differently: "Therefore if anyone is in Christ, he is a new creation; the old has passed away, behold the new has come" (RSV); "So if anyone is in Christ, there is a new creation; everything old has passed away; see, everything has become new!" (NRSV). Though either translation is possible in the Greek, the larger context of the paragraph and the chapter suggests that the NRSV is closer to Paul's thought. What Paul proclaims is not just the individual reconciled to God — an individual who is a new creation. What Paul proclaims is the world reconciled to God — a cosmos created anew.[2] Indeed, even the NRSV may underplay the nuance of delight and surprise with which Paul declares his good news. A more wooden but perhaps vivid translation is: "Therefore if anyone is in Christ — new creation!" It's rather like saying: "Therefore if anyone is in Christ — Christmas morning!" The sentence is not so much descriptive as exclamatory. The imperative that follows close upon this phrase underlines the exclamatory mode: "See! Everything has become new."

Paul's claims about new creation move beyond the personal toward the universal but do not (yet) represent a claim that God's redemption includes the whole universe. It is not just that the believer is a new creation, but that the believer confronts a new creation, larger and more intransigent than the simple self.

Yet even this does not point all the way toward a universal view of redemption. On the one hand, there is the universal claim: "God in Christ was reconciling the world to himself." The world here is understood not as the whole universe of created things, but as the human world. When God reconciles the world, God "does not count their trespasses against them."[3] So what is here redeemed in Jesus Christ is the world of persons — those who are capable of sinning and capable, too, of having amnesty declared on their sins. The scope of the new creation is apparently limited further. Either it is only those who are "in Christ" who partake of the new creation, or it is only those "in Christ" who recognize the new creation whose scope in fact includes all of humankind. Paul does not use the term "Christian" for the believers to whom he writes; the most usual phrase for believers is those who are "in Christ." The phrase may have deeper and richer meanings than "Christian," but it at least means that. "For Christians, there is a new creation."

One suspects that for Paul the scope of "new creation" is limited in 2 Corinthians because here he writes of the new creation as a present reality. In the same world where God creates anew, many refuse to believe in

2. For a discussion of the proper translation of the verse, see Victor Paul Furnish, *II Corinthians*, AB 32A (Garden City, NY: Doubleday, 1984), pp. 314-15. Furnish also provides on these pages a list of some of the uses of the phrase "new creation" in apocalyptic Judaism.

3. Though Furnish thinks that here, already, "new creation" refers to the whole cosmos (*II Corinthians*, p. 314).

the gospel and others set out to follow the false "super" apostles. It may be that for Paul new creation is both a gift and a promise. In 2 Corinthians he emphasizes the gift, which is as yet incomplete. For the shape of the promise we will need to look elsewhere in Paul's writings.

In each case where Paul writes about creation and new creation, he appears to be interpreting the story of creation in Genesis. Behind the proclamations there is an implicit narrative (more explicit in Romans). The narrative has at least these four acts.

Act One: God creates the world as good.
Act Two: Sin mars God's good creation.
Act Three: God acts in Jesus Christ to redeem the world.
Act Four: The lost good of creation is (will be) restored — purer and brighter than before.

Act One. In each "new creation" passage Paul suggests the shape of the good that God created; at the very least it is implied by the shape of the good that typifies the new creation. In 2 Corinthians 5, what marks the new creation is the fact that people — at the very least believing people — are reconciled to God. Without much stretch of the imagination one can read this as Paul's gloss on Genesis 2, when Adam and Eve lived in the garden unafraid of God and unashamed before one another.

Act Two. In this passage sin is defined as trespass, stepping out of bounds. Surely this is a gloss on Genesis 3, where the man and the woman overstepped the fence God built around the tree in the middle of the garden. From that day until almost the moment Paul writes his letter, God has counted that trespass against all of humankind.

Act Three. For Paul, God overcomes the sin always and only through Jesus Christ. In a multitude of passages that good news is declared in a multitude of ways. Here are the packed, complex, affirmations of 2 Corinthians 5:21: "The one who knew no sin, for our sake God made into sin itself, in order that in him we might become God's righteousness." There is a switch. Righteous Christ turns into sin; sinful humankind turns righteous. New creation is more astonishing than the first creation. Now it is not innocent humankind created out of dust but righteous humankind created out of sinners. Christmas morning.

Act Four. What does new creation look like? It looks like old creation, only more so. It is not just innocence; it is righteousness. It is not just peace; it is reconciliation, peace bought at a price. It's like coming home after a journey to a far country, or as T. S. Eliot says of the sacred journey, "the end of all our exploring/Will be to arrive where we started/And know the place for the first time."[4]

Because it deals with the present, not yet complete reconciliation of humankind, the reconciliation of humankind and not of the universe, and because it is evident only to those who are "in Christ," the new creation of 2 Corinthians 5 does not entirely move toward the pole of new creation as the redemption of all that God has created. This passage is, however, a long way from the individual pietism implied by the older translation: "If anyone is in Christ, he is a new creation."

As in each of the other passages on new creation, this word on reconciliation has implications for the life of the church and its mission in the world. When Paul tells the Corinthians that God has "entrusted the message of reconciliation to us," he means first of all that God has entrusted the message of reconciliation to Paul and the apostles who share his understanding of the gospel. But he also means that God has entrusted the message of reconciliation to the church. To be the church is to be the community that knows that trespasses are no longer counted against it and that it is reconciled to God through Christ. To be the church is also to be the ones who bring that message to those who do not yet believe.

II. Galatians

A much briefer reference to "new creation" is found in Paul's letter to the Galatians. In some ways we are clearer on the context of this letter than we are on the context of 2 Corinthians.

Again, as in Corinth, other preachers have arrived among the Galatian churches after Paul, and they are preaching what he calls a "different" or "alien" gospel, a gospel which is not really good news (Gal. 1:6-7). We are not sure what theological principles these Christians espouse, but we know what practice they are imposing. They want to insist that male Gentile believers submit to circumcision, and there is some evidence that they are citing the so-called pillars of the Jerusalem Church, that is, Peter and Jesus' brother

---

4. T. S. Eliot, *The Four Quartets,* in *The Complete Poems and Plays of T. S. Eliot* (New York: Harcourt, Brace & World, 1962), p. 145.

James, to make their case. Paul tells them that if they are to take on the requirement of circumcision, they are obligated to take on the whole law. But in the light of God's action in Jesus Christ believers no longer live under the law. The letter reaches its climax in Paul's ringing affirmation:

> For freedom Christ has set us free. Stand firm, therefore, and do not submit again to a yoke of slavery. Listen! I, Paul, am telling you that if you let yourselves be circumcised, Christ will be of no benefit to you. Once again I testify to every man who lets himself be circumcised that he is obliged to obey the entire law. You who want to be justified by the law have cut yourselves off from Christ; you have fallen away from grace. For through the Spirit, by faith, we eagerly wait for the hope of righteousness. For in Christ Jesus neither circumcision nor uncircumcision counts for anything; the only thing that counts is faith working through love. (Gal. 5:1-6)

The last verse corresponds almost exactly to the claim Paul makes about new creation in the final exhortation of the letter: "For neither is circumcision anything, nor uncircumcision, but new creation" (Gal. 6:15).

We hear Paul wrongly if we imagine him sitting there with a first-century Greek thesaurus finding equivalent expressions for the claim he wants to make about a circumcision-free community: new creation is not simply equivalent to faith working through love. But in the larger context of the epistle the two phrases are certainly congruent; the one illumines the other.

In his commentary on Galatians Hans Dieter Betz suggests that the Galatian Christians must have known just what Paul meant by "new creation" because he alludes to it here so briefly but does so in such a way that he seems to think it proves his case.[5] To be sure, the phrase is not elaborated upon here as it is in 2 Corinthians, but we can detect behind the phrase another interpretation on creation not unlike the interpretation in 2 Corinthians.

Act One. God creates the world as good. In Galatians we can assume from the description of the new creation that the first creation was marked by the absence of any distinction between circumcision and uncircumcision. Circumcision is a mark of life after the garden; it does not belong to the original good order of creation.

---

5. Hans Dieter Betz, *Galatians* (Philadelphia: Fortress, 1979), p. 319 n. 79. The discussion on pp. 310-19 helpfully sets the Galatians passage in the larger context of Pauline themes.

It needs to be noted that this is a minor theme in Galatians. In Galatians Paul makes something of the same point by insisting that circumcision belongs to the law, and that the law is later than Abraham. For Abraham in Genesis 15:6 it was faith, not law keeping or circumcision, that was counted as righteousness. The contrast between Abraham and the law with its attendant circumcision is much more central to Galatians than the contrast between creation and the law.

However, two other passages may also help us imagine Paul's vision of the creation that has been restored in Jesus Christ. We have already seen that Galatians 5:6 is in many ways parallel to Galatians 6:15. What counts is not circumcision or uncircumcision but new creation (6:15), not circumcision or uncircumcision but faith working through love (5:6). Perhaps "faith working through love" is another way of reading the gifts of the original creation. As in 2 Corinthians, Paul sees Adam and Eve as being close to God before their trespass estranged them, so here perhaps the first days of creation are days of faith (the man and the woman walk with God). They are also days of love (the man and the woman dwell together naked and unashamed). Faith is violated when the man and the woman disobey. Love is violated when they turn away from each other in shame and anger.

Galatians 3:28 is probably a baptismal formula, or so the introduction in 3:27 would suggest. Yet implicit in the formula is the vision of a restored creation: "There is no longer Jew or Greek (that is, circumcised or uncircumcised), there is no longer slave or free, there is no longer male and female; for all of you are one in Christ Jesus." If (as in Romans and 1 Corinthians) Christ is implicitly the new Adam who includes all of humankind in himself, then in him (as in the first Adam) all of humankind is one. In Galatians 4 the immediate move is to Abraham, and the unity that all Christians have in him through the promise of faith. Abraham's faith is the main theme; creation and our unity in Adam comprise the minor, but no less important, theme.

Act Two. Sin mars God's good creation. Here what mars the creation with its freedom from distinction between the circumcised and the uncircumcised is not so much sin as the law. The law, of course, is intimately related to sin: "Why then the law? It was added because of transgressions" (Gal. 3:19a); "But the scripture imprisoned all things under the power of sin" (Gal. 3:22a). For Paul humankind was twice imprisoned. We were imprisoned by sin, and we were imprisoned by the law. Sin bound us because it did harm. Law bound us because it could not do the good we craved and needed; it could not free us from sin.

Act Three. God acts in Christ to free the world. If we are twice imprisoned then in Christ we are freed twice over. In Christ faith overcomes the bondage of sin: "But the scripture has imprisoned all things under the power of sin, so that what was promised through faith in Jesus Christ might be given to those who believe" (Gal. 3:22). In Christ God overcomes human bondage to the law.

> Christ redeemed us from the curse of the law by becoming a curse for us — for it is written, "Cursed is everyone who hangs on a tree" — in order that in Christ Jesus the blessing of Abraham might come to the Gentiles, so that we might receive the promise of the Spirit through faith. (Gal. 3:13-14)

Note how close this is to the claim of 2 Corinthians 5:21: "God made him to be sin who knew no sin," so that we might be righteous. Here God curses him who deserved no curse so that we might be blessed. Paul develops no full doctrine of substitutionary atonement, but again and again there is an image of Christ bearing what he did not deserve so that God might give us what we did not deserve either — abundant mercy, lasting grace.

Act Four. The lost good of creation is restored, brighter and purer than before. Christians are returned to the time when there is neither slave nor free, male nor female — and especially in this context, no Jew or Greek, no distinction between circumcised and uncircumcised, no advantage to being circumcised. Christians are one in the second Adam as all creation was one in the first Adam. But now humans are not only God's creatures but God's children — adopted in the second Adam to become part of Christ's own family, through God's own Son made sons and daughters of God: "But when the fullness of time had come, God sent his Son, born of a woman, born under the law, in order to redeem those who were under the law, so that we might receive adoption as children" (Gal. 4:4-5).

In Galatians there is yet another way to distinguish between the old that is passing away and the new creation that has come. The old was the age of the flesh; the new is the age of the Spirit. That sin and the law of circumcision belong to the flesh is clear enough literally as well as metaphorically. Does Paul also remember the Spirit over the face of the deep at the beginning of creation? Did the Spirit leave for the long years in between, the years of sin and law, to return with Christ who gives the Spirit to those who believe? This is to wonder more than we can know (see Gal. 5:6).[6]

As Hans Dieter Betz notes, we notice that in Galatians 6:15-16 Paul draws the implications of his call to the new creation: "For neither circumcision nor uncircumcision is anything; but a new creation is everything! As for those who will follow this rule — peace be upon them, and mercy, and upon the Israel of God." New creation is not only a description, not only the good news and surprise of 2 Corinthians, it is now the rule — the canon — by which believers live. What kind of canon? Surely it is a rule to be distinguished from the law. The law divides; the new creation unites. The law curses; the new creation blesses. Perhaps it is the canon hinted at by Galatians 5:6, which closely corresponds to Galatians 6:15. In new creation faith works through love. Faith provides access to the righteousness we have in Christ; love works out that righteousness in right relationships with our brothers and sisters.

In Galatians, how universal is this new creation? Again it is a reality for humans and among humans, for believers. If it is the firstfruits of a renewed cosmos, we do not know that from what Paul tells us in this letter. Perhaps in other sermons he told the Galatians that second Adam restores what first Adam marred, that one day God will be everything to everyone. But we do not hear that sermon in this letter. Perhaps Paul is too busy trying to restore new creation in Galatia to envision new creation for the whole world.

The image of the new creation has implications for the life of the church. A church that lives under the new creation is not divided by the distinctions between male and female or between slave and free. The issue that Paul addresses, however, is not simply that circumcised people are claiming to be truer believers than uncircumcised people; it is that circumcised men are trying to persuade the uncircumcised that they should be circumcised too. If the Galatians only realized that their relationship to God is received through faith and not through circumcision or any other pious act, the circumcised would not feel compelled to bolster their own self-confidence by forcing other people to be like themselves (see Gal.

---

6. Paul also draws the contrast between seeing the world according to the flesh and seeing the world in some other way, presumably according to the Spirit, when he writes of new creation in 2 Corinthians. See Gal. 5:16.

5:26). The uncircumcised would not have to strengthen their case for inclusion in God's people by adding on this other, extraneous rite. The congregation would live by faith, and faith would work, not through psychological coercion, but through love. The congregation would not live by the flesh (worrying about such fleshly matters as the foreskin) but by the Spirit, with "love, joy, patience, kindness, generosity, faithfulness, gentleness and self-control" (Gal. 5:22-23).

III. Romans

Perhaps in Romans we do get the kind of theology that provides the basis for his message in Galatians. Certainly Paul cannot here assume that the Roman Christians know "his" gospel, because he has not yet visited them. He writes this letter to prepare them for his coming visit, establishing his right to speak to them and the righteousness of what he has to say.

As in Galatians, one of the great issues that Paul addresses in Romans is the way in which God deals with Gentiles as well as Jews. Whether or not Paul's gospel turns out to provide a universal promise of redemption, it certainly provides a universal opportunity: an opportunity that transcends the barriers between Jews and Gentiles. In Jesus Christ the one God who created all people offers all people justification, a right relationship with God. Because justification must be a possibility for all people (since God is the God of all), justification cannot be provided through the law, because the law is God's gift to Israel alone. Justification comes through faith, faith that is available to every human being, Jew and Gentile alike.

The first three chapters of Romans exhibit two interlocking motifs. First, every human being is in need of being made right with God. Second, every human being has access to that righteousness through Jesus Christ.

> For there is no distinction, since all have sinned and fall short of the glory of God; they are now justified by his grace as a gift, through the redemption that is in Christ Jesus, whom God put forward as a sacrifice of atonement by his blood, effective through faith. (Rom. 3:22b-25a)

While in Galatians the debate seems to be whether Gentiles can be redeemed apart from obedience to the Jewish law, a debate between Pauline Christians and Judaizers, in Romans the issue is that of the relationship between Jews and Gentiles in the community of faith and in God's plan of redemption. As in Galatians the great exemplar of the justification that comes from faith is Abraham. Those who follow Christ, Jews and Gentiles alike, are children of Abraham, because, like Abraham, they trust in God, and that trust counts as their righteousness (Rom. 4).

What is only hinted at in Galatians 6:15 now becomes the theme of a major section of the epistle to the Romans (chs. 5–8), the new creation made available in Jesus Christ. In Galatians the phrase "new creation" is without much supporting theological framework. Romans provides the framework, but Paul never uses the exact phrase.

Romans 5–8 has a kind of circular structure; it begins and ends with Paul's claims about creation and new creation. In the middle Paul addresses an imagined objector who is particularly concerned with the role of law in this new world that Paul proclaims. Both chapters 5 and 8 push the image of redemption beyond the redemption of the individual and even beyond the redemption of Christian believers toward a more universal promise. Romans 5 deals with the creation and re-creation of humankind. Romans 8 builds on that and pushes even further to the creation and re-creation of the whole cosmos.

Again both the claims of Romans 5 and the claims of Romans 8 can be seen as growing out of Paul's reading of the creation story in Genesis and of the great redemptive drama that follows. We look first at that drama as it is understood in Romans 5.

Act One. God creates the world as good. This is only implicit in Romans 5, but it is explicit in the larger argument of Romans. In Romans 1 the creation is a manifestation not only of its own goodness but of the very majesty of God: "Ever since the creation of the world [God's] eternal power and divine nature, invisible though they are, have been understood and seen through the things [God] has made" (Rom. 1:20a).

Act Two. Sin mars God's good creation. The sin to which Romans 5 refers is the sin of Adam, the disobedient eating of the fruit. Even though those who follow Adam may disobey God in different ways — breaking different commandments — all of them have followed the tragic pattern that he set; all trespass the boundaries God has ordained.

Furthermore sin brings with it the terrible consequence, death. Just as every human being sins, so every human being is subject to death. All are mortal as Adam was mortal. Here surely Paul reads Genesis 2:15-17:

The Lord God took the man and put him in the garden of Eden to till it and keep it. And the Lord God commanded the man, "You may freely eat of every tree of the garden; but of the tree of the knowledge of good and evil you shall not eat, for in the day that you eat of it you shall die."

Paul reads this as the writers of Genesis must have intended it, not as God's promise that within twenty-four hours of eating the fruit Adam will die, but as God's promise that, having eaten of the fruit, Adam will be subject to death, mortal. Paul's words to the Romans provide his reading of the Genesis text and its universal significance:

> Therefore, just as sin came into the world through one man, and death came through sin, and so death spread to all because all have sinned — sin was indeed in the world before the law, but sin is not reckoned when there is no law. Yet death exercised dominion from Adam to Moses, even over those whose sins were not like the transgression of Adam, who is a type of the one who was to come. (Rom. 5:12-14)

Act Three. God acts in Jesus Christ to redeem the world. In 2 Corinthians and Galatians God's act in Jesus Christ is explicitly identified with the cross. Here the identification is more implicit, but any reading of Paul's letters will indicate that it is the cross where Jesus Christ acts out his full obedience to God. So Adam's disobedience is countered by Christ's obedience; the loss in the garden is trumped by the loss, the gain, of the cross.

Act Four. The lost good of creation is (will be) restored, deeper and richer than before. Again the language is not the language of innocence or purity, but the language of justification and life. The new creation is even richer than the old, because in it the power of sin and death is not simply evaded, it is conquered. "But the free gift is not like the trespass. For if the many died through the one man's trespass, much more surely have the grace of God and the free gift in the grace of the one man, Jesus Christ, abounded for the many" (Rom. 5:15).

It may be that Paul also plays on another text from the Genesis story. In the original creation, God gives humankind dominion over creation (Gen. 1:28). But then, in Paul's reading, when Adam sins he can no longer exercise dominion, he falls under the dominion of death; he can no longer rule because death rules him. In the new creation, man and woman are restored to their primal authority: "If, because of the one man's trespass,

240

death exercised dominion through that one, much more surely will those who receive the abundance of grace and the free gift of righteousness exercise dominion in life through the one man, Jesus Christ" (Rom. 5:17).[7]

Now with a clarity beyond even that of 2 Corinthians 5, the passage from Romans raises the question of universality. The fact that Paul sometimes refers to "all" who sin and are redeemed and sometimes to "many" does not represent a confusion in this passage. The idiom in which Paul writes "many" can refer to all the members of a particular category, not just to a large number of members. When Paul writes in Romans 5:15 "For if the many died through the one man's trespass, much more surely have the grace of God and the free gift in the grace of the one man, Jesus Christ, abounded for the many," he surely does not mean that only a number of people have been subject to mortality through Adam's sin; mortality is universal. So, in this passage, we can presume that the free gift abounds for "all" as well.[8] Of course this does not tell us whether in Jesus Christ God makes redemption available for all or whether in Jesus Christ God works redemption for all. Verse 18 certainly points in the more inclusive direction: "Therefore just as one man's trespass led to condemnation for all, so one man's act of righteousness leads to justification and life for all." Certainly the logic of the contrast between the first and second Adam, between Adam and Christ, would suggest that if the power of sin was great enough to condemn all of Adam's children, the power of grace is strong enough to make righteous all of Jesus' brothers and sisters.

As Sibley Towner points out in the passage quoted at the beginning of this article, there are sections aplenty in Paul where the faith in Jesus seems to be a precondition for redemption (e.g., Rom. 3:21-16; 9:22). Yet over against that confessional rigor and ethical realism there is this other picture as a counterpoint, the picture of a grace so strong (see Rom. 5:15) that finally it works its irresistible mercy on all of humankind.

One fairly similar passage requires brief attention. In 1 Corinthians 15 Paul compares the harm wrought in the first Adam and the redemption wrought in the second:

7. I would be more confident in this reading if the term for "dominion" in Rom. 5 were the same as the Septuagint term in Gen. 1. Ernst Käsemann suggests this interpretation also (*Commentary on Romans,* trans. Geoffrey W. Bromiley [Grand Rapids: Eerdmans, 1980], pp. 155-56).

8. See Paul J. Achtemeier, *Romans,* IntBC (Atlanta: John Knox, 1985), p. 98. His discussion of this passage (pp. 95-101) is very helpful.

But in fact Christ has been raised from the dead, the first fruits of those who have died. For since death came through a human being, the resurrection of the dead has also come through a human being; for as all die in Adam, so all will be made alive in Christ. But each in his own order: Christ the first fruits, then at his coming those who belong to Christ. Then comes the end, when he hands over the kingdom to God the Father, after he has destroyed every ruler and every authority and power. . . . The last enemy to be destroyed is death. For "God has put all things in subjection under his feet." . . . When all things are subjected to him, then the Son himself will also be subjected to the one who put all things in subjection under him, so that God may be all in all. (1 Cor. 15:20-28)

Again we can see here a reading of the Genesis story in the light of God's redemption in Jesus Christ. What is emphasized is the relationship between disobedience and mortality: "You may freely eat of every tree of the garden; but of the tree of the knowledge of good and evil you shall not eat, for in the day that you eat of it you shall die" (Gen. 2:16-17), as that promise is confirmed in the curse: "By the sweat of your face you shall eat bread until you return to the ground, for out of it you were taken; you are dust, and to dust you shall return" (Gen. 3:19). The polarity, or the counterbalance, between Adam and Christ is presented somewhat differently here, however. In Romans 5 Adam represents disobedience and, consequently, death; Christ represents obedience and, consequently, life. It is obedient death that opens justification and life. In 1 Corinthians 15 Adam represents death — the disobedience is only implicit — and Christ represents life. Atonement is only implicit; it is resurrection that brings life to all.

Here, if anything, the universalism presented in Romans 5 is even more explicit: "As all die in Adam, so will all be made alive in Christ" (1 Cor. 15:22). Though the passage is entirely cryptic, one wonders whether Paul's allusion in 1 Corinthians 15:29 to the Corinthian Christian practice of being baptized for the dead does not suggest that hope beyond the grave is universal and not just for those who have been baptized believers during their (first) earthly lives.

The universalism pushes even broader and deeper in 1 Corinthians 15:28: "When all things are subjected to [the Son], then the Son himself will also be subjected to the one who put all things in subjection under him, so that God may be all in all." That last phrase "all in all" might mean "so that God might be all things to all people." In that case the verse seems

242

to imply universal redemption for the human race. It also might mean "so that God might be all things to everything." The language is that of poetry not of proposition: Does God become God of all that is, or do all things get taken up into God? In either case the verse is congruent with the material in Romans 8.

The hints of universal redemption in Romans 5 are reiterated, deepened, and expanded in Romans 8. Now it is not only humans who move between creation and new creation, it is the whole universe.

> I consider that the sufferings of this present time are not worth comparing with the glory that is about to be revealed to us. For the creation waits with eager longing for the revealing of the children of God; for the creation was subjected to futility, not of its own will but by the will of the one who subjected it, in hope that the creation itself will be set free from its bondage to decay and will obtain the freedom of the glory of the children of God. We know that the whole creation has been groaning in labor pains until now; and not only the creation, but we ourselves, who have the first fruits of the Spirit, groan inwardly while we wait for adoption, the redemption of our bodies. For in hope we were saved. Now hope that is seen is not hope. For who hopes for what is seen? But if we hope for what we do not see, we wait for it with patience. (Rom. 8:18-25)

Again this is a reading of the Genesis story in light of Paul's questions.

Act One. God creates the world as good. The shape of the good creation is more implicit than explicit. Creation before Adam's disobedience was not subject to bondage, to futility, to decay; it was free, purposeful, spared the threats of mortality. Further, since the present age is marked above all by suffering (Rom. 8:18), we can assume that in the first creation humankind was spared that suffering.

Act Two. Sin mars God's good creation. Here I think Paul provides an audacious reading of the curse God pronounces on Adam and Eve before they are driven forth from the garden. Paul applies two aspects of the curse to the world between creation and new creation. The first aspect is fairly straightforward. In Genesis 3:17b-18 God says to Adam, "Cursed is the ground because of you . . . thorns and thistles it shall bring forth for you." Adam's curse, the harshness of his labor, is replicated in the earth's curse — the harsh and unyielding soil, creation subject to decay.

243

The second way in which Paul applies the curse of Genesis is bolder. Paul takes the curse that God pronounces on the woman and expands it to apply to the whole created world: "To the woman [God] said, 'I will greatly increase your pangs in childbearing; in pain you shall bring forth children'" (Gen. 3:16). Just as the harshness of Adam's toil is reflected in the harshness of the created order, so the birth pangs Eve experiences infect all of nature; not woman alone but all of creation is in travail. However, the curse is also promise: the pains of childbirth bring forth children, even as the harsh soil brings forth some fruit. God's curse is never absolute. Creation's birth pangs will bring forth the revealing of the children of God. Then the image circles around again: Eve's birth pangs become creation's birth pangs, which become the birth pangs of all the children of Adam and Eve who await not childbirth but their own adoption. Adoption is the birth God gives, not by the flesh but by the Spirit.

Act Three. God acts in Jesus Christ to redeem the world. In Romans 8 a feature of God's act in Jesus Christ becomes absolutely clear. Though God's redemptive activity has begun decisively in Christ's death and resurrection, the fullness of that redemption is yet to come. The cross is absolutely essential for God's work of redemption, but the reconciliation begun there still points ahead to a glory yet to be revealed when not one thing will come between God and God's children. And that glory (just as much as the present reconciliation) God will accomplish through Jesus Christ (Rom. 8:31-39).

Act Four. The lost good of creation is (will be) restored purer and brighter than before. Just as the earth (the creation) is cursed because of Adam — Adam's fall is the firstfruits of creation's fall — so the creation can be redeemed only through Adam's redemption. The adoption of humans is the firstfruits of the restoration of the whole creation. Creation waits with eager longing for the revealing of God's children, because the revealing of God's children is the promise to creation that after the curse on *Adam* (the man) has been lifted, the curse on *Adamah* (the earth) will be lifted, too. Though Adam and Eve thought themselves separated from God, hiding from God, banished from God's garden; through Jesus Christ nothing can separate Christ's brothers and sisters from the God who loves them. Though the phrase is not used, this too is "new creation."

Paul has yet another set of images that deal with the continuity and distinction between the old and new creation. Paul draws on the images of flesh and spirit. As a reader of the Genesis story, Paul remembers that when creation began, God's *pneuma* (spirit) swept over the face of the waters (Gen. 1:2). As an apostle and believer, Paul has seen God's spirit enliven and illumine the churches he has founded, and the resulting gifts of the new creation are even richer than the gifts of the first creation. Now the Spirit is named not only God's spirit but Christ's spirit. The Spirit not only creates, the Spirit creates God's family. It is the gift of the Spirit that enables Christians to call God by name — Abba, father. Through the Spirit Christians are adopted as Christ's brothers and sisters. Through the Spirit believers receive not only the breath of life but the gift of life eternal (see Rom. 8:9-17).

The time between creation and new creation, between the spirit that creates and the Spirit that creates family, between the spirit that gives life and the Spirit that gives life eternal — this is the time of the flesh. The time of the flesh is the time marked by sin, law, and death. Sin is flesh because it turns us away from the God who is Spirit; law is flesh because it does not avail to bring us back to God; death is flesh because mortality is the sign and substance of our fleshiness: dust to dust.

In Romans 8 we see the universalist pole of the Pauline tension between particular and universal redemption at its fullest. Not only are Jews and Gentiles, slaves and free, men and women and maybe even those who believe and those who do not yet believe all caught up into the coming glory, but now also the whole creation. Now lilies of the field and birds of the air, cucumbers and caterpillars wait for the glory that will include them. When Christians cry "Abba! Father," they lay hold of the hope of glory for all that God has made. New creation is not just a code for new humankind. New creation is new *creation*.

One more word needs to be said about the argument of Romans 5–8. Crucial to the argument is Paul's discussion with an (imaginary?) opponent in Romans 6–7. There we find his most complete and complex discussion of the relationship among sin, law, and righteousness. It lies beyond the scope of this paper to discuss this difficult material, but it needs to be noted that in the fourfold drama of redemption that lies behind much of Paul's exposition, the law clearly belongs to the second act of the drama. It has no place in the original blessing of creation (Act One) or in the redemptive work of Christ (Act Three). Moreover, the new creation is marked by neither torah nor new torah. The law is a feature of the second act of this drama, that period marked by Adam's sin and human mortality. In Romans the law serves two functions during this period. The law entices to sin, just as Adam and Eve were enticed to eat the fruit of the tree by the very commandment that forbade the eating (Rom. 7:7-12). The law increases sin: it is bad enough to do wrong, worse yet to do wrong against God's specific commandment (Rom. 7:13-14). The law is not sinful, but where the law obtains, sin is both elicited and deepened.

Paul's suggestions for the shape of the obedient life in the Roman churches in part reflect his hope for the redemption of humankind and of creation. The one God will bring all people and all the world to God's own self. In part Paul uses this assurance to provide hope and courage amid suffering. Whether he knows of particular tribulations suffered in Rome or knows only that Christians are bound to undergo their share of pain, Paul promises that today's sufferings will be overcome by God's final victory when creation is redeemed from its curse. Paul may very well intend the promise of a new creation, where all are brought to life through Jesus Christ, as a way of countering the apparent divisions within the Roman Church — divisions between "weak" and "strong" believers and perhaps between Gentile and Jewish congregations. Because the new creation is God's promise for all people, all Christians are to live in harmony as they await the new creation: "Welcome one another, therefore, just as Christ has welcomed you, for the glory of God" (Rom. 15:7). Finally, the whole affirmation that the restored creation will include both humankind and the rest of the created universe may help Christians today to think more responsibly about our relationship to the rest of nature. Before the curse in Eden we tended the earth with loving care. At the end, humankind and nature will again be joined, freed from our bondage to decay. As we look hopefully to that day, we will want to attend more lovingly to the world, a world that is not only "nature" but, like us, "creation."[9]

IV. Synoptics: Divorce

Though the theme of new creation is strongest in Paul's writings, a similar motif is found in the synoptic tradition, in the pericope about divorce. Though this tradition does not carry with it all the remarkable affirmations about the work of redemption that we find in Paul, there is a similar

---

9. For further discussion of Paul's hope for the Roman churches, see David L. Bartlett, *Romans,* Westminster Bible Companion (Louisville: Westminster/John Knox, 1995).

pattern: creation, call (the time of sin and law), and new creation. Here is the pericope in Mark's version:

> Some Pharisees came, and to test him they asked, "Is it lawful for a man to divorce his wife?" He answered them, "What did Moses command you?" They said, "Moses allowed a man to write a certificate of dismissal and to divorce her." But Jesus said to them, "Because of the hardness of your heart he wrote this commandment for you. But from the beginning of creation, 'God made them male and female.' For this reason a man shall leave his father and mother and be joined to his wife, and they shall become one flesh.' So they are no longer two, but one flesh. Therefore, what God has joined together, let no one separate." (10:2-9)

Behind this word of Jesus to the Pharisees is the picture of human history passing through three stages. The first stage is creation, where man and woman are one flesh. The second stage is the stage marked first by hardness of heart and second by the Mosaic commandment. The third stage is the new age, in which the conditions of the creation apply once again. Now man and woman are again inseparably one flesh.

The overall pattern recalls the structure of Romans 5. There is a period of blessedness. Then sin enters human history with its companion, the law. Then comes the new age or creation where the law is no longer binding and where sin no longer has dominion. Galatians 2–3, where the law serves as a guardian until humankind is grown up enough to live by grace, provides a somewhat similar scenario. Morna Hooker is surely right that Mark's Gospel here does not make a radical disjunction within the Old Testament, as if Genesis were God's gift and Deuteronomy (where the word about divorce is found) were only burden and curse. Mark (and Jesus) surely thought that Genesis and Deuteronomy alike came from Moses and alike were part of God's good law.[10] Nonetheless, just as Paul can use the Torah to talk about those blessed ages before the commandments — the age in the garden, the age of Abraham — so Mark or the tradition he draws upon makes a distinction within the larger torah between the original blessedness and the stipulations that were not blessings but concessions, responses to human sinfulness.

A few features of the Markan story further underline the richness of

---

10. Morna D. Hooker, *The Gospel According to Saint Mark,* Black's New Testament Commentary (Peabody, MA: Hendrickson, 1991), p. 236.

nuance here. That man and woman were joined together "from the beginning of creation" indicates what the rest of the text makes ineluctably clear, that Jesus grounds his understanding of marriage in a reading of Genesis, where in Genesis 1:1 we have "the beginning" of creation.

The fall from creation, from the original blessedness, is marked by the reminder that the Pharisees (and presumably all of Israel) suffered from "hardness of heart." Though the compound noun "hardness of heart" appears in the New Testament only here and in the parallel passage in Matthew 19:8, Paul expresses a somewhat similar idea in Romans 2:5 and 9:18.

In the latter verse Paul suggests that many in Israel have shown hardness of heart by their unwillingness to trust the promise of God in Jesus Christ. In a stunning example of exegetical role reversal, Paul quotes God's word to Pharaoh, "I have raised you up for the very purpose of showing my power." For the reader who knows the exodus story, this will recall the time when God hardened the heart of Pharaoh against Moses and his people. But now, Paul suggests, it is not Pharaoh whose heart is hardened; it is those Israelites themselves who do not recognize this new liberation from bondage that God is working in Jesus Christ. In Romans 2:4-5, therefore, where Paul is accusing his (presumably Jewish) interlocutor of noticing Gentile sins while ignoring his own trespasses, Paul says to this opponent: "Or do you despise the riches of [God's] kindness and forbearance and patience? Do you not realize that God's kindness is meant to lead you to repentance? By your hard and impenitent heart you are storing up wrath for yourself on the day of wrath, when God's righteous judgment will be revealed."

Because of this hardness of heart Moses had conceded to human sinfulness by making provision for divorce, according to the Markan passage. Law is concession here, not part of the original goodness of creation. This understanding of law recalls not so much Romans, where the law finally multiplies sin, as Galatians, where the law "was our disciplinarian until Christ came" (Gal. 3:24). Law was there to keep the lid on for the time between creation and new creation.

In Mark, now that Christ has come, man and woman are joined together. This is not far from that picture of new creation conveyed in Galatians, where circumcision and uncircumcision do not separate faithful people from one another. Now maleness and femaleness with all the difference they entail do not keep people from the original blessing of creation, two becoming one.

As is so often the case in Paul's descriptions of creation and new creation there are clear ethical implications for the life of the Christian community: "Therefore what God has joined together, let no one separate." Does this mean, what God has joined together let the human Pharisees (who are raising the issue) not separate? Does it mean, what God has joined together let Moses not separate, with his permission for a decree of divorce? In either case Jesus claims that believers are back in the realm of creation. They live under God's direct jurisdiction and blessing, and human stipulations about divorce do not hold. As in 2 Corinthians 5, new creation is reconciliation. As in Galatians, new creation is the restoration of an earlier unity. As in Romans, Christians welcome one another; spouses welcome one another.

It is perhaps impossible to know whether this discussion of creation, divorce, and new creation goes back to Jesus, or to the early church, or to Mark's own creativity. The fact that Paul may know something of this divorce tradition in a different form suggests that some version of the material on divorce was very early (see 1 Cor. 7:10-11). Even if the saying is early, it is not likely that Paul's much more elaborate discussion of creation, sin, law, and new creation goes back to this material attributed to Jesus. Nonetheless, it is striking that in two rather diverse strains of early Christian tradition the claim is made that in Jesus Christ the original conditions of creation obtain again. Whatever the law permitted in the age in between, in the new creation husband and wife are one, as long as they both shall live.

V. Conclusion

In Mark and in Paul, then, there is a fairly consistent pattern that compares and contrasts the time of creation with the time of redemption, new creation. Neither in the Gospels nor in Paul's writing is this the only or even the most pervasive way to talk about what God has done for humankind in Jesus Christ, but in each case the pattern plays with other motifs to enrich our understanding of how the creator God redeems creation.

Different features of the original blessedness are highlighted in different accounts: reconciliation, freedom from the distinction between circumcised and uncircumcised, harmony between men and women, freedom from death, and freedom from suffering. The "fall" from that original state of blessedness is described in terms appropriate to the blessing that has been lost: reconciliation becomes separation; the unity of humankind falls apart with the distinction between those who are circumcised and those who are not; the goodness of unity between the sexes is marred by divorce; creation cries out in pain; and humans suffer mortality. In Galatians, Romans, and Mark 10, there is also the clear sense that the law is one of the conditions of the time between Eden and God's redemption in Jesus Christ.

The redemption is always wrought in Jesus Christ. That is explicit in Paul's writing. His obedience undoes Adam's disobedience; his cross reconciles those who have not been reconciled; his resurrection brings life to the dead. It is implicit in Mark's Gospel where the one who declares that God's reign is at hand (Mark 1:14-15) also declares that men and women now live under the orders of creation, not of law.

Sometimes "new creation" seems to be a gift for the faithful and sometimes a promise for all humankind, even a promise for the whole cosmos. When new creation represents a present reality, life in the community of believers, its scope seems limited, as the community is limited. It is Christians who no longer live under the Mosaic law and permit divorce; it is Christians who are building a community where neither circumcision nor uncircumcision counts for anything; it is a new creation where faith works through love.

In 2 Corinthians 5 it is not certain whether the new creation is a gift for believers or a hope for all humankind. "For anyone who is in Christ there is a new creation" might mean that it is Christians who receive the gift, or it might mean that Christians recognize the gift, or the promise, of a whole world reconciled to God.

Elsewhere, though the exact term is not used, the motif of new creation is surely the promise of the completion of God's work, a promise not yet fulfilled in the time of the New Testament, nor in our own. In Romans 5 and 1 Corinthians 15:22, Paul at least holds out the possibility that Christ will overcome death for all of humankind. In Romans 8 and 1 Corinthians 15:28, Paul suggests that God through Christ will redeem the whole creation.

Perhaps this all-encompassing vision is a mark of Christian hope. For Paul, hope is the mode by which the faithful attend to God's eschatological promises (see Rom. 5:1; 8:24-25). Now we see in a glass darkly, but then face to face. In that light it is hard to see how Pauline Christianity can evade the lure of a universalistic vision. To this day, Christians may believe that God will do something less than redeem the whole creation. But how, in Christ's name, can we *hope* for anything less?

Creation and Apocalypse

John T. Carroll

The book of Revelation arrests the reader with stunning sights and sounds pointing to the approaching end of the world as we know it. Images of violence and destruction are cosmic in scale. Surely this is the last place one would expect to find a theological vision that affirms the world as God's creation, or that supports a responsible environmental ethic. Yet John the seer is full of surprises! This essay pays tribute to Sibley Towner by addressing a concern about which he has written and spoken with eloquent passion: the relationship between creation — as God's gracious activity, but only with human partnership — and apocalyptic hope.[1]

---

1. See most recently W. Sibley Towner, "The Future of Nature," *Int* 50 (1996): 27-35. Towner's affirmation of the theological priority of redemption over retribution (*How God Deals with Evil* [Philadelphia: Westminster, 1976]) has also informed this reflection on Revelation. On the topic of this essay, see also David M. Russell, *The "New Heavens and New Earth": Hope for the Creation in Jewish Apocalyptic and the New Testament* (Philadelphia: Visionary Press, 1996); Gale Z. Heide, "What Is New about the New Heaven and the New Earth? A Theology of Creation from Revelation 21 and 2 Peter 3," *JEvTS* 40 (1997): 37-56; M. Eugene Boring, "Revelation 19-21: End without Closure," *PSB* Sup 3 (1994): 57-84; A. Truesdale, "Last Things First: The Impact of Eschatology on Ecology," *Perspectives on Science and Christian Faith* 46 (1994): 118-20; R. J. Raja, "As it was in the beginning . . . (Eco-spirituality in the Book of Revelation)," *Bible bhashyam* 19 (1993): 210-30; Adela Yarbro Collins, "The Physical World in the Book of Revelation," *Bible Today* 26 (1988): 156-59; Donald E. Gowan, "The Fall and Redemption of the Material World in Apocalyptic Literature," *HBT* 7 (1985): 83-103.

I. God the Creator

Revelation contains not a single explicit quotation from the Jewish Scriptures, yet biblical allusions and echoes pervade John's Apocalypse. Among the notes sounded is the biblical affirmation of God as creator. In the foundational heavenly throne scene of chs. 4 and 5, John listens in on the heavenly liturgy. Parallel hymns of praise are addressed to God (4:11) and to the Lamb (5:9-10; cf. v. 12). God is praised for the work of creation, and the Lamb of God for the work of redemption:

Worthy are you, our Lord and God, to receive glory and honor and power,	Worthy are you, to receive the scroll and open its seals,
because you have created all things, and by your will they have been created. (4:11)	because you were slaughtered and by your blood you have bought [a people] for God from every tribe and language and people and nation; and you have made of them a royal realm and priests, and they will reign on earth. (5:9-10)

Joining the twenty-four elders in these hymns celebrating the divine work of creation and redemption are four living creatures (zōa) reminiscent of Ezekiel's throne vision (Ezek. 1), and perhaps representing the domain of created animals (lion, ox, human, eagle). If they "symbolize the created cosmos," John is privileged to overhear "the unceasing song of nature in praise of its Creator."[2]

The angel who holds the second revelatory scroll (the "little scroll" of Rev. 10), according to the vision narrator, returns to the theme of divine creativity. The completion of divine judgment is imminent. How can one be sure? The oath by which the angel gives assurance that "there will be no more delay" links eschatological judgment to creation: "He swore by the one who lives forever, who created heaven and the things in it, the earth and the things in it, and the sea and the things in it . . ." (10:6).

---

2. Wilfrid J. Harrington, *Revelation*, SP 16 (Collegeville, MN: Liturgical Press, 1993), p. 82.

Later, another angel-revealer, proclaiming a message of universal appeal, connects the imagery of imminent judgment, divine creation, and worship (14:7). Glory is due God because judgment is at hand; worship is offered God "who made heaven and earth, sea and springs of water." Clearly, creation and justice or vindication are closely aligned in Revelation.

II. The Created World in the Drama of Divine Judgment and Redemption

In the vision cycles that depict divine judgment against evil (e.g., the septets: seven seals, seven trumpets, and seven bowls in chs. 6, 8–9, 16), the created world is a key player. Repeatedly, God's creation is the instrument of divine justice, and typically in ways that evoke memories of the exodus from Egypt.

As the four horsemen inaugurate the judgment cycles (6:1-8), God's creation serves God's purpose of judgment. Much of the damage stems from the ravages of human warfare, but famine, plague, and wild animals do their part as well (v. 8). At the breaking of the scroll's sixth seal, earthquake and cosmic distress extending to sun, moon, and stars intensify the images of destruction (vv. 12-14).

The created world contributes to the divine activity of judgment again in the trumpet septet (chs. 8–9) and in the bowl septet (ch. 16), with clear echoes of the plagues in Egypt (Exod. 7–12). Hail and fire raining from the sky destroy one-third of the earth (Rev. 8:7; cf. 16:8-9, 20-21; Exod. 9:22-26). The sea turns into blood, as one-third of ocean life dies (Rev. 8:8-9; cf. 16:3, where all sea life dies; and Exod. 7:20-21). Rivers and springs become polluted ("bitter") and a source of death (Rev. 8:10-11). At the fourth trumpet, sun, moon, and stars are diminished (8:12; cf. 16:10; Exod. 10:21-23) — again by one-third, the pattern that marks the trumpet sequence as a whole. Locusts with the destructive capability of scorpions (Rev. 9:3-10; cf. Joel 2:1-11), earthquakes (Rev. 8:5; 16:18), and a cavalry that deploys lethal horses (9:16-19) fill out the grim picture of destruction. Still, those who survive the ordeals refuse to repent of their evil (9:20-21; cf. 16:9, 11; Exod. 7:13, 22; 8:15). The severity of these plagues, coupled with humanity's stubborn refusal to repent, displays the tenacity and the power of evil in the world. In the face of such evil, creation itself becomes the vehicle of divine justice.

While the role of nature in the execution of justice is especially prominent in the visions of Revelation, on occasion earth plays the part of protector of God's people. Assuring the seer of the blessing that awaits all who remain faithful through persecution, one of the twenty-four elders promises that the sun will not harm them and springs of living water will nourish them (Rev. 7:16-17). In a later vision, the woman who gives birth to the Messiah is pursued by the dragon but finds shelter and nourishment in the desert (12:6, 14); in fact, when the dragon sends a flood of water to drown her, earth comes to her aid and devours the flood waters (12:16). These images of nature supporting and protecting God's people prepare the reader for the culminating vision of John's Apocalypse, which draws together city and garden, and people and nature, in a glorious and harmonious order superintended by none other than God.

III. New Creation and Paradise Restored

The first of the messages to the seven churches of Asia (2:1–3:22) introduces the motif of "conquest," which receives such rich and paradoxical development in Revelation.[3] One conquers through persevering fidelity to God, and in John's world that means active, though nonviolent, resistance to the Roman system even to the point of surrendering life itself. Conquest, that is, comes not by wielding coercive power, not by submitting to its claims to authority, but by resisting out of undying allegiance to God who — despite all appearances — is sovereign. The first promise held out to those who conquer harks back to Genesis and the primeval garden: "To the one who conquers I will give to eat from the tree of life, which is in the paradise of God" (2:7). Already John signals that the consummation of history will fulfill the promise and potential present in the beginning of the human story. Yet the End recalls, but does not simply recapitulate, the Beginning. The fruit of the "tree of life" went uneaten in the primeval paradise (Gen. 3:22-23), but now in Revelation it symbolizes the gift of eternal life to God's faithful people, and they will eat.

---

3. For "one who conquers" in Revelation, see 2:7, 11, 17, 26; 3:5, 12, 21; 21:7; cf. 5:5; 12:11; 15:2. On this theme, see further C. Freeman Sleeper, *The Victorious Christ: A Study of the Book of Revelation* (Louisville: Westminster John Knox, 1996), pp. 117-21; M. Eugene Boring, *Revelation*, IntBC (Louisville: John Knox, 1989), pp. 89-91; idem, "The Theology of Revelation: 'The Lord Our God the Almighty Reigns,'" *Int* 40 (1986): 267.

The tree of life reappears in the magnificent closing vision of the book (Rev. 22:2). After the forces of evil have finally been vanquished, the new Jerusalem descends from heaven. The garden of Eden gives way to the city of God. A river flows from the throne shared by God and the Lamb; between its banks courses the "water of life" (22:1).[4] No wonder, then, that on either side of the river the "tree of life" grows. The picture from Genesis is embellished with imagery drawn from Ezekiel 47. This life-giving tree[5] bears fruit continuously, each month producing a different fruit. Its leaves offer healing to the nations, the very nations whose demise the earlier visions of judgment have pictured.[6] For all the wrenching conflict and destruction of the previous visions, John composes a culminating vision marked by healing and restoration. In this city of God the created order serves up not judgment but healing and life to humankind.

John's visionary excursion to the eschatological Jerusalem is in important respects a return to paradise. The "new heaven and new earth" fashioned by God who "makes all things new" (Rev. 21:1, 5, echoing Isa. 43:19; 65:17; 66:22) still works with the raw materials of the old cosmos. The new creation improves the old but does not substitute one cosmos for another.[7] Yet the city's heavenly origin signals impressive discontinuities as well. Several features of the old order are conspicuous by their absence. Death will no longer exist (and with it, crying or pain: Rev. 21:2), a reality symbolized by the presence of the tree and water of life. There will be no

4. John plays here with Ezekiel's vision of the eschatological temple (47:1-12), in which the river's source is the temple. In Revelation, of course, there is no temple, for the city itself is the temple. In this holy city, no building is needed to house the divine.

5. Apparently, that is, the "tree of life" on each side of the river.

6. Several details — trees on both sides of the river, bearing fruit continuously, with leaves that provide healing — are borrowed from Ezek. 47:12. In Revelation, however, the leaves on the tree of life bring healing *to the nations*. This embellishment of Ezek. 47 only heightens the tension between the vision of the new Jerusalem and the earlier visions of worldwide destruction. If the visions of the Apocalypse are read literally, as predictions of historical events in a linear sequence, then they are contradictory. The seer John, however, delights in paradoxical images. While taking seriously the conflict between the world-as-experienced and the coming world of God's re-creation, and while asserting the accountability of the nations and their rulers for their opposition to the ways of God, John nevertheless also affirms the universal reach of God's redemptive, healing work.

7. Compare Jürgen Roloff, *The Revelation of John: A Continental Commentary*, trans. John E. Alsup (Minneapolis: Fortress, 1991), p. 226: "The new creation is not denial and abandonment of the old, but rather the surpassing of it." See also Pablo Richard, *Apocalypse: A People's Commentary on the Book of Revelation* (Maryknoll, NY: Orbis, 1995), pp. 161-62.

need for a temple to contain the divine *shekinah* (21:22) in a city permeated with purity and holiness (21:8; 22:3). The sun and moon will no longer be needed, and there will be no more night, because light will perpetually emanate from God or from the Lamb (21:23; 22:5) and will illuminate the nations. The panoramic field of the seer's vision of salvation is again striking.

Another prominent feature of the first creation is missing from the "new heaven and new earth": there will be no sea (21:1). The sea — emblematic of the primeval waters of chaos, which God's creative hand must restrain, and home to the "beast" that embodied enmity to the ways of God (13:1) — now has given up the dead hidden beneath its waves (20:13) and, in a universe entirely under divine sway, has no further role to play.[8] In the new creation, elements of the cosmos that symbolized threat to humankind and implacable opposition to the divine creative purposes — sea, night, and death — disappear.

In a sense, the seer's report that he observed heaven and earth fleeing from the great white throne of judgment (20:11) clears the deck and prepares for the arrival of the new creation (21:1). Yet it is misleading to suggest that the old world is simply replaced by a new and perfect one. In John's narration of his vision, the attempt of heaven and earth to escape divine justice by fleeing the throne is unsuccessful: "[E]arth and heaven *began to flee*[9] [from the presence of the one seated on the great white throne], and yet *no place was found for them* [to hide]." Heaven and earth do not vanish but — with humankind — must face the cosmic judge. The point therefore is that there is no escaping divine justice.[10] All God's creation is accountable to the creator. The first heaven and earth "depart," and the new heaven and earth come into view (21:1), but the meaning is that the present creation of God is renewed, not replaced. The implications of this interpretive move for the construction of an ecological ethic are enormous and claim our attention in the closing section of the essay.

---

8. Compare Harrington, *Revelation*, p. 207; Heide, "What Is New?" pp. 44-45; Richard, *Apocalypse*, p. 160.

9. The expression "and yet no place was found for them" indicates that the aorist verb *ephygen* ("began to flee") should be construed as ingressive. Heaven and earth were attempting to flee (but could not do so).

10. See Heide, "What Is New?" pp. 41-42.

IV. Apocalypse and Ecological Responsibility

James Watt, Secretary of the Interior during the administration of Ronald Reagan, captured headlines when he appealed to his own belief that the end of the world was at hand in support of a relaxed concern with environmental issues.[11] After all, if the world as we know it is destined for imminent destruction, and if the future world is entirely God's new creation *ex nihilo*, then why be overly concerned about decimation of tropical rain forests, or global warming, or ozone layer depletion, or pollution of streams and rivers, or the disappearance of endangered species? The new world is a fresh start, so why be troubled with the saving of this world, hopelessly contaminated as it is by human sin? Why not adopt a strictly utilitarian approach to the nonhuman environment, using it in whatever way supports human welfare and economic growth? Questions of ecological sustainability may then simply be dismissed.

Regardless of how one handles apocalyptic texts such as the book of Revelation, careful reading of Genesis, the Psalter, the Wisdom Literature, and Paul's epistles (especially Rom. 8) points toward a quite different approach to the created world, one that emphasizes human responsibility to tend and keep, to nurture and manage wisely, the world entrusted to our care.[12] But rather than develop here that alternative biblical theology of creation, I confine my remarks to the framing of an appropriate response to the book of Revelation itself. When we attend to the role of creation in the Apocalypse of John, this visionary work does not undermine but strongly supports responsible ecological engagement by people of faith.[13]

At the very center of Revelation, the climactic seventh trumpet opens onto a portion of the heavenly liturgy featuring acclamation of God and thanksgiving (11:15-18). The acclamation boldly asserts that the world has

---

11. See Jim Castelli, "The Environmental Gospel According to James Watt," *Chicago Tribune*, October 25, 1981, p. B2; cf. Stephen O'Leary, *Arguing the Apocalypse: A Theory of Millennial Rhetoric* (New York: Oxford University Press, 1994), p. 182.

12. In this vein, see the essays by Gene M. Tucker, David L. Petersen, James L. Mays, Patrick D. Miller, Jr., and David L. Bartlett in this volume.

13. Compare Harrington, *Revelation*, p. 210: "[T]he promise of a new world implies a radical questioning of our present relationship with the world. . . . It is a reminder that we human beings have sinned grievously against God's world, which was committed to our responsible care. . . . We are summoned to *metanoia*, called to work towards the new world held in prospect."

257

become even now the dominion of God and of the Messiah (v. 15). This is the central (and subversive!) theo-political claim of the book.[14] The thanksgiving hymn sung next by the twenty-four elders picks up this note — God has begun to reign — and links it to the working out of justice for both the living and the dead (vv. 17-18). God will judge the nations, among other things, for their abuse of the world they inhabit: destruction from God will fall upon "those who destroy the earth" (v. 18). Oppression of God's people is a serious matter (e.g., 6:9-11), but so too is violation of God's good creation.

Moreover, God delivers justice with active participation from both the vindicated people of God and the nonhuman creation. Oppression of God's faithful gives way to the millennial reign of the martyrs (20:4-6). In a similar fashion, the created order contributes materially to God's judgment against evil, as we have already seen.[15] If we human beings claim mastery of the earth, the visions of Revelation expose such confidence as illusory. We will answer for our infidelity to the creator, whether expressed in abuse of others or in contempt for creation, and nature itself may be our judge. Our treatment of the ecosphere is never without consequence, though the effects of our actions may remain long concealed. Environmentalists would not be the first to observe, "What you sow, that you will also reap."

For John the visionary, God — the eternal one, the one "who was and is and is to come" — is the creator of the universe. All of space-time is in the hands of God the *Pantokrator* (Rev. 1:8; 4:8; 11:17; 15:3; 16:7, 14; 19:6, 15; 21:22),[16] who exercises dominion over all that is and all that will be. Creation itself serves the sovereign purposes of God, extending healing, protection, and redemption to God's faithful, but holding accountable all who oppose the ways of God. Affirming God the creator, Revelation affirms God's good creation as well. Whatever pessimism may mark this text's response to the world, it is worlds removed (pardon the pun) from a gnostic devaluation of the cosmic realm.

Like other apocalyptic writings, the book of Revelation — for all its concern with faithful human response to the working of God — includes within God's sphere of concern the whole universe.[17] John does not pre-

---

14. Compare Boring, "Theology of Revelation," pp. 257-69.
15. Part two of this essay.
16. See Boring, "Theology of Revelation," pp. 259-61.
17. *1 Enoch* reflects especially deep and sustained interest in the created order. The

sent an anthropocentric vision but a radically theocentric vision that encompasses all the created world. Obstacles remain, however, to a reading of apocalyptic texts that would point toward a constructive ecological ethic for our time. In closing these reflections, I address two of these obstacles: (1) the notion that there is a caesura between the old and new creations; and (2) the view that God, not humankind, accomplishes the work of creation and re-creation.

In the end time, do "heaven and earth" pass away in order to make way for the new creation?[18] Does God really fashion a new world only after discarding the old one? Given John's evaluation of the world under Roman domination, it is scarcely surprising that he favors imagery suggesting radical discontinuity between the present age and the age to come. The power and tenacity of evil's operation in the world are not easily countered. Only processes involving deep and fundamental transformation will do. Yet, as we have seen, the future John imagines brings about the restoration of the beauty and grandeur of the original creation. The old world may seek to escape God, but God will not give it up. Rather, God allows it to realize its full promise. Pictures of cosmic transformation in Revelation do not give humankind a license to neglect or destroy the earth.

With jarring dissonance between the world as John now experiences it and the coming world of which the creator is the architect, Revelation, to be sure, sharply accents the divine role in the new creation. A number of prominent features of the book express or reinforce this claim, among them the heavenly throne from which God — with the Lamb — exercises sovereign rule over the nations; the pivotal role played by the Lamb (and his faithful witness to the point of death) in the formation and redemption of the people of God;[19] and the decisive intervention by God and by the Messiah-Lamb in scenes of judgment and military victory. Only God can repair what has gone wrong with the world that John — and we — know. This conviction shared by Revelation with many other apocalyptic writings lends itself to dangerous caricature and distortion. Simply put, apocalyptic literature (in

---

cosmos faithfully follows the patterns laid down by God, and this stands in stark contrast to the perfidy of humankind (e.g., *1 Enoch* 2–5, 72–79). So the nonhuman creation highlights the culpability of human beings. For discussion of the place of the cosmos in apocalyptic literature, see Russell, *New Heavens;* Gowan, "Fall and Redemption."

18. In addition to Rev. 21:1, see, e.g., *1 Enoch* 91:16-17; *Jub.* 1:29; 23:18.

19. See John T. Carroll and Joel B. Green, *The Death of Jesus in Early Christianity* (Peabody, MA: Hendrickson, 1995), pp. 142-47.

this view) leaves the future to God; no real place remains for ethical engagement, since we cannot build the new world for God.

While recognizing the central and determinative role Revelation and other apocalyptic texts assign to God in the work of re-creation, we must also honor the moral seriousness of these writings. Human fidelity to covenant, persevering commitment to the ways of God, active resistance to powerful systems that oppress the needy — these are part and parcel of the moral vision commended by John and kindred visionaries. This moral vision was counter-cultural in John's day, and it is no less so in ours. One lives now in the light of, and toward, the future world God is fashioning. Apocalyptic texts like Revelation exhort readers to that kind of faithful living, even if it means facing great personal risk, and assure and comfort those who do encounter danger and adversity because of their religious commitment.

If we take our cue from the pictures of creation and new creation in John's Apocalypse, the life of faith sustained by this book will express itself in faithful, responsible, and creative care of the earth. To be sure, the magnificent eschatological city that reopens paradise for human enjoyment descends from heaven, which is to say it comes as God's gracious gift. But who knows what crucial part we may yet play as agents and partners of God in that work of re-creation?

Ebenezer Scrooge, confronted by the "Ghost of Christmas Yet to Come" with the terrifying prospect of a lonely and loveless death, asks in desperation: "Are these the shadows of the things that Will be or are they shadows of the things that May be, only?"[20] Reflecting on the fearful pictures of cosmic devastation painted by John the seer, it is fair to ask the same question of the interpreter of Revelation.[21] These images do not show us what will be; Revelation does not predict with precision the events of the future. Like Scrooge's "angel," however, John moves us to change course before it is too late, before destruction falls upon those who, in our day, "destroy the earth." People of faith, drawing inspiration, courage, and hope from John's bold vision of the future and living already in the present from and toward the substance of that awaited future, may yet make peace with the earth, God's good creation.

20. Charles Dickens, *A Christmas Carol* (reprint; New York: Pocket Books, 1963), p. 196.
21. Compare O'Leary, *Arguing the Apocalypse.*

Index of Scripture and Other Ancient Texts

17:7	25	41:23	148	8:15	253
17:7-14	25-26	41:46-57	28	9:13-16	28n.65
17:15-19	26n.58	44:9	139	9:22-26	253
17:20	24n.53	45:12	140	9:30	8n.10
17:20-27	26n.58	45:18-19	139	10:21-23	253
18:1-15	25n.56	46:3-4	24n.53	12:9	173
18:18	23n.51, 24	47:1-27	28	12:12	18n.36
18:19	25	47:10	26	14:13-14	30
20:1-18	48	47:27	28	14:16	145n.21
21:8-21	48	48:3-4	8n.12	14:21	145n.21
22:1-19	25n.56	48:4	24n.53, 26	14:30-31	28n.65
22:14	10n.17	48:13	139n.8, 140	14:31	31
22:15-18	26n.58	48:15	25	15:1-12	30
22:16-18	25	49:1-28	27	15:1-18	28n.62, 144-45
22:17-18	23n.51	50:19-21	28	15:18	11
22:18	24			15:22-25	146, 148
24:3	9n.13	**Exodus**		17:1-7	146, 148
25:12	4n.1	1:7	28, 172n.3	18	27
25:18	179	2:24	25n.55	18:10-11	28n.65
25:19	4n.1	2:25	10n.17	19:1	27
25:21-26	26	3	55	19:3-5	137
26:3-5	23n.51	3:1–4:17	30	19:3-6	18, 28n.65
26:4	24	3:1	27	19:3-8	29, 38
26:5	25	3:7	10n.17	19:5-6	11n.20, 137
27:27-29	26	3:7-8	137	19:7-9	9n.15
27:39-40	26	3:8	36	20:4-6	11n.21
28:3	26	3:16-17	36	20:5	34n.80
28:3-4	8n.12, 24n.53	3:20	113n.26	20:8-11	32n.75, 49
28:13	24n.53	4:10-16	9n.15	20:22	9n.15
28:14	23n.51, 24	4:21-23	28n.65	24:3-8	29
29:31-32	10n.17	4:22-23	43	24:10	15n.28
30:26-28	26	6:1-8	30	25–40	12n.22
33:1-17	26	6:2-5	25n.55	25–31	15
35:9-15	8n.12	6:2-8	8n.12	25–27	182
35:11-12	24n.53	6:7	137	26:36	111n.20
35:22-26	26	6:16-25	35n.82	27:16	111n.20
36:1	4n.1	6:28–7:1	11n.20	28:39	111n.20
36:1-41	26	7–12	253	29:4-9	33
36:9	4n.1	7:1	31	29:43-46	31
37–50	28	7:4-5	28n.65	31:12-17	32
37:1	26	7:13	253	31:18	31
37:2	4, 26	7:20-21	253	32–34	29, 35-36,
40:24	139n.8	7:22	253		34n.80
41:6	148	8:3	172n.3	32	29, 31n.73, 48